HOPSCOTCH & HANDBAGS

The Essential Guide to Being a Girl

HOPSCOTCH & HANDBAGS

The Essential Guide to Being a Girl

Lucy Mangan

headline
review

First published in 2007

by HEADLINE REVIEW

An imprint of Headline Publishing Group

2

Cataloguing in Publication Data is available from the British Library

ISBN 978-0-7553-1647-2

Designed and typeset by Ben Cracknell Studios

Printed and bound in Great Britain by Clays

Illustrations by Alice Tait

HEADLINE PUBLISHING GROUP
An Hachette Livre UK Company
338 Euston Road
London NW1 3BH

www.reviewbooks.co.uk

www.hodderheadline.com

Contents

For my parents, of course.

Acknowledgements

Thank you to all at Headline, especially my editor Andrea Henry, to my agent Euan Thorneycroft and to my sister Emily and all the friends who read bits of the manuscript, laughed in the right places and encouraged me to keep going. You're all in here somewhere, so I hope you like it.

CHAPTER 1

Different for Girls

Picture the scene. A draughty church hall filled with semi-feral children, a dozen splintery little chairs, a pile of mismatched bricks, assorted strains of impetigo and a handful of hungover, disaffected supervisors likely to burn you with their fags if you got too close. It's an unlikely place for an epiphany. But it was here, during my first day at playgroup, that I first realised that the world was divided into two different strains of humanity.

There were those who sat around chatting and playing quietly with tattered board games or ancient and quadruply amputated dolls. They wore skirts or pastel-coloured trousers and took care not to damage either. They were girls.

The others careened round the hall making ack-ack noises and beating each other over the head with blunt objects. They seemed to consider it a day wasted if nobody was hospitalised or dismembered. They never wore skirts, only trousers, and always shredded them by lunchtime. They were boys.

The girls watched them with pity, contempt, fatigue and fascination. The boys didn't watch the girls at all, in case they were blindsided by a fellow pre-schooler with a nail-studded baseball bat he had hidden inside the wee-filled sandpit.

If you had seen exactly how they filled the sandpit with wee, of course, you were already well on the way to understanding what made you female and them male. Physically, it all boils down to a bobbing acorn of flesh in a place where you are as smooth and neat as a nectarine.

But even if you don't spy a penis early on, there are a number of other signs that give the game away, certain characteristics that are only to be found in those who have the XX chromosome.

You know you're a girl when …

1. … you do all the talking.

Your own family and circle of acquaintances will probably provide you with ample illustration of the fact that the world is full of garrulous women and silent men. This is the reason the standard template for the weekly phone call to the parents looks like this:

```
PHONE RINGS
DAD: Hello?
DUTIFUL DAUGHTER: Hi Dad!
DAD: I'll get your mother.
DAD [muffled mumbling]: I don't know. I think
   it's one of those daughter things we had.
MUM: Hellodarlingnowdidyougetthoseshoesintheend …
DD: … Icouldn'tgetawayfromworkandbythetimeIgot-
   thereattheweekendtheyonlyhadtheminthebrown …
```

MUM:… becauseIwasthinkingyoucouldgettheminbrown-
    andthenthey'dgowiththeskirtwegotwhenwesawthe-
    manwiththethingonhisneck …
DD:… andIwouldhaveboughtthemtogowiththeskirtwegot-
    whenwebumpedintothatmanwiththegoitredoyouremem-
    berbutItooktbackbecauseIstoppedgoingtothegymso-
    nowI'venoshoesandnoskirt …
MUM:… butbeforeIforgetdoyouwanttocomeroundonFri-
    daybecauseI'veaccidentallyboughtabigchicken …

It's also the reason retirement homes are filled with the song of game
old birds while the blokes just shuffle around looking exhausted and
trying to find a quiet corner for dominoes where they will be free from
aural assault. My grandma – who moved into such a home at a relatively
young age because she needed to cart her enormous Les Dawsonesque
bosom around in a trolley, which made it hard to negotiate stairs – was
typical of the breed in her dedication to contextual speaking. In other
words, she couldn't tell a story in less than five hours because they all
began like this:

'That Mrs Postlethwaite over there – you know, the one that used to
have the garden until there was all that trouble with Mrs Ogglethwaite –
she were the one who taught at the school that had that fête that Russell
Harty nearly opened until they found out he was a bit funny and asked
Alma Cogan's cousin instead, which were daft really because no one
were coming to t'fête anyway because it were the Saturday before t'Great
Garstang Victuallers' Whippet Roasting and Clog Dance, although they
were holding it in Pendle that year because Mrs Evenmoreridiculousfirst-
twosyllablesthwaite had to stand on a hill because one of her legs were
that short after t'accident, which was when we all had to whitewash the
street's lavvies or be fined three and six when Albert the Privywatcher
came round …'

By this point, you had either learned to fortify yourself with medication or lie back and enjoy the soothing narrative waves, as constant and unstoppable as the sea. The only chance you had of interrupting her was if the forty-eight packets of cigarettes she smoked a day ('for the protein') suddenly asserted themselves and she had to stop to cough up a lung. But if she – and you – did make it to the end of the story, it always finished the same way. 'Well, *her*, over there,' she would conclude triumphantly, 'her son's a lesbian.'

No man has this limitless capacity for conversation in old age, or at any other age for that matter. They are simply wired differently. After all, how many times have you gone to a party with a boyfriend and discovered more information about his best mate in one evening than he has gleaned in fourteen years of friendship with him? Perhaps it is evolutionary: while we were out gathering roots and berries, we learned to engage in conversation in order to stave off what must otherwise have been a quite stultifying level of boredom.

'Found another berry.'

'Really? So have I.'

'I've found a seed.'

'Have you?'

'Oh – no, it's a berry.'

'Anyone found a root?'

'Yes. And a berry.'

It would surely not be long before you were driven to evolve the capacity for finding the minutiae of other people's lives worthy of discussion and an ability to store the data for later retrieval, in order to while away quieter hours and long evenings of – oh, I don't know – cooking roots and stewing berries, perhaps. Or seeds.

Men, on the other hand, I can see would have had enough to deal with trying to bring down mastodons with a handful of flint chips and spears. That's a lifestyle that lends itself to short, sharp commands – brief exclamations of surprise maybe – not meandering discussion or emotional probing. Cut to eight million years later, and while they have made some progress, they are still by and large happy to exist without much in the way of the detailed conversation and happy volubility on which their female counterparts thrive.

2. ... *you would rather read than fight.*

Yes, you will get the occasional boy that reads, and the occasional girl that fights. But by and large it is girls who are the most committed, passionate readers and boys who are the most committed, passionate pugilists. And even the most voracious boy readers rarely open books intended for girls. Thus there is a world of literature that is known and loved only by girls, certain books that every female takes to heart at a young age, and adores forever after.

It can be noted, not without irony, that any woman who later in life finds her beloved characters or stories being traduced by someone will happily beat the offender bloody with her handbag. This remains true even though she knows deep down that few of them stand up to adult scrutiny.

The 10 Most Beloved Books

NUMBER 1: THE LITTLE HOUSE ON THE PRAIRIE BOOKS

Ah, the Ingalls – what a family! They can't go two pages without stopping to exercise once more their boundless resourcefulness by building a log cabin, making pokebonnets out of grasshoppers and slough grass, or butchering a hog and using the bones to make new eyes for Mary. And who's at the centre of everything? Why, Laura, of course, and her 800 sisters. Well, okay, three sisters. But her mother's always there too, and although Pa's nominally the head of the household, he spends so much time away from home working on railroads, getting stuck in snowdrifts and growing his whiskers that in effect they live in a total gynocracy. As a result, the *Little House* books give due weight to the importance of dolls that your mother should never, ever be allowed to give away to ungrateful guests who then leave them in puddles on the way home, the gleaming beauty of coloured sweeties and the evilness of completely heinous bitches like Nellie Oleson.

NUMBER 2: MILLY MOLLY MANDY

When you read the stories as a child, you long for the life of Millicent Margaret Amanda. It is a delightful existence in thirties England, in the Nice White Cottage with the Thatched Roof, largely taken up by stripping village fête stalls of homemade cakes courtesy of the sixpence bestowed by a munificent Grandpa, going on intrepid fishing expeditions with Little Friend Susan and Billy Blunt and having picnics in hollow tree trunks. The books are testimony to how very little girls require in the way of narrative thrust or adventure. Milly Molly Mandy can get twenty pages out of spending a penny on mustard and cress seeds or winning a fairy doll at a party without anyone giving even the gentlest sigh of frustration. God knows what would happen if she broke her leg or Grandma got pissed on whisky sours – the resulting account would look like the *Encyclopaedia Britannica*.

Reading them as an adult, you realise that at least one of the six grown-up members of the family living there would have cottoned on to the commercial value of the Nice White Cottage with the Thatched Roof and sold it to developers and razed to the ground before you could say eggs-for-Muvver. The village fêtes will have long since given way to a juvenile heroin problem and the stream turned to a bubbling stew of chemicals and toxic waste. And the hollow tree trunk is now a Tesco Express.

It will also not escape your adult eye that Milly Molly Mandy is a child who owns only one (pink-and-white-striped) dress. She probably stinks and spends every playtime crying in the loos. Which is still better than the weekends that she has to spend being molested by one of the village shop owners when she goes on her interminable errands.

But you must defend MMM and her (non) adventures to the death if anyone else points out these disheartening facts.

NUMBER 3: THE SECRET GARDEN

Orphaned Mary finds a secret garden, an invalid boy and a proto-sex god called Dickon! Honestly! What more could you ask from a story?

NUMBER 4: LITTLE WOMEN

The tale of four sisters competing to see who can be the most saintly, the most sickly, the most striking and the most sensible. Beth wins by being relentlessly angelic AND dying first.

It is an enduring favourite with girls because there is someone for everyone. Stay-at-home types can take comfort in Meg's story. She is the oldest sister and therefore the most sensible, except for one chapter when she suddenly throws caution to the wind and lets Sally Moffat lend her a fancy dress and earrings and curl her hair. She even gets her shoulders out for the lads. After an evening of waving her fan and drinking a glass of champagne like a total slag, however, she resumes her customary role and settles down with John Brooke and a linen cupboard.

True slags admire Amy, although these days, unlike her, they will probably be able to get a nose job instead of sleeping every night with a clothes peg attached to their faces.

Tomboys adopt Jo as their hero/heroine. From her they learn that they can make money in unfeminine ways like writing, as long as they a) spend all their hard-earned cash on sending their consumptive sisters to the seaside and b) eventually stop it in order to marry ancient German men with beards and open orphanages for boys, in a not-very-subtle exercise in sublimated wish-fulfilment.

Those who like dying, of course, can take Beth. And are welcome to her.

NUMBER 5: BALLET SHOES

Ballet Shoes satisfies every little girl's ravening lust for stardom. Three orphan sisters claw their way up from nothing but a comfortable, upper-middle–class, post-war background to become a renowned actress, dancer and – er – engineer. Again, something for everyone, as well as the stirring message that every girl has a talent if she just looks for it and works hard enough. Oh, and enjoys a fantastically improbable combination of circumstances that see her end up at Madame Fidolia's Academy of Dance and Stage Training. Otherwise, truth be told, you can *plié* around the house all you want and still never get that lifechanging call from the Bolshoi.

NUMBER 6: WHITE BOOTS

Just like *Ballet Shoes*, but on ice skates.

NUMBER 7: GIRLS' COMICS

Obviously, these are not books. But while there have been tomes and essays aplenty attesting to the vital cultural importance of boys' comics, there has been precious little said about the glorious delights of *Twinkle* (with Nurse Nancy and her Dolls' Hospital! Easily replicable with your own teddy bears and shoeboxes for beds!), *Bunty* (with the Four Marys!), *Mandy* (with the mysterious Valda and her amazing youth-restoring crystal!) and *Judy* (nobody remembers anything about *Judy* – it was just the one that didn't have Valda and the Four Marys. Sorry, Joods.)

Bunty and *Mandy* were for slightly older girls who were just waking up to the fact that there is written into female DNA an almost insatiable appetite for vicarious suffering. So they were full of stories with titles like 'The Guardian Tree' (oldest sister of nine orphaned siblings must hide them in a cave under a gnarled oak and find innovative ways to feed and clothe them without being discovered by the cruel, cruel gentry who would hit them with riding crops and put them in the workhouse), 'I Must Fall Out With Mary!' (sister must fall out with other sister to keep Mum and Dad from thinking they would support each other if Mum and Dad went through with the planned divorce – what twisted mind thought up this stuff?) and 'Oh, Woe Is Me, I Wish I Was Dead' (orphaned, deaf-mute Victorian girl who is now just a scarred head after a terrible mill accident is kicked around the streets by uncaring villagers until she is taken in by a poor but honest couple who are killed by a runaway horse, who becomes the girl's only friend until it is caught and turned into glue by the ugly, wicked factory owner who uses his product to stick the girl's eyes together to make her the perfect blind, dumb, deaf wife. The End.)

And all for between 18p and 22p a week.

NUMBER 8: MALORY TOWERS

Boarding school gels, midnight feasts, japes in the dorm, the honour of the school, guilty secrets, Lacrosse matches, the beautiful third former and her ugly friend, misunderstandings, reputations damaged and restored, friendships fractured and repaired – all of female life is here, writ small.

NUMBER 9: ST CLARE'S

See *Malory Towers*, but with a set of twins and a girl secretly from the circus!

NUMBER 10: WHAT KATY DID

You know how we talked about girls' infinite appetite for vicarious suffering? Here it is again: Katy Carr ignores clear instructions not to play on the new swing. Katy swings high. Too high. Astute reader spots metaphor. The swing, and very shortly thereafter Katy's back, breaks. She lies in bed for years, being a right mardy cow just because she can't use her legs, until her equally paralysed Cousin Helen wheels herself up to Katy's bed of pain. Yes, lucky reader – two Connecticut paraplegics for the price of one! She teaches Katy to be patient and have faith in God, though presumably not the same God who let her splinter her spine half a lifetime ago. And one day an older, wiser Katy, who has learned to choke down her black, seething rage and bitterness and present a passive, smiling face to the world, can walk again. Hurrah!

3. ... *you invest your dad with magical powers.*

Your mother holds no intrigue for you. For one thing, her talkativeness is such that you have never known her to have an unexpressed thought, and for another, she is just another girl like you, albeit bigger and with access to gin. Even from a young age, you realise at some level that she is you and you is she and that you both, for better or worse, are locked in an unbreakable circle of shared thoughts, experiences and a fundamental comprehension of each other. Your dad – the Silent Other – however, is an international man of mystery.

* • • ✦ • ' •

I was four and we were walking along the Golden Mile in
Blackpool, eating fish and chips, when my father first spoke to
me directly. He was handing down chips and flakes of cod in
golden batter from on high as we strolled, Gipsy Petulengros
to our right, raw sewage to our left, the Scylla and Charybdis
of late seventies holidaymaking. Our mutual contentment
swelled and he was eventually moved to speech. 'It doesn't,'
he said thoughtfully, 'get much better than this.' Mouth agape
at this unprecedented burst of prolixity and heedless of the
half-masticated potato on display therein, I gave a vigorous,
vinegary nod of agreement.

Naturally, I thought of my father as the repository of all
knowledge and the fount of all wisdom, not yet realising that
this is only true as long as the subjects under discussion are
Preston North End and pork belly. I believed that he had come
to this conclusion as he looked back on a life stuffed with
exotic adventures that conceivably stretched back until the
dawn of time. In fact, at the time of our Blackpool bonding
Dad would have been about three years older than I am now
and had already curtailed his career as an exotic adventurer by
marrying the girl next door and moving to a crappy corner of
south-east London in order to provide their two forthcoming
daughters with a better quality of lead poisoning. Ah well.

He crumpled the fish and chip papers, fell silent again and
remained so for the next twenty-five years. And counting.

• • • ✦ • ' •

You have to invest your father with an air of intrigue, otherwise he just becomes a dull stranger who disappears to the office every morning and comes back every evening just in time to eat tea, watch the news, feign interest in your mother's account of the day's dealings with recalcitrant children, boilers and domestic appliances and go to bed.

The key thing to point out – or rather to spotlight and illuminate so thoroughly that there can be no possible shadow of a misunderstanding anywhere – is not to believe him too fascinating. Otherwise you can become that most freakish and frightening of creatures: the Daddy's Girl.

The Daddy's Girl

These are girls who hero-worship their fathers and spend all their time trying to attract his attention and approval. Which would be fine, were it not for the stomach-churning tendency of the breed to go about this not by building kit cars, making a killing on the stock market or doing something spectacular like blasting his likeness into Mount Rushmore, but by flirting. Flirting! With their own fathers! Yeeuch! As they get older, they find themselves unable to talk in an adult fashion to anyone with a penis and spend their entire lives searching for male laps to squirm on. As they get older still, this results first in socially awkward situations and finally in civil suits.

If you have never met a Daddy's Girl, then you probably are one. A quick quiz should show us which way your psychological land lies:

QUESTION 1

Do you call your father...

a   once a month
b   once a week
c   once a day, or
d   Big Boy?

QUESTION 2

Do you lick your dad's face when you need...

a   a laugh
b   the salt
c   money, or
d   a shag?

QUESTION 3

When you are out together do people think you and your father are...

a   cute
b   a cute couple
c   acutely embarrassing, or
d   illegal?

QUESTION 4

Does your son have...

a   your eyes
b   his dad's eyes
c   your dad's eyes, or
d   all of the above?

QUESTION 5

When you were growing up, was your mother...

a   at home
b   at work
c   at the chemist, refilling her anti-depressant prescription, or
d   surplus to requirements?

QUESTION 6

Do you find Catherine Zeta Jones' relationship with Michael Douglas...

a   faintly boring
b   faintly disturbing
c   faintly arousing, or
d   inspirational?

QUESTION 7

Do you like a man to give you...

a   flowers
b   diamonds
c   teddy bears, or
d   siblings?

QUESTION 8

Did your dad teach you how to...

a   read
b   ride a bike
c   dance, or
d   lap dance?

If you answered mostly (d), you are in all kinds of trouble. And so's he.

4. ... you can make a towel turban for wet hair.

Nobody teaches you. One day you just step out of the shower, tip your head down, wrap your towel around it in one fluid motion and stand back up complete with a delightful and practical towel turban. Boys neither learn this trick spontaneously nor can be taught it. Hours of intensive tutoring from successive girlfriends will be of no avail. Their post-ablution heads must go forever cold and wet. Perhaps this is God's way of making up for the fact that they can wee standing up.

5. ...you are plagued by a strange feeling that you are an inherent disappointment to somebody, somewhere.

We are living in the modern age. Years – generations – have passed since the abolition of the various primogeniture laws and customs that once stalked this and other lands, but for some strange and unfathomable reason, people – friends, strangers and just about anyone in between – still assume that a pregnant woman or daughter-toting parent is secretly hankering after a son. Often this is just something you absorb unconsciously from the culture around you, in much the same way as you breathe in air pollutants on the way to school, but occasionally this odd but persistent belief is made explicit with a sorrowing look or a patronising word. I don't know about you, but I think this is Weird and Depressing. And, frankly, Rude.

You can understand the desire to see sons born in the days when without them and their big muscles the family farm would go unploughed and the family itself would therefore starve. Or when women couldn't go out to work and the best return you could hope to get on your investment in a daughter was to have her marry a multi-millionaire or stay a spinster forever and be on hand to nurse you in your dotage, so that you didn't have to hire a nurse from the lower orders who would give you lice and steal the silver. But the fact that such a desire still lingers today is a testament to the power of folk memory. So if and when you are pregnant and confronted in such a way, simply smile sweetly and say, 'Absolutely! We just don't know what we're going to do with the entailed estate and attendant patrilineal grouse-shooting rights otherwise! Isn't the orderly transmission of property a bugger without boys?' and graciously steer the conversation onto less controversial topics, like buttonhooks and the appalling price of petticoats. Or you can point out that we are not living in Regency England and that in the modern absence of heavily circumscribed inheritance laws, it becomes unquestionably better to have daughters than sons, as even the most cursory reckoning of the genders' respective attributes will show.

Boy or Girl?

- *You can dress girls nicely. Let's face it, the whole point of having a baby is so that you can dress it in lovely, floral, smocky things or, if your mother forbade you them throughout your youth, lovely, glittery, flouncy, sequinny things in pink. Pink, pink, pink, pink, pink. And pink. No woman really wants to have a baby that she has to dress in trousers and mud-coloured t-shirts. Have you been round the boys' section in Gap or Mothercare? It's enough to make you want to kill yourself.*

- *You can change a girl's nappy in five minutes. One smooth wipe round her neat little nether regions and you're good to go. Getting poo out of all a boy's cracks and crevices takes nine hours. And in the end you have to use your fingernails. And while his little peanut willy is amusing, peeling his sweaty scrotum off his bum quickly loses its charm.*

- *And the peanut willy will shoot a jet of pee into your face as soon as you think you've finished. Girls funnel it thoughtfully away.*

- *Girls develop faster. By the time a girl is two and a half, you can hold an interesting conversation with her about her pets,* her toys and her array of real and imaginary friends. She will watch you with bright, alert eyes and give due consideration and full, impassioned answers to all your questions. The average two-and-a-half-year-old boy, by contrast, is virtually indistinguishable from a bag of soil.

- If your attention is distracted for a moment while you are looking after a girl, when you refocus you will find her roughly where you left her, playing contentedly with the toy you gave her, and the rest of the room much as you left it. Turn your back on a boy for three seconds and you will turn back to find him smeared in rabbit blood, naked to the waist and howling war cries from the top of the curtains while he surveys a roomful of splintered floorboards, broken toys and dead pets. Boys are bellicose little bastards and girls are not. This is cruelly reductive generalisation, and absolutely true.

There are only two drawbacks to having a girl. One is that it makes it that much easier to repeat history and turn immediately into your mother. The second is that you are condemned to relive all the most painful parts of childhood through your daughter's eyes – the murderous playground cliques and the misguided love of overpriced tat and unsuitable men – and be as unable to save her as you were unable to save yourself.

Still, it's either that or three years of peeling reluctant scrotums off backsides. Up to you.

6. ... you think keeping your clothes clean is the entire point of your existence.

While boys, as already noted, devote their lives to reducing their clothes to rags by the end of every battle-filled day, girls' lives are full of the sound of women shouting, 'Why can't you be more careful! Mind your dress/top/skirt/shoes on that floor/rusty nail/powdered marshmallow/ kitten tail!' It frequently seems as though nothing would make them happier than to see you safely housed in an iron lung, where your outfit could remain pristine all day, untouched by the perils of, say, brushing past a dusty surface, being creased during a hedonistic bout of sitting down or becoming infinitesimally scuffed on the pavement during a careless walk down the street, all of which causes the ever-present adult female contingent to go into paroxysms of horror and start grating away at your tender person with balled-up tissues and spit.

If you had patent leather shoes, the need to keep their glowing patina unblemished meant your life was effectively over.

7. ... you discover a talent for undetectable cruelty.

If you are an only child, you may have to wait until you are of a fairly advanced age and at school before you realise quite how fantastically nasty you can be. How you can size up people's strengths and weaknesses and manipulate and exploit them to your own advantage. How you can discern and analyse people's hopes, desires, intentions and motivations and then bend them remorselessly to your will.

If you have brothers and sisters, however, you can start exercising this gift as soon as they are old enough to have strengths, weaknesses et al and understand your simple, concise and entirely self-serving instructions. Sibling rivalry is a wonderful spur to a girl's emotional and mental development.

It makes sound evolutionary sense to hate any sibling, of course. Lodged deep in the primitive parts of our brains and only patchily overlaid with a veneer of civilisation is the knowledge that parental resources are customarily scarce and best concentrated on – how can I put this? Oh yes – me! Me! I was here first! Me!

When that sibling is a sister, it makes even more sense because she is even more direct competition. Hardwired into her are the same charms and tricks you have for getting round your parents and securing more than your fair share of stuff. You may have worked out that you are not huddled beneath wolfskins in a Cornish cave, wishing someone would hurry up and invent fire, but comfortably ensconced in a centrally heated terraced house in an affluent, post-industrial world, but your primordial instincts will smoothly focus instead on securing luxuries like sweets and favouritism now that the basic necessities for survival have been met.

Rivalrous brothers have things relatively simple. They wrestle (literally) for dominance throughout childhood and the one who ends up the biggest/ tallest/most heavily muscled/sexually experienced adult wins. Throw a sister – or worse, two – into the mix and things lose such enviable clarity.

I was modestly resentful of my sister, but my depredations upon her person* were, I discover now, as nothing to the roiling hatred other girls brought to bear upon new interloping siblings. You think Amy throwing the only copy of Jo's handwritten manuscript on the fire was an admirably perceptive and economical way to wreak her revenge? Then

---

* I invented the Drinking Game. It is intended to cause the younger sister's death by drowning and works like this:

Younger Sister lies in bed.

Older Sister says, 'Let's play the Drinking Game.'

Younger Sister has played the Drinking Game before, but is on a very gentle learning curve and so agrees to participate again.

Older Sister holds the two bottom corners of the pillow under Younger Sister's chin, essentially trapping her head in a noose-cum-vice.

She reminds Younger Sister that in this game Younger Sister is not allowed to move her arms.

Younger Sister agrees.

Older Sister reflects briefly on fathomless stupidity of Younger.

Older Sister proceeds to feed water from plastic cup into Younger Sister's mouth.

Older Sister speeds up process of feeding water into Younger Sister's mouth until Younger Sister is desperate, choking head in sodden pillow-vice.

Older Sister becomes so weak with laughter that she is unfortunately required to desist before Younger Sister actually drowns.

Younger Sister spends next few hours clearing water from her lungs and the rest of the night sleeping in a puddle. Older Sister initially regrets failure to drown her, but in later years comes to appreciate a lifetime not spent at Her Majesty's Pleasure.

you can only admire the youthful achievement of the work colleague who once told me that she covered her sister's soft toys with an inch-thick layer of grease from the garage. 'I told her I'd waterproofed them for her, but really it was so that she couldn't hug them,' she said. So she not only devastated her sister but put herself beyond punishment or reproach in the process. Amy, you are but an amateur in the field. 'How very inventive of you,' I replied appreciatively, making a mental note never to piss her off lest she skewer my cats, pin them to the front door and claim that she was saving me litter money. Another friend has a story about how every night she used to open the window of the room she shared with her little sister and then sleep outside on the landing, hoping that the toddler would be stolen by a burglar in the night. In the morning she would close the window and be back in bed before her parents got up.

So, brothers quickly establish the day's pecking order by bashing each other a few times, while sisters concoct plans for family domination via Swarfega-covered rabbits, burglar baiting and rudimentary forms of Chinese water torture. This is the dark side of the famed emotional intelligence of the female, I suppose. More fun though.

Nowadays, as I get older and can see more clearly into the black chasm of mortality that confronts us all, I am actively pleased to have a sister. In fact, I'd quite like to have more – more people to help maintain a sense of continuity through life, more hands to pull you back from the brink at those times when you feel yourself about to fall into the abyss, shared keepers of the collective cache of childhood memories. On the other hand of course, you may feel that a second person with knowledge of the collection of woes, humiliations, unrequited loves and misguided hairstylings that make up the average girl's youth is easily one person too many, especially if you haven't guarded yourself against unauthorised dissemination of such information by terrorising her into silence or cutting her tongue out beforehand.

8. ... you are persuaded that activities of mind-numbing tedium are a valuable and appropriate use of your time.

Looking back on the average girl's childhood from an adult perspective frequently ends in loud howls of pain. Severe mental distress can occur when you think of the vast tracts of time spent labouring at the 'hobbies' adults decreed should fill a young girl's days. Listed below are the main enforced pastimes which bounded a girl's life experiences as effectively as Valium did for the women a generation before us – it's a cut-out-and-keep guide in case you ever have daughters of your own and wish to pass on the gift of wasted hours.

FRENCH KNITTING

Hooking wool over a four-pronged bobbin until you go cross-eyed with boredom produces a long, knitted worm. And that. Is. It. No one has ever found a consequent use for this and I suspect the whole procedure was invented by a man in ages past as a way of keeping girls occupied when they might otherwise have been learning to read, agitating for votes, splitting the atom or curing cancer. One friend of mine insists that if you coil the worms up and add a few stitches here and there they make good coasters, but this sounds to me like the desperate ramblings of a woman driven mad by overexposure to the bobbin from hell.

POMPOM-MAKING

You take two doughnut rings of card and wind wool round them. As the hole gets smaller, it becomes more difficult to pass the wool through. Weak-minded girls will begin to weep with frustration at this point and must be cajoled or beaten – with a bobbin if the beater is truly sadistically inclined – in order to finish.

When the hole is gone, you cut the wool at the outer edges of the ring, tie a length between the rings, pull the pieces of cardboard off and lo! You have a pompom and a pointless life. I suppose an enterprising child these days could stick them in a basket, call it Monument to Futility and win herself the Turner Prize, but Emily and I just used to stare at them for a while and give them to Grandma next time she came down. When she died a few years ago, my greatest fear was that she had left them all to us in her will, but luckily she left us a million pounds each instead. No, not really. I got the bread bin and Emily got the cheeseboard, which was great as it enabled us to fulfil a long-held ambition to found the Museum of Damaged 1950s Culinary Artefacts.

FLOWER PRESSING

This was a favourite occupation of young Victorian ladies. They needed blotting paper, some heavy books and TB. These days the TB is optional, but your daughters will need to find out from the internet what blotting paper and books are, order some and within five to seven working days, they will be ready to press flowers.

You've got them? Excellent. Put one book on the floor. Put a sheet of blotting paper on top. Put your flower on top of that. If you haven't got a flower, you really should have thought of that before you started.

Right. Put another sheet of blotting paper on top of your stupid flower. Put on top of that as many heavy books as you can find. Now wait. I know this is hard in an age in which MTV defines attention spans in terms of picoseconds, but in my day we would happily wait weeks for excitement to come along, even if it did tend to be confined to the appearance of Tufty the Road Safety Squirrel at a local fête.

After a month or so, remove the books and blotting paper and take out your flower. Disappointing, isn't it? Just be grateful you're not coughing up blood.

MAKING A WENDY HOUSE

A few sheets of yellow, blue and red plastic, a handful of hollow plastic rods and eight or nine weeks of half-hearted labour from the nearest adult was all it took to erect this monument to domesticity.

Because at this point political correctness and the dangers of imposing sexual stereotypes on innocent children had yet to be invented, every playgroup (and a few lucky homes) had a Wendy house. Girls flocked to it and the boys hurled Plasticine at it from the climbing frame and pretended it gave you the lurgy.

Very lucky Wendy House owners (I never met one – I thought of them as mythical beasts, like unicorns or sober grandmothers) had theirs fully equipped with a tea set, a pretend oven and a copious supply of flour and water dough with which to make pretend buns, loaves and – if it was a pathologically imaginative child – pork chops to serve to envious friends.

MAKING A TELEPHONE

Take two yoghurt pots and a piece of string. Put the string inside the yoghurt pots and throw the lot in the bin. The string telephone has never worked in the history of time and it is a mystery how it ever came to be a staple activity of even the most chronically entertainment-deprived, pre-electronic childhood.

Instead, children today would be better advised to take two drink cartons – low sugar Ribena, Sainsbury's fruit juice or Sunny D, depending on how little attention your parents pay to your nutritional intake – stick the straws in and draw buttons on the front of the boxes. Go to a crowded public place and shout into your fake Nokia Twat1000 as loudly as you can. By the time you get a real mobile phone, you will be a pro.

CAT'S CRADLE

Take a loop of string or a shoelace. If you don't know what a shoelace is because all you have ever known are Velcro fastenings on trainers (tomboys) or strappy shoes with diamanté buckles (embryonic slag), ask your gran. She ate a lot of them during the war and will still be stockpiling them in case of future shortages.

Wind the loop round your hands twice. Put your middle finger through the opposite band, do something else and then do something else and you will have had an experience that will teach you much about the tangled nature of life and the essential futility of existence. If you require further proof, you can always try making Chinese lanterns.

THE BROWNIES

You join the Brownies for one of two reasons. Either all your friends are doing it and you want to do it too (the kind of reasoning that will see you giving handjobs to not very good-looking adolescent boys in nightclubs just a few short years later), or your parents notice that you have no friends, never stopping to think that this might have something to do with the fact that they have spent the last few years convincing you that a set of yoghurt pots on a string are all you need to construct a wholly fulfilling existence, and you will look up from your pompoms to find yourself in another draughty church hall filled with splintery chairs and cold children* wearing little brown dresses, big brown belts and an assortment of regimental decoration.

---

* Everybody's childhood was punctuated with these places. First playgroup, then Brownies and not long after that it would be host to that brutal adolescent boxing ring, the youth club. No wonder our generation never took to religion.

· · ✴ · · ·

Displaying an unexpected predilection for the trappings of pseudo-military organisations, I took to the little yellow tie and chunky metal trefoil straight away. Wearing them was easy, seemed to please people and got me counted as one of a gang – albeit a gang that spent an inordinate amount of time sitting round a plaster toadstool – with minimal effort on my part, so why not? I daresay that's the kind of attitude that in a different place and time would have led me into hemming shirts for the Reichstag, but fortunately any fascists that existed in early-eighties Lewisham had yet to mobilise themselves into a cohesive corps.

Actually, I would probably have been saved from becoming a war criminal by my inability to care about badges, those sturdy triangles of webbed-backed fabric that you could earn for knot-tying, campfire-building and tea-making. Of course, some concessions to the modern age and non-rural location had to be made. Nobody in our unrelentingly suburban environment got to try for the campfire badge. I remember a Sixer trying to argue that watching her dad bleed a radiator should count towards it, but Brown Owl was a woman of limited vision and passionate attachment to the letter rather than the spirit of the Brownie handbook and busted her down to Seconder for insubordination. There's a life lesson or two, right there.

· · ✴ · · ·

Once the novelty of the uniform and trefoil wears off, however, a girl's underlying temperament will reassert itself. If you are the active, gregarious type, you will throw yourself into Brownie life – visiting old people, going on educative and character-building weekend trips, cheerfully letting yourself be used as cheap labour by Brown Owl when she needs her garden digging or bathroom regrouting – and soon you will earn enough badges to render you unable to lift your arms from your sides. Then you join the Guides and start all over again, but in blue.

The rest – in which, I confess, I must include my team-spiritless and badge-free self – last about a month. By the end of those four weeks, I was spending the ninety-minute session huddled under the toadstool, a little brown lump as solid and immobile as a turd and marginally less rewarding to have around, so I was asked to leave.

I understand that things are quite different in the Brownies these days. For a start, it's all yellow sweatshirts with screen-printed trefoils, brown trousers and trainers. God knows what they get badges for. Tying knots in local paedophiles' genitalia and making Slippery Nipple cocktails instead of tea, I suspect. And I assume they carry hip flasks of WKD Blue instead of emergency ten pence pieces in their money belts. I can't help but feel something's been lost.

9. ... your early attempts at socialising fail.

Ironically, the occasions on which you broke free of your cat's cradle responsibilities and streaked out into the world, eager to drink of its delights, frequently became the stuff of nightmares. This is because you were leaving the house to attend another girl's birthday party. Few are without the psychic wounds inflicted by their first attendance at such an event.

The trauma begins a week before, when your mother takes you to buy party shoes. Not, it turns out, the strappy, pink, diamanté confections you hold in your mind's eye, but the kind of indestructible, black patent leather efforts from Clarks that remind you only of the callipers worn by all the saintly crippled orphans in your *Mandy* stories. You may admire the look on Angel the Consumptive Guardian of Eighty-two Workhouse Refugees in a Stable, but legitimately doubt its appropriateness for a lengthy game of musical chairs. Add to this your mother's idea of party clothes – itchy kilt and woolly tights up to the armpits, topped off with a polyester polo-neck to make sure that sweat drips non-stop from every pore – and you begin to sense that the day cannot end well.

You arrive at the house of fun and are tipped into a back garden full of little girls who are more bow than hair, more flounce than flesh and more delighted with the arrival of the kilt-clad cretin in their midst than words can say. They encircle you like wolves round a limping fawn. To this day, I remember the rising sound of mocking giggles. 'That's ... nice,' said some little tyke whose name eludes me, although the hatred remains as fresh today as it was in that moment. Her friend – Alice Bitchface-McFarthead I believe was her name – moved forward and tugged my jumper. 'My dress,' she said loudly, 'is *pretty*.' 'Yes,' I wish I'd replied. 'But you have a face like a bum.' But I didn't. I sat in the corner for the rest of the afternoon instead, trying in vain to get drunk on Panda Pops, while the frilly tribe carried on their celebrations without me.

This, in a nutshell, is the problem with girls. An oddly dressed boy would either have been punched by his peers until he reached a state of bearable dishevelment, or mercifully ignored for the duration. Girls revert to bitchery as soon as an opportunity presents itself. Little boys have to be monitored 24-7 because unsupervised they'll kill each other. Girls have to be watched constantly in case they drive each other to suicide.

All in all, it was a relief when the weekends and evenings ended and it was time to go back to school or bed. I perhaps wouldn't have minded the enforced wool-work if we had been unable to see from the sitting room window all the neighbourhood boys our age* careening round on their BMXs, setting up dens in the crumbling house on the corner and generally making a vibrant noise and taking up space, while we were forever being encouraged to sit properly and keep quiet. I firmly believe that it is pompoms and French knitting that are to blame for most of the sexual inequities that pervade later life. Why do women still get paid less than men for doing the same jobs? Because part of us is secretly, eternally so grateful to have the chance to be frigging about with spreadsheets instead of yarn for eight hours a day that we will put up with anything. In addition, everyone knows that pay rises and promotions go to those who shout loudest for them. Years spent hunched over cat's cradles and waiting for flowers to dehydrate is hardly the best preparation for barging to the front of the career queue and making our feelings known.

This is an exaggeration, of course. There is no direct connection between girls' hobbies and the glass ceiling. But there is an indirect one, even if it's only that girls who put up with this mind-numbing tedium (like me) will put up with a lot more crap at work and elsewhere when they grow up. Forget – according to your age and nationality – the Eleven-plus, end-of-year exams, SAT scores and all the academically diagnostic rest. I bet you can tell at least as much about a girl's chances of success in the future by the amount of time she can spend playing cat's cradle before trying to hang herself with it from the doorknob instead.

---

* That makes it sound like there were hundreds of them. There were, in fact, only a handful – it was a quiet terraced street in suburban England after all, not a scene from *The Kids of Degrassi Street* – but enough to incur a certain amount of jealousy and frustration if you were on the wrong side of the net curtains.

10. ... you have a complicated relationship with your idols.

Boys admire superheroes, footballers and aeroplanes – things with measurable, visible, concrete, indisputable, universally recognised talents. This is why they collect comics, Panini stickers and Top Trumps, and this is where the relationship begins and ends. Where is a girl to look for idols and heroines? Even the best of the options on display over the years seem flawed in various important ways.

The Top 10 Heroines

NUMBER 1: WONDER WOMAN

Boys get Batman, Spiderman, Superman, the X-Men, the Hulk and Captain America, who can leap tall buildings in a single bound, see through walls, burn things with their laser eyebeams, drive heavily accessorised Batmobiles, live in Fortresses of Solitude, possess self-healing properties allowing near-immortality, razor-sharp retractable claws, super-soldierdom, super-athletic prowess and the ability to shoot webs from their very flesh, to the awe and amazement of generations. They are reinvented according to the needs of each new age and immortalised in print, multitudinous films and internationally-renowned television series.

What do we have? Wonder Woman and her Lasso of Truth and bullet-proof bracelets. She is essentially a woman with Kevlar accessories and a piece of rope. No wonder the only time she ever really penetrated the public consciousness was during the seventies TV show starring Lynda Carter, and that was only because dads slavered over Carter, while their daughters became enraptured with the twirling Diana Prince morphing into a woman with a fabulous bustier and golden accoutrements. It falls a little short of being encouraged to feel that you too could become the living embodiment of truth, justice and the American way.

On the other hand, there's no denying the fact that, given a straight choice, most women would prefer to be able to carry off high-heeled boots and a tiara than save the world. A world in which you cannot accessorise successfully is, after all, hardly a world worth saving.

NUMBERS 2–4: CHARLIE'S ANGELS

Three female private investigators get sent on undercover missions by an
unseen yet all-powerful boss. They use a combination of peerless mastery of
data (gathered to help them blend into their new situation as roller girls/beauty
pageant contestants/denim hotpants testers/curling tong spokesmodels) and
going bra-less in order to succeed. These are not the most enlightened messages
to be sending to impressionable young female viewers, but when you happen to
have cast three women who look so very good in denim hotpants, it does seem a
waste not to use the fact.

The Angels did teach us one genuinely valuable lesson, however – namely that
where any three women are gathered together in a group, one will be labeled
the sexy one, another the pretty one and the brownest-haired the ugly one. Thus
the viewer can learn early the value of staying far away from other women at all
times and of hitting the peroxide bottle as soon as possible.

NUMBER 5: ALEXIS COLBY

Or, to give her her full name, Alexis Morrell Carrington Colby Dexter. Unlike
drunk and quivery Sue Ellen Ewing in Dallas or her fellow *Dynasty* star Krystle
'Total Drip' Carrington, Alexis MCCD was in many ways an excellent role model –
ruthless, no-nonsense, entrepreneurial, a nice line in mocking condescension
and entirely without mercy to anyone younger, weaker or poorer than she. But
she did suggest that you could only get away with this if your shoulders were
wider than you were tall, you spent half your income and working day reapplying
eyeliner and lip gloss with a hose and didn't move your neck. It remains to be
calculated how many working hours were lost to injury by real women who tried
to emulate her trademark full-body pivot on four-inch heels whenever anyone
came in the door, instead of simply turning their heads, but it must run into the
millions. Icons should be aware of the extent of their power and use it for good,
not osteopathic evil.

NUMBER 6: BUFFY SUMMERS

Some say she is a feminist icon, an action heroine blessed with magical physical
strength, deadly martial arts skills and a higher calling to save mankind, not
just from individual villains, but from ancient malevolences bent on apocalyptic

destruction. She is also odds-on favourite every year for the Dana Scully Athleticism and Accessories award for her ability to pursue supernatural beasts through chiaroscuro sewers in three-inch heels and still change outfits eighteen times an hour.

Others insist that she is an academically underachieving, chronically underweight popsy whose preferred ambition of high-school popularity has only been thwarted by the unwanted advent of her special slayer powers. If she's the designated aspirational figure for young women, they say, we're just going to end up with an awful lot of broken ankles and disillusioned schoolgirls.

However, while Buffy may have her issues, we must lob into the mix:

- Her loyalty: her friends may rip her out of heaven, murder people by tearing off their skins in a Wiccan frenzy in the woods and in Angel/David Boreanaz's case insist on hanging around long after his neck has grown disconcertingly thicker than his head, but Buffy will stand by them.
- Her ability to betray sacred callings by having repeated sex with vampires, which speaks of an admirable independence of spirit and immunity to peer and watcher pressure.
- Her hair – which is just lovely.

On balance, I think we can all agree, Buffy is a girl who seems more than most to be coping with the complex nature and multiplicity of responsibilities and obligations that dog a lady's life these days, and for this we must salute her. Even if we do not always agree with her choice of thickly-lashed freshmen shags.

NUMBER 7: DANA SCULLY

Well, she can't have an award named after her without her being a heroine in her own right. Doctor Dana Scully, for your services to scepticism, for your valiant attempts to prick the bubbles of Mulder's ego hard and often, for the gradual evolution of your style, from oversized pastel blazers and voluminous skirts in the pilot to Armani suits and boots by season five, for your cool intelligence, your fearlessness, your implacable, empirical evidence-gathering nature, your refusal to use feminine wiles or change your facial expression under any circumstances, we salute you even more than we do Buffy, as you do all this not only without ever (or almost without ever) giving in to your partner's virile animal magnetism, but also without a murmur of complaint ever passing your lips about the burden of gingerdom that you so stoically bear.

NUMBER 8: MARILYN MONROE

She's all women had in the fifties, you know. Abused, crazed, idolised, exploited, talented, tragic Marilyn. So gorgeous that it made your eyes hurt to look at her, manipulative as Machiavelli, vulnerable as a skinned rabbit. An ordinary woman couldn't live up to her in a million lifetimes. She was the greatest star of her or any other age, the embodiment of female sexuality and male fantasy. If she'd just been slightly less unhinged, she could have conquered the world.

NUMBER 9: MADONNA

She conquered the eighties and most of the nineties. She's got more money and muscles than God. She has been in complete control of her entire life since she left the womb. It's not a bad way to be. You might want to leave out the Kabbalah though. It works better in California than Croydon.

NUMBER 10: DOLLY PARTON

A few facts about Dolly.

- She's been playing guitar and writing songs since she was one of twelve barefoot Parton toddlers running round a one-room shack in the Smokey Mountains, Tennessee.
- She's been a star since she was ten.
- With no business training, she knew enough from day one to keep the rights to every song she ever wrote, even turning down Elvis Presley when he wanted to record 'I Will Always Love You' in 1974 because his manager insisted that Elvis always got half the rights to anything he covered. This has made her a multi-multi-multi-millionaire and earned her the nickname 'The Iron Butterfly' – a fine soubriquet to which we should all aspire.
- She is a songwriting genius.
- She built a theme park in her hometown to provide work for her family and bring money to the region. And she called it Dollywood.
- She has been married to the same man, Carl Dean, for forty years. When asked for her secret to a happy marriage, she replied, 'I stay gone!', a valuable corrective to all those tweeting fools who would have us believe that a state of complete interdependence and physical proximity at all times offers the only true happiness in a relationship, when in fact it is the one thing guaranteed to make you want to pistolwhip each other til the blood flows in rivers.

- If you look closely and have a reasonable comprehension of the basic laws of physics, you can see that her commitment to breast augmentation and six-inch heels means that she now stays upright through sheer force of will alone.
- She is entirely magnificent in every way.

Overall, however, I think we can agree that while life as a girl has its problems and its pitfalls, it still beats being a boy by a comfortable margin. You might have to make do with Farrah Fawcett instead of Captain America and spend your early years wrestling with woolly worms, but at least you will never have to go to war or spend your entire life trying to communicate through the medium of hitting and Top Trumps. We, in short and in all the ways that really matter, rule.

CHAPTER 2

Mother, Dear

For girls, life is divided between having a mother and being a mother, each a state of affairs frequently so appalling it is a wonder we don't make our way en masse to the woods every night to howl in pain at the moon.

10 Lies Your Mother Tells You

1. It doesn't hurt
2. It's only a game
3. Debbie's mother doesn't let her stay up to watch *Maverick*
4. It's a lovely party dress and everybody will want one
5. It's all perfectly normal
6. They'll grow
7. I never made this kind of fuss when I was growing up
8. You'll look back on this when you're older and laugh
9. He's out there somewhere
10. You'll meet him when the time is right

So, one way or another, maternity is going to cast a dark shadow over your entire life. From the first moment of consciousness, the looming, all-seeing, all-knowing form of your own mother dominates. From the minute you are born she can see directly into your soul and use whatever she finds there to bend you to her will for the next fifteen years until you and your hormones eventually begin to assert themselves. From then on you are firmly locked in a bitter psychological struggle for independence and supremacy.

If you are lucky, you may enjoy a few brief years of freedom from the grasping tentacles of motherlove before they begin to stir somewhere in the fathomless primaeval depths of your own psyche and you start casting round for someone with whom to produce a baby of your own so that the whole infernal circle can start again.

Let us begin, therefore, with the mother–daughter relationship as we first experience it – from the bottom.

Mothers and daughters

As any sociology, psychology or self-help book will tell you, the relationship between a child and its mother is the most powerful and influential one you will ever have. And how could it not be? She is, after all, responsible for bringing you into the world after eighteen hours of agonising labour (this period will expand and contract over the years, depending on whether you are in or out of favour at the time) and you spend the first few years of the life she graciously bestowed upon you entirely dependent on her. She controls the food supplies, the nappy supplies and the central heating. It is on her that you rely for shelter, teaching and protection and without her there is every possibility that you will starve to death at the hands of a loving but clueless father.

That's if my own is anything to go by. Legend has it that Mum once left my six-month-old self in Dad's care for a few hours while she went to John Lewis, or to solve the Middle East peace crisis or something, and came back to find him trying to feed me egg and chips as I lay in my pram looking frankly perturbed by the disquieting turn life had suddenly taken and the likelihood of it ending imminently in a flurry of choking sounds and infant convulsions.

Just what kind of food, shelter, teachings and protection are on offer depends on the type of mother you have been vouchsafed by whatever whimsical god it is who is in charge of these things.

Earth Mother

Earth Mother has overlong hair, a baby a year till her uterus prolapses, and a tendency towards hairy facial warts in later life. She wears homemade skirts with elasticated waists and sports floury streaks about her person at all times, which say proudly to the world, 'I've just finished making sixteen batches of caraway and rye bread, kneading my overflowing maternal instinct into each softly yielding loaf and baking them in the warm Aga of my soul. And what have you done today, Mrs Sunblest?'

These powdery badges of honour are the only dry things about her. Her hair is permanently greasy because she's too busy being available to her children to wash it, and she is always leaking from one orifice or another. Either she's nursing a new arrival or she's crying over the beauty of nature/the suffering of the planet/the purity of little Hummusella's tinkling laugh or she's menstruating heavily (earth mothers can bleed for Britain) and only using looped towels because a) tampons are unnatural and b) she's an idiot.

The bread, incidentally, goes with her homemade soups, all of which her children hate, partly because they taste foul and partly because lumpy soup with visible veg means that they cannot have friends round for tea without becoming the outcasts of Tyke Primary. Wait till they find out it's all made with placenta stock.

Neurotic Mother

She has one child. She is slightly thinner than the carrot sticks she nibbles all day. She can't eat because she is in a constant state of panic. Her mind is crowded with images of disaster befalling her precious infant. She buys smoke alarms and baby monitors by the dozen and uses the latter until her child is thirty-two.

If she has a son, he rebels against this by becoming a knife-juggling bungee jumper. If she has a daughter, she internalises her mother's anxieties and spends her life developing an obsessive-compulsive disorder and waiting for a jet engine to fall onto the house from a passing plane.

Feminist Mother

It probably does a girl good to be raised by one of these, provided that she can control her missionary zeal and in the rush to start dismantling the patriarchal order does not take the empowerment of her daughter too far. It's disconcerting to be confronted by a five-year-old pointing at her knickers and saying proudly, 'That's my vagina.' If presented with such a situation, immediate correction is required. 'No, it's not,' you reply firmly. 'It's your foo-foo. And it's disgusting. Now go away.'

Martyr Mother

Her mantra is 'After all I've done for you … !' Martyr Mummy's children are in no doubt as to the extent of the sacrifices she has made for them. These may be real – perhaps she did indeed give up a lucrative career in oil derivatives or wave goodbye to a fabulously glamorous yacht-and-international-playboy-based lifestyle – but more often than not they are entirely imagined. The dedicated MM convinces herself (and more importantly, her children) that she turned her back on a Hollywood career, a Royal marriage and multi-million-dollar modelling contracts in order to bring them forth into the world, and makes them pay for it in the coin of guilt and awe for the rest of their lives.

Most of said children end up killing themselves or their mothers unless they find themselves a very good therapist very early on.

Yummy Mummy

While the Yummy Mummy may be wholly admirable from an adult point of view (why, after all, should a woman abandon her sexuality and allure just because she has produced a few anklebiters along the way if she has been blessed with that rare mix of energy and elasticity that enables her to bounce back from the procedure?), her children are a mess. An overly attractive mother, whether deliberately so or in a just-can't-help-myself-I-was-born-this-femme-fataley-way, is an impossible burden for a child. Her sons are destined to spend their teenage years surrounded by friends who, fifteen-year-old testosterone levels being what they are, clearly want to shag her, which is more than enough to drive him into the sweet embrace of drink and drugs.

For the daughter of a Yummy Mummy, things are naturally much worse. She labours forever under the multiple psychological burdens induced by having a mother who looks better in a bikini than she does and the deeply corrosive knowledge that if Yummy M so chose, she could pluck her boyfriend from her in a heartbeat. There are enough sexual complexities in life without having to compete for male attention with your mother. It seems only fair that by the time you are entering into adolescence either her face or her libido (and ideally both) should have collapsed, leaving you to take part in a fair fight with your peers in the sexual arena.

The only thing a girl in this situation can do is either remove herself from the competition entirely, via heavy tattooing, disturbing piercings and the careful cultivation of a pungent body odour, or take the fight directly to Yummy M by embarking on a rigorous programme of seducing every middle-aged man within a twenty-mile radius. This is likely to result in either a police investigation or the kind of internecine sexual feuding that makes the Borgias look like the Waltons, but at least either will add some spice to the traditional dish of adolescent tantrums.

Still, even the yummiest mummies have it less easy than they once did. In this, as in so much else, celebrities have raised the bar almost beyond the reach of mere mortals.

Celebrity Mother

Of course a celebrity may avoid the physical imperfections traditionally associated with pregnancy and childbirth by choosing not to incubate a baby herself, but to write a cheque to an African orphanage or pop one in her handbag as she passes through Hanoi on a comeback tour instead. But others* step out six weeks after the birth, having spent longer with the personal trainer than with the wailing newborn, with concave stomachs, breasts pointing to the stars instead of their ankles and less subcutaneous fat than you would find on a Quorn chop. In

---

* With the ever honourable exceptions of Kate Winslet and Catherine Zeta Jones, who alone insist that even famous new mothers are allowed the odd bag of crisps now and again.

fact, I've had bananas with a higher BMI than most celebrities emerging from Portland Place ten minutes after expelling their babies from the womb.

Good celebrity mothering mostly involves securing Elton John as godfather, giving your child the kind of name that under ordinary circumstances would constitute child abuse (Apple, for Christ's sake? *Apple?*), establishing a trust fund that will take care of its future educational, wardrobe and rehab needs and getting the timing of baby's first photoshoot right. This can be tricky. Too soon and you look desperate and exploitative, à la Geri Halliwell, who had Bluebell Madonna (really, did no one call Social Services about that? No one?) wiped down, buffed up and plastered over 867 pages of *Hello!* before the infant had managed her first feed. Proper celebrities – by which I mean, of course, American celebrities – withhold the baby from the public gaze until it has lost that dazed and crumpled look of someone recently wrenched from uterine safety, curiosity has reached fever pitch and they can then generously release a handful of carefully vetted shots to the highest bidder.

After that, the Celebrity Mother just has to maintain her good reputation by repeating a handful of stock phrases to magazines over the years and hope that no one ever translates them accurately:

'Motherhood has taught me so much about life/love/myself.'

MOTHERHOOD HAS TAUGHT ME THAT I CAN GET STRETCH MARKS LIKE ANY MERE MORTAL AND I RUE THE DAY I EVER LET MY PERSONAL TRAINER TOUCH ME WITH ANYTHING OTHER THAN PROFESSIONAL DISINTEREST.

'I just feel so much more deeply connected to the world.'

I'VE HAD TO STOP TAKING DRUGS.

'I've stopped working because I can't bear to be away from her.'

NO ONE WILL HIRE ME BECAUSE THEY THINK I AM A WALKING BAG OF FAT AND HORMONES, EVEN THOUGH IN FACT I HAD BOTH SUCKED OUT WHILE THE BABY WAS HAVING ITS FIRST NAPPY CHANGE.

'I've always told her not to go into the business, but she's such an incredible actress. I could not be more proud.'

I'VE ALWAYS TOLD HER NOT TO GO INTO THE BUSINESS BECAUSE THE THREAT OF HER SUPPLANTING ME AS A SCREEN ICON AWAKENS THE SCREAMING EGOMANIACAL BEAST WITHIN WHICH WILL ONE DAY SLIP THE TATTERED LEASH OF MY CONSCIOUS CONTROL, LEAP OUT AND TEAR HER LIMB FROM LIMB. I COULD NOT BE MORE TENUOUSLY LINKED TO SANITY.

Economy Mother

Some mothers, of course, are thrifty through force of circumstance. My grandma, for example, was widowed at thirty-three. As she and her late husband had been single-income practicing Catholics, she was left with eighty-two fatherless children under seven and half a crown to feed them with until they were old enough to work their own Spinning Jennies down t'mill. She fed them mince and oxtail for the next twelve years and at Christmas wrapped up the week's groceries as presents and put them back in the larder on Boxing Day.

My Auntie Judy still reminisces mistily about the pound of sugar she once owned for twenty-four hours, but then she's not had a happy life. Instead of money, Grandma used her ingenuity and impressive powers of persuasion to supply the family entertainments. She convinced her own children that there could be no greater pleasure wrung from the summer holidays than by digging a giant hole in the garden and filling it in again. They danced Scottish reels while she played the piano and churned butter with her feet. She organised endless family competitions and obstacle races in the garden. The lucky winners got a drink of water from the unchipped mug, and a look at the butter.

For others, however, raising children without spending any money is a choice and assumes the form of a moral imperative. Just as Shakespeare imposed the challenge of iambic pentameter on himself – so that he was forced to come up with: 'My salad days, when I was green in judgment, cold in blood to say as I said then!' for Cleopatra, rather than: 'Christ, if I'd known then what I know now, I'd do things a bit fucking differently, eh, Charmian?' – the self-confessed Economy Mum bravely refuses to let any financial ease and security obscure the opportunities to teach her children valuable life lessons. Thus, during my childhood, ruled as it was by the Economy Mum par excellence, butter was for grown-ups and margarine was for kids. In this way, her daughters were gently schooled in the knowledge of their inferior citizenry and able to look forward to that great day when they would not only be allowed to vote but also start stoking their cholesterol levels with dollops of the good stuff. An indispensable lesson in deferred gratification, without which, as I'm sure you're all aware, there can be no true enjoyment of life.

ECONOMY MOTHER RECIPES

These family recipes, scratched by my distaff relatives on the backs of used envelopes and social workers' reports, have been handed down through three generations of pathologically parsimonious women. Enjoy.

Pork in Tomato

Buy some pork.
  Add a tin of Campbell's condensed tomato soup.
  Don't add seasoning. The children's tears will salt it sufficiently.
  Serve with potatoes to howling screams of protest.

Mince in Oxtail

First, catch your mince.

If you've got visitors, brown the mince and add a chopped onion and carrot. If not, don't bother browning and sell the veg.

Add a tin of Campbell's condensed oxtail soup.

Cook for four hours or until the children faint from lack of nourishment.

Feeds five children for between three and eight days, depending on whether the rent's due. If it starts to leak out of their ears before then, switch to:

Chicken in Mushroom

Kill the nearest chicken.

Get the butcher to joint it in return for a look at your ankles. Or bra strap if you've bad ankles or it's a big chicken.

Add bacon pieces if it's Christmas or the butcher got overexcited by the bra strap.

Add a tin of Campbell's condensed mushroom soup.

Buy shares in Campbell's.

Serve with potatoes and the promise of a better life far, far away from here.

Economy Mums are a dying breed now. As children become more label-conscious, assertive and, oh yes, greedy, getting away with buying own brand cola (or, for those who are less concerned with their children's salt levels than with their continuing moral development, water with a spoonful of gravy browning in it) or biscuits (or no biscuits at all until they're eighteen and can buy their own) becomes more difficult. As they watch more and more adverts for credit cards, consolidated loans and AVA agreements to save you from bankruptcy if things do go tits up, it becomes impossible to convince them that you really can't afford something. Unless, of course, you are an Economy Mum to the very marrow, in which case you will have long ago sold the television and put your children to work in the fields.

Control Freak Mother

This is the mother who thinks of the house less as a place where the family can range in happy domesticity than as a form of open prison in which the inhabitants and their activities can be under her constant surveillance. She cruises the floors continuously in order to assuage the fear that one of her charges might one day leave and develop a mind of its own. Her children either become voracious readers, escaping into the gloriously unbounded world of books, or they become mental cases.

I first realised how large a streak of control freakery ran through my own mother when I was seven years old and cut my head open, as seven-year-olds will, on the corner of the drinks cabinet. With a loud squawk, I collapsed to the ground in a haze of blood and pain as Mum came pounding in from the garden. 'Don't get blood on the carpet!' she screamed. 'I don't do floors till Thursday!' I have a dim recollection of her dragging me outside and letting me bleed freely in the garden because it was good for the soil, but as I was all but comatose by then, I can't be sure.

Other signs that your mother is an unregenerate control freak:

❧ *She can have an apoplectic fit over the fact that the napkins on the breakfast table are facing the wrong way. 'Rambling rose motif faces north-north-west, you mangy curs! How many times do I have to tell you?' will be her epitaph.*

❧ *And you look forward to the day you have to carve it.*

❧ *The napkins are there because the table is laid for breakfast shortly before lunch, which you have to eat over the sink at midday or, ideally, throw straight in the bin to avoid dirtying the plates.*

❧ *You are not allowed pets because they mess up the house.*

❧ *You are not allowed friends because they mess up the house AND undermine the tyrant's power by having you round to tea at their houses, which reveals to you that a life in which you don't have complete Form 43a in triplicate and submit it on the third Monday of the month to the House Crumb-producing Activities Committee before you unwrap a Crunchie not only exists but does not necessarily lead to international chaos and global anarchy.*

❦ *You admire her energy even as you cleave to the certainty that it could be better spent doing almost anything other than folding said rose-embroidered napkins with a ruler and a set square.*

❦ *You dream not of going to university or becoming famous but of living under an assumed name at an undisclosed address where she can never find you again and where you will raise your children as free and independent beings, while remembering always that although consistency and discipline may be the hallmarks of good mothering, this need not mean dragging a semi-conscious child through the house and leaving her to bleed copiously from head wounds in the herbaceous border.*

Supermum

You can recognise this type of mother by the fact that they habitually greet their children home from school with strangely glittering eyes and a buzzing aura of delight. In others this might denote copious drug use, but in Supermum it merely signals that she has reached multitasking nirvana by having:

A load of washing on

While a load of washing dries

While the dishwasher's on

While she mows the lawn

While the fridge defrosts

While the dinner cooks

Which will be ready to eat
When she's finished the lawn.
She will eat her dinner
While the washing finishes
Which will be ready to peg out
By the time
The first washing is dry
While the dishwasher cools down
While she re-fills the fridge
After which she will empty the dishwasher
And fill it with dinner plates
Before she decides to dig up the lawn
And replace it with Astroturf
To cut next Thursday's list by 21.4 minutes
So she can re-plumb the toilet instead.

If she had been born a generation later, Supermum would have become a management consultant, a human dynamo sweeping into global corporations, identifying problems and wastage in nanoseconds and ruthlessly stripping out the dead wood before knocking up a chicken casserole for the forty-two remaining employees who had survived the cull. Concentrated in the home, however, such tireless efficiency can have some counterproductive effects.

Partly because they know that they can never measure up to the fearsomely competent woman before them and partly because their mother's powers of anticipation and pre-emptive problem-solving prevent them from ever needing to develop the capacity for independent thought, Supermum's children become as dull and lazy as mud turtles. Supermum stares with incomprehension and despair at the lumpen fools she has produced. The lumpen fools stare back. Supermum sublimates her rage and disappointment into attaining yet higher levels of hyper-efficiency until she eventually creates her own Supermum event horizon and implodes, leaving only a freezerful of home-baked quiches and a colour-coordinated knicker drawer behind.

Whatever kind of mother you have, whatever kind of warping of her offspring's characters she provides and whatever particular forms of madness she is intent on passing on, there is one thing you can be sure of: as a daughter, this is only the beginning of your problems. As you grow up, you realise that, unlike your brothers or any other male children of your acquaintance, you have been gifted a deluxe set of extra emotional issues which will bind you and your mother together for eternity in a bitter, neverending battle from which there is no escape, no court of appeal against decisions made, no possibility of divorce or amicable separation. Or, if you prefer, like a couple of animals with their teeth embedded in each other's necks, who cannot call a truce and let go without bleeding to death.

The Issues

1. Persistent mental invasion

Not only do you have the blood-and-guts connection with her, she will also purport to be able to read your mind all your life. This is because she 'went through exactly the same thing at your age'. This, to the young, impressionable mind, appears logical, but in fact it is not quite as true as it seems. Mothers of previous generations usefully handed down valuable bits of wisdom about dealing with rakes who tried to impugn a young girl's honour by sitting too close to her on the chaise longue, passed on helpful remedies to deal with that difficult time of the month and tips on how to bury the screaming frustrations of domestic life beneath a veneer of civility and a light dusting of face powder. Nowadays, however, times change too fast and the generation gap is consequently growing at a breathtaking rate. Take, for example, a mother who grew up anywhere in England in the fifties. She wouldn't even have known she was a teenager, for God's sake, and her idea of a good night out for anyone under the age of twenty was a shared bottle of Dandelion and Burdock in the park, a quick game of hunt the meat-and-potato pie – which wasn't even a euphemism – and home before the gas shilling ran out at 10 p.m. When it comes to issuing you with advice on negotiating the more complicated social and sexual mores of, say, eighties London ('Mum, Anne-Marie says that if a boy buys you anything in Pizza Hut, you have to suck him off. What does she mean and do you still have to do it if it's Pizza Express?'), she's going to be at a loss. Although she could place a ban on any more nights round at Anne-Marie's house.

And what will you do when confronted by your own daughter, who arrives home from school saying, 'Kelly-Marie's got a photo on her phone of me taking it up the bum from Simon – Herpes Simon, not HIV Simon – in geography and says she's going to put it on Myspace unless I deposit 38,000 euros in her Swiss account by the end of playtime tomorrow. Have you got anything I can sell on eBay?' You'll probably be even more useless. 'Well, we'll just have to sew your bottom closed so this sort of thing can't happen again, won't we, my girl?'

2. The turning wheel

Although we are now comfortably into the third millennium, there is still more truth than any female offspring would like in the old saw: 'A son's a son till he takes a wife, a daughter's a daughter for all her life.' In other words, boys will always have a blessed degree of distance from their mothers, and mothers spend their entire lives preparing and practising for the day when they will have to let them go, but as a daughter you are your mother's alpha and omega, and she is yours.

You remember how the boys were riding their BMXs round the block while you went cross-eyed over bobbins? Forty years later and this has translated into your mother sending cheery Christmas cards to your brother and his brood in Australia, while putting in six daily phone calls to you to check that you're coming over to watch Where the Heart Is *with her on Sunday. Every Sunday. Twenty years after that, when the old bag's started to go batty as well? It's not your brothers that will be wiping her bum, finding a care home or desperately searching for a sympathetic doctor with a fatal dose of morphine going begging, it'll be you.*

3. Mirror imagery

As that much neglected philosopher Ally Sheedy said in *The Breakfast Club*, we all turn into our parents: 'It's inevitable. Your heart dies.' That's a little extreme, but she was probably suffering from low-grade eyeliner poisoning at the time, so we must forgive her. The wider point is valid. We're all going to turn into our mothers.

Psychotherapists say it's because we internalise the way our mothers relate to the world. The lay person says it's simply a particularly far-reaching case of monkey see, monkey do. The more religiously inclined say it's a sick joke perpetrated upon the innocent by a phalanx of surpassingly cruel and malevolent gods. I say it's all of the above, but with a particularly heavy dash of the third, because more often than not, the victim is aware of the transformation as it is happening and yet is powerless to stop it. And because, with a final twist of the divine dagger, the gods have made it so that you never become like your mother in any good or useful way. Succumb to any tendencies towards neuroticism, alcoholism, hysteria and obsessive-compulsive disorder, yes. Inherit anything in the way of kindly practicality, commonsense, musicality, flashes of creative genius or whatever else she has to leaven the daily bread of existence, no.

The upshot of all of this, of course, is that your mother, as the person you love most unconditionally, in whose image you have – whatever later conscious efforts have been assayed to undo the damage – been moulded and yet somehow failed to fit satisfactorily, in whom you can see all the sources of your successes and failures, your flaws and … more flaws reflected and magnified, is also the person who can drive you most swiftly round the bend, up the wall and round the corner to the nearest establishment offering neat gin by the pint glass.

And with this heartwarming thought, it is time to turn to the second half of the life equation: becoming a mother.

10 Things You Should Make Sure You Crave During Pregnancy

1. Money
2. A new dishwasher
3, Uninhibited sex with your husband's attractive best friend
4. Uninhibited sex with your own attractive best friend
5. Jewellery

6. An unlimited account at Whistles
7. Rather expensive holidays ...
8. On your own ...
9. Without the kids ...
10. For at least three months a year till they turn 18

It is now easier than ever to become a mother. You can be married or single, gay or straight. You can squeeze kids out of your loins in the traditional manner or pluck them out of Third World orphanages. You can have sex or be artificially inseminated. You can use your own eggs, a stranger's, your sister's or your cousin's and collect sperm from a lover, a donor, a gay best friend or a barman whose name you didn't quite catch before you ended up having filthy monkey sex in the storeroom. You can use your own uterus or a surrogate's – your sister again perhaps, if she really owes you, a paid professional or even your mother, although you should be aware that having your mother give birth to your baby will certainly make it harder to stick her in a home in years to come. 'Thanks very much for everything you've done, Mum, up to and including – through great personal sacrifice, considerable risk to your own health and forty-eight hours of unimaginably painful labour thirty years after you must have thought yourself forever safe from a repeat of such agony – enabling me to fulfil my own maternal destiny. But you're starting to smell a bit, so I'm moving you to a not-very-expensive institution in Bedford so I don't have to see you dribble away to nothingness and mess up the front room. Cheerie-bye!'

It is, however, increasingly hard to be a good mother.

Go back a century or two and things were simpler. Not for the ladies of yesteryear a plethora of competing maternity books or barrage of advice from doctors, supernannies, newspapers, chatrooms or specialists. Your great-great-grandmother's mothering To Do list would have looked like this:

1. *Survive various forms of disease, pox and galloping organ-rot currently thriving in all parts of the land thanks to no one having a buggering clue about germs or sanitation and husbands thinking there's nothing untoward about porking a noseless prostitute and bearing syphilis back to marital bed.*

2. *Reach childbearing age.*

3. *Give birth without dying.*

4. *And without baby dying.*

5. *Keep child alive for next six years till old enough to send down the mines or to boarding school, depending on class.*

6. *Congratulate self on job well done.*

You didn't even have to like your children very much. In seventeenth-century France, *mignotage* – excessive affection towards your offspring – was considered unreasonable and dangerous. Then again, look how the French have turned out. It might be better to throw the occasional friendly glance in your kid's direction, in case it too grows up to be a wartime coward with an unwarranted and yet unshakeable core of arrogant self-belief. It's up to you.

Everything has changed now. Delivering a healthy baby and keeping it so until chimney-sweeping age is no longer enough. The current motherhood rulebook looks something like this:

Before pregnancy

Up to about eight years before you actually get around to throwing away the condoms and yelling 'Impregnate me!' at the nearest set of male genitalia, the thought will pass fleetingly across your mind: 'I might like to have a baby someday.' As soon as this happens, you must start eating nothing but nuts, berries, leafy green vegetables and folic acid tablets by the fistful, or you will be a bad pre-mother and end up giving birth to a baby that has no head.

Then you must consider whether you are ready to have a baby and whether the multitudinous mental, physical and spiritual agonies children put you through over the years are worth the potential rewards they bring.

The best way to decide is either by catching a bus filled with screaming teenagers at the end of the school day, visiting a supermarket peppered with tearful toddlers or turning on the television to see semi-feral youngsters of all ages doing their best to lay waste to their desperate parents, which will ensure that you keep swilling down the Microgynon until the menopause and beyond. Or you can use the following carefully designed quiz to assess your fitness for maternal purpose.

Are you fit to be a mother?

1. When you ask your boyfriend if you should have a baby, does he:
   a say, 'Yes, yes, a thousand times yes. I can think of no better way to spend our brief and easily inglorious span on this earth than by uniting in love and perpetuating the genes which have conspired to make something as wondrous, beguiling, beautiful and essential to my happiness as you'
   b say yes wholeheartedly, because he thinks it is like a puppy with clothes, or
   c make a high-pitched squealing sound and break down the door in his rush to vacate the premises?

2. When you visualise your ovaries, do you see them as:
   a two plump, juicy balls of promise waiting to jump into action
   b line drawings from your sixth-form biology class five years ago
   c a brace of knobbly, desiccated lumps that are but days away from starting to rattle round your withering body like despairing marbles, or
   d the enemy?

3. When you ask your mother if you should have a baby, does she respond:
   a 'As a child you never failed to delight and entertain me. I can only wish for you half the pleasure and happiness that having you as a daughter has visited upon me over the years'
   b 'No, you should wait for two years until I retire and need to find new ways to use my time productively. And what could be more productive than colonising the minds of future generations? It has been a long time since I ruled uncontested over a pre-verbal subject, but I'm sure my powers remain strong.'
   c 'No, you should be forcibly sterilised as you are barely capable of looking after yourself, never mind the next generation. The damage you would inflict on an innocent newborn makes my heart convulse with fear.' or
   d with hysterical laughter?

4. Complete the following sentence. My life currently lacks:
   a the opportunity to rediscover the world through fresh eyes
   b entertainment
   c a source of unconditional love, or
   d a sense of achievement, purpose, meaning, something for me to grab on to during long, dark nights of the soul.

5. Does the world seem to you to be:
   a a repository of hope and opportunity for coming generations
   b flawed but bearable
   c laughable,
      or
   d bordering upon the apocalyptic?

6. When a friend invites you to coo over her new baby do you:
   a pretend it's yours
   b pretend it's cake
   c pretend it's shoes,
      or
   d pretend you have an appointment?

7. When you imagine giving birth, do you:
   a dilate
   b feel your entire being suffused with a sense of belonging to something larger and more significant than yourself, something woven deep within the fabric of space and time itself, connecting you to every woman who ever lived and who is to come and become suddenly, irrevocably and profoundly aware of a new consciousness that reveals that all living things are interconnected, so that when a butterfly flaps its wings in Borneo, a breeze flutters over your baby's face in Barnsley
   c scream,
      or
   d faint?

8. Would you rather:
   a smell of shit and sick all day and spend your nights hovering over a sleeping infant in case it stops breathing or is stolen by burglars until your eyes roll back in your head and the ability to form complete sentences seems but a delightful dream you once had
   b party
   c sleep,
      or
   d have sex ever again?

9. Complete the following sentence: The best thing about having children is:
   a the clothes in Baby Gap
   b that they eventually grow up and start earning
   c being able to do everything for them that my mother did for me,
      or
   d being able to do everything to them that my mother did to me.

During pregnancy

Once you are actually pregnant, you must:

- go to eighteen pre-natal classes a day
- join the National Childbirth Trust (and the National Trust while you're there. What are you going to do, let Orlando and Arabella watch television instead of going on improving trips to Hampton Court and Penshurst Place, where they can learn about Elizabethan quatrefoils and Tudor politics instead of enjoying themselves?)
- exercise – but not too much
- get plenty of sleep – but not too much, and finally
- try to ignore the fact that a few months from now you are going to experience a degree of pain that in any other context would cause anyone with a modicum of human decency and compassion to inject you with every opiate known to science, but in this one instance will only prompt them to lean over you with wholesome and encouraging smiles and say, 'Just breathe through it, dear, just breathe through it.'

If, incidentally, you have a Caesarean in order to sidestep the suffering engendered by nature's greatest design flaw, you are a selfish coward who now has so many debits in the mothering ledger that you might as well give up now and leave the baby on a hillside to be cared for by wolves.

After pregnancy

Now that you have managed the equivalent of pushing a bowling ball through a hosepipe, the mental torture begins.

Once the child is born, you must devote your life to its care and interests, subsume your being within its and never be without guilt, shame or worry that you are failing in this for the next thirty years. You will manage most of this yourself, thanks to the fact that the birth will have transformed you into a raging clutch of hormones that take around a decade to settle down to manageable proportions, but in case you can't, there will be plenty of people around to undermine your confidence. Once you have a child, everyone's a critic. Complete strangers will think nothing of coming up to you and offering advice on feeding, clothing, holding, cleaning, weaning and raising it. And in your weakened post-partum state, you will only be able to nod, smile and burst into tears, instead of gently but firmly re-establishing the boundaries that should be maintained between all members of a civilised society – i.e. by saying quite politely, 'I'm so sorry, my mind's all over the place. Did I inadvertently ask for your opinion? No? Then fuck off, twat.'

As the child grows up, the good mother must be calm, beatifically patient, non-judgemental, an attentive listener, a provider of uncon-ditional love without being suffocating, able to wrap her offspring in a warm blanket of security while still granting them their own space to grow into independent, autonomous beings, able to guide them with the gentle hand of discipline while remaining permissive and child-centred at all times and always burying the consequent screams of frustration and empty gin bottles every night in her pillow and at the bottom of the garden respectively.

Fail in any of these basics and you are a Bad Mother. And remember – they are just the basics. There are plenty of other ways, according to the papers, who seize on the 800 surveys a week published by researchers at the Smethick Sociological Institute of Fannying About to Justify Our Grant Money to fill their news pages and induce panic in their female readers.

What The Daily Crap *says:*
OLDER MOTHERS BAD FOR BABIES!

Your eggs become splintery balls of decayed DNA, resulting in defective babies. You will be deliberately bringing suffering mites into the world unless you get pregnant now, do you hear me? Now!

What The Daily Crap *means:*

No one wants to look at disabled kids. And certainly no one wants to pay for them. Cripples never earn their weight in tax revenue, but drain the NHS of resources that could be better spent stapling the stomachs of compulsive overeaters and giving women better tits.

What The Daily Crap *says:*
YOUNG MOTHERS BAD FOR BABIES!

You will have healthy eggs, but feral children.

What The Daily Crap *means:*

Young mums = stupid mums. Either because they believed our story about old mums having gnarled and twisted babies or because they are teenagers who are, y'know, just stupid.

Also, all teenagers live on council estates. I am frightened of teenagers. And council estates. Anyone born on a council estate is a criminal. We have enough criminals arriving as 'asylum seekers'. We do not need to breed our own.

What The Daily Crap *says:*
RICH MOTHERS BAD FOR BABIES!

If you have lots of money, you will be tempted to pay for a nanny or au pair and your child will grow up neglected by its own mother, unable to form proper relationships, living a kind of shadowy half-life, pursued by pain and forever vainly trying to fill the mummy-shaped hole left in its heart. Shame on you, madam, shame on you!

What The Daily Crap *means:*

I don't like the idea of women being rich. It's weird and wrong. How can we make them think it's a bad idea? I know! Pretend it makes them heartless bitches! Tah-daah!

What The Daily Crap *says:*
POOR MOTHERS BAD FOR BABIES!

If you can't afford a nanny or au pair to help you with your children, you will be too stressed to be a good mother. You will be bitter, irritable, unkind and probably violent.

If you can't pay for dance classes, tutors, must-have Christmas toys, a nice house, a big garden, music lessons and gymnastics clubs, you are denying your child the right to reach his or her full potential, condemning him or her to a lifetime of thwarted ambition and quiet desperation. How can you be so cruel? How?

What The Daily Crap *means:*

If you are poor, it probably means that you are a teenager on a council estate, and we all know what happens then. You and your kids will live off my taxes and then mug me on the streets for cash to buy drugs and hoodies. I'm so frightened.

What The Daily Crap *says:*

FAT MOTHERS BAD FOR BABIES!

Fat women jeopardise their own health by having babies. And then they teach their children bad eating habits, resulting in a family of morbidly obese people who all have to be winched out of the house by the fire brigade when they die.

What The Daily Crap *means:*

We don't want to look at fat women. Yuck! How can we make them lose weight?

What The Daily Crap *says:*

THIN MOTHERS BAD FOR BABIES!

Thin women risk infertility and often have eating disorders which they can pass on to their children.

What The Daily Crap *means:*

Obviously, thin women are better than fat women, but we mustn't let them get complacent. They might stop buying stuff.

Also, remember that women are all stupid, so thin ones will probably feed babies skimmed breast milk and sushi and make them die. It's only our warnings that can keep these children alive.

What The Daily Crap *says:*

MOTHERS WITHOUT DEGREES BAD FOR BABIES!

If you are undereducated, you will forget to get up in the morning, won't know how to make cereal or get the children off to that big brick building at the end of the road which is called a school. You won't be able to help them with their homework, although you will be able to point at the television and say 'Pretty colours! Pretty colours!' You won't be able to remember the number for an ambulance if they have an accident. They will grow up dim, savage or dead. All because of you.

What The Daily Crap *means:*

Thick people go at it like rabbits and spread their thick genes everywhere unless you scare 'em, and scare 'em good.

What The Daily Crap *says:*

MOTHERS WITH DEGREES BAD FOR BABIES!

If you know too many facts, they push out all the mothering instincts and you start trying to dress your children in protractors and set squares and make them eat books instead of food. You won't be able to cuddle them because your arms will be so heavy with the weight of knowledge and you will make them do sums instead of football. They will be sad and weird and killed in the playground.

What The Daily Crap *means:*

Women who know stuff! They scare me! I hate them! Stop them!

What The Daily Crap *says:*

WORKING MOTHERS BAD FOR BABIES!

Your child will be like one of those monkey experiments, hugging your laptop for surrogate maternal warmth.

What The Daily Crap *means:*
Successful women are women who don't want to sleep with me. I can't afford to encourage that.

What The Daily Crap *says:*

STAY-AT-HOME MOTHERS BAD FOR BABIES!

You will be a bad role model for your child. Your lack of ambition will pass down the generations until your great-grandchildren can do no more than roll around the floor like giant grubs. Do you want that on your conscience? Well, do you?

What The Daily Crap *means:*
No one wants your welfare-state-leeching type to breed.

If you were to take all these stories to heart, you would rapidly discover that the only way you could avoid giving birth to the next Jeffrey Dahmer would be to lose a stone while taking an extra six A-levels and getting pregnant a week last Tuesday during an interview for a part-time job that came with a six-figure salary and personal trainer and dietician.

So just listen to your heart and do it when it feels right for you. Of course, if this also coincides with what feels right for your bank manager and credit card providers, so much the better.

10 Signs That Your Mother Is Ready For You To Have Children

1. She is retired
2. She is accumulating cats at the rate of eight a week
3. She has converted the loft into a nursery
4. She has taken up crochet
5. She is crocheting baby matinée jackets

6. And the babies to put in them
7. She has been giving you folic acid for Christmas
8. And birthdays. Since you were 28
9. She starts rewriting history and claiming that giving birth to you was not the forty-eight hours of screaming agony she has led you to believe for the past three decades but more akin to shelling a particularly tiny pea
10. She offers to pay for the baby's nappies/food/education/surrogate mother

Grandmotherhood

Perhaps the best reason for having children of your own is that science has yet to yield a more foolproof method for becoming a grandmother in later life. And even the most objective observer can see that grandmotherhood is a riot. You get all of the pleasures and none of the responsibilities. You can mess with your daughter's head by indulging her kids at every turn, instead of draining the joy and spontaneity out of everything, as you did for her. The buffer of age and distance means that you are the treat, the special visitor, the hotly anticipated guest star and will receive the kind of untrammelled, uncomplicated love and affection that can never exist between mothers and daughters. Instead of spending your declining years staring dully at the wallpaper and necking anti-depressants or becoming the kind of tyrannous old bag before whom entire villages cower in fear, you can bask and flower in the family spotlight whenever you choose.

To be a successful grandma, you need only a few key features:

1. A large bosom

Symbol of maternal kindness, generosity of spirit and certain refuge for granddaughters living through the 'Mum just doesn't underSTAND me!' years. The naturally skinny should strap pillows judiciously about their persons if they wish to be truly loved by the next generation.

2. Mild eccentricities

The refusal to buy a vacuum cleaner, say, and the professed preference for crawling about on the floor picking up bits of fluff with sticky labels from the shopping. Or an abiding belief that champagne cocktails are good for children. Or a gambling problem. My own beloved grandma taught us to play gin rummy, three-card brag, pontoon and Newmarket as soon as we were old enough to wrap our pudgy fingers round a deck of cards and calculate some basic odds. The first thing we did when we walked through her front door for the summer holidays was empty onto the hall table the little copper mountains of coins from the special purses we had carefully fed all year and announce, 'Bring it on, old bag.' She would settle her green-visored cap on her head and the gaming would begin.

3. An utter disregard for parental rules

If the mother has a thing for cleanliness, Grandma should ensure that the children have access at all times to a large, muddy field and orders to tramp mud through the grandparental home as often as possible. If she believes that television is hell's own poison, Grandma should buy a forty-foot plasma screen and let the kids watch it until their eyes shrivel. If the mother forbids chips and sweets, a week at Grandma's should mean a week of flirting with Type 2 diabetes, as she lays tray after tray of Penguins and orange Club biscuits before her grandchildren and encourages them to eat their own bodyweight in Bakewell slices while she peels a sack of potatoes for the next meal. Happy, happy days.

4. A special talent

Something that separates you from the mundane and quotidian and makes those visits sparkle. A removable glass eye or other body part is always a winner. The ability – and repeated willingness – to fit 784 winegums in your mouth by distending your jaw like an African snake will also do nicely. My grandma could play the piano. In fact, provided there was someone on hand to top up the petrol drum containing that day's libation of choice, she could play 'Bobby Shaftoe' for five days straight, and frequently did, her iron willpower enabling her to disregard both the calls of nature and those of her exhausted grandchildren, who were forced to march to the militaristic lyrics until their soft, young joints compacted into rigid agony. By gum, it were grand.

5. Location, location, location

Grandmas must live somewhere different in kind from their grandchildren – a rural idyll if they are feral urbanites, a concrete estate if they hail from thatched-cottagey, chocolate-boxy splendour. One of the nicest things about children is that they are stupid enough to endow anything out of their ordinary experience with charm and romance, no matter how unremittingly ugly or free from actual interest it may be.

Again, my grandma came up trumps. We lived in a London suburb, she lived near Blackpool. Thus we enjoyed countless perfect summer holidays following her into every arcade on the Golden Mile while she lost our inheritance on the one-armed bandits. It's not easy to feed a set of stainless-steel cutlery and a framed photo of Frankie Vaughan into a slot more obviously designed for two pence pieces, especially when you've been smashed on crème de menthe since 10.30 that morning, but she managed it. She was a hell of a woman.

I recently found myself acting as one of the 8,000 chaperones required in these heavily regulated times by my teacher friend (who now works at my old school and, incidentally, has officially changed her name to Miss! Miss!) to enable her to take the disadvantaged but ebullient thirteen-year-old girls from her English class on a trip to the Shakespeare's Globe Theatre ("Oos Globe Fee-a-uh, Miss?' 'Shakespeare's.' "Oo?' 'The man who wrote the plays that Mel Gibson's *Hamlet* and Baz Luhrmann's *Romeo + Juliet* were based on.' 'Isn't he quite boring though, Miss?' 'Shut up and get on the train.')

In the grand tradition of school trips, it goes without saying that easily the best part of the day was lunchtime. I sat on a bench eating sandwiches with the three girls whom Miss! Miss! had designated my particular responsibility and discussing what they planned to be when they grew up. One wanted to be a supermodel – 'And I won't get out of bed unless Prada and Versace offer me, like, thousands of pounds!' she shrieked.

Her less volatile friend, who had the face of a natural tragedian, sat stolidly munching her Dairylea Dunkers. 'Yeah?' she said, raising deliberately mournful eyes with perfect timing. 'And what about when Primark calls?'

They collapsed as one into a hysterical lump and I suddenly remembered what fun it could be to be thirteen en masse.

Just then, another girl came up, a look of outrage on her face. 'Michelle just said, "Your Mum!" to me!'

The lump straightened immediately and its component parts reacted with shock, sympathy and promises to do Michelle damage if called upon. Marcelle gave me to understand that the unabbreviated version of the insult was not fit for my delicate adult ears, though under close and careful questioning eventually revealed that it could be completed either by the phrase 'gives bangs' or the even more evocative 'does heads'.

'Does this mean what I think it means?' I said with my best serious face on, wondering how teachers get through the days without laughing or weeping at the occasional pockets of naïveté that survive in even their toughest charges.

Marcelle nodded, wide-eyed with horror.

I was, to the outward eye, dutifully appalled. But inside I was thinking what a testimony it was to the enduring power of the mother–child relationship that such an insult – well, not even an insult, half an insult, a suggested insult, an implied insult – still had such power to wound and outrage.*

---

* And not just amongst children. Zinedine Zidane had that summer head-butted Marco Materazzi in the World Cup final for impugning his mother's sexual integrity, and David Beckham had received a red card during a Spanish game for calling a linesman an '*hijo de puta*' (although opinion was divided as to whether he actually knew this meant 'son of a whore' or, if so, appreciated that in continental Catholic countries, it carries more weight than an English or US 'sonofabitch'). The resulting media coverage also unearthed mother-dissing versions from other cultures: in Finland you can cause people to rock back on their snowshoes with '*Aitisi nai poroja*' – your mother copulates with reindeer – and if you ever want to upset a Mandarin Chinese speaker, there is apparently no better way than to fling '*Nide muchin shr ega da wukwei!*' at them – your mother is a big turtle – because, duh, turtles are promiscuous.

Edukashun, Edukashun, Edukashun

Cast your mind back to the first day of school, the playground awash with fibrillating children in the grip of extreme emotion. Some were furious at having been dragged from the easeful life of home, some were scared of being left in the care of an unknown teacher – most were both.

Some mothers cried too, for the end of those few brief, precious years when they were their children's entire world, at the end of innocence that comes with exposure to other children and other influences, for the sheer emotional wrench that comes with leaving your tiny four-year-old to institutional mercies.

Mine cried for the loss of cheap labour she would now suffer between the hours of 8.50 a.m. and 3.30 p.m. – who else would she find who would adhere so closely to the fourteen pages of regulations required to make a bed correctly? – and the sudden comprehension that I would now spend most of the week beyond the reach of her iron will. While she pounded her fists to a bloody pulp against the playground wall in frustration, I skipped blithely into the classroom without a backward glance. I was rewarded almost instantly by the sight of my first penis – Tommy Docherty's, to be precise. He had arrived early with another boy and they had been allowed to play with a decrepit game of Buckaroo. I had arrived at a moment of victory and high excitement, which had caused him to stand on a table and pull down his polyester pants as the only means of expressing his joy. It was more a point of interest than a pleasure, I suppose, but neither traumatic nor – for any Freudians out there – the occasion of any sort of envy. But I did think it beat staying at home.

Primary School

Once upon a time, primary schooling was a matter of walking twenty miles to classes, where you would be beaten daily for failing to learn your Latin primer, until you were eight and it was time to go to work in the potato fields.

Except for girls, of course, it didn't even mean that. Only boys got to go to school (even if it was largely just to be flogged for the crime of being seven years old and unable to pray in dead languages). We stayed at home, sewing, washing, stirring porridge, spinning and carding (that's the medieval equivalent of French knitting, by the way, with the crucial difference that you could sell the results and buy salt pork instead of simply staring at woolly worms in dismay). If you were lucky enough to have a lettered mother who had not died in childbirth, she might teach you to read from the Bible if your calloused hands could still turn the pages.

Fortunately, by September 1979 things had changed and the early eighties seemed to me a fine time to be alive and the recipient of its pedagogic charms. I mean, who didn't love primary school? It is the first place you ever enter in which the furniture is made for people your size – tiny desks, miniature chairs, low chests full of plastic drawers for you to keep your work and the Unibricks in – and you are eased gently into the day by the soothing ritual of the register (which takes ten minutes if the boys are paying attention, twenty if they are not and forty if Stinky Pete has forgotten where the classroom is and his surname again) and assembly.

Assembly has become a rather fraught business over the years. People objected to it using only Christian hymns and stories, then to it having any religious overtones at all, and then back to the all-inclusive argument again. But it was possible to bumble along quite happily, hearing a story about Jonah and the whale here, a tale of Anansi the spider man there, enjoying a taste of unleavened bread at Passover, sweets at Diwali or an explanation of Eid and Ramadan whenever the time came. And then we would have a hymn, folk song or chant, with the words handwritten on a giant scroll of paper pinned to a classroom door*. To the best of my knowledge, nobody's

---

* Do you ever feel the weight of the years suddenly pressing down upon you, despite what is still your relative youthfulness? Overhead projectors didn't even exist at this stage. The year above me probably remembers slates and wax tablets. Perhaps an inability to download tracks onto our iPods shouldn't be a source of shame. We have clearly done well enough just by being able to use a phone and type.

spiritual sensibilities (or self-esteem) were damaged. This is partly, I am sure, because the teachers went to great efforts behind the scenes to ensure that all ethnic groups were fairly represented – and partly, I am equally sure, because no child has ever paid the slightest attention to what goes on in assembly. It is an opportunity for the boys to pick it, lick it, roll it and flick it for twenty minutes and for the girls to do each other's hair. Experts in their respective fields can render a bogey airworthy and boing it the width of the hall or French plait a shoulder-length bob in the time it takes to sing 'Kumbaya, My Lord'. No one, I assure you, had any time to ponder issues of wider religious significance.

After assembly, it was time for some real education. Scientific experiments usually had to be attended to first, by which I mean of course adding water to the jam jars stuffed with broad beans and blotting paper, measuring the tap roots of the ones kept in the dark, the ones in the light, the ones kept moist, the ones kept dry and the one Stinky Pete kept spitting in, then filling in the growth charts the teacher has drawn before finally concluding – if memory serves – that broad beans seem to respond best to light and water and not to darkness and the glutinous phlegm of deprived children.

After that it would be time for some heavy work, in the form of sums on the blackboard. Girls bent their heads instantly to work; the boys when they had been told collectively and individually six times to settle down, stop dead-legging and punching each other in the head and cease from making the farting noise with their hands, even though it is clearly The Funniest Thing Ever Invented.

After sums, some spellings on the blackboard. The girls generally managed to cope with the switch from numbers to letters, but it would always have a profoundly stimulating effect on the boys. They would become overexcited once more and it always took another bout of threats to make them concentrate. Ninety per cent of life in the classroom was spent waiting for the boys to settle down.

If you had told the seven-, eight- or nine-year-old girls that fifteen years later boys would be getting better degrees, better jobs and better pay than their female peers, they would not have believed you. And if you'd told them that this irrational state of affairs would persist well into the third millennium, they would have been frankly appalled, especially once you had explained to them what 'millennium' meant. It would have struck them as the grossest injustice ever perpetrated upon a gender.

Thanks to Miss!'s morning lessons, I still know that 6 × 6 is 36, that a verb is a doing word and that it's 'i' before 'e' except after 'c'. This soupçon of knowledge can actually get you a surprisingly long way in life, mainly because at some point very early on in my school career, people stopped teaching children the basics. I think mine must have been amongst the last years to have received even the lightest instruction in grammar and spelling, and I even have dim memories of handwriting lessons and being forced to contain my 'a's within red lines and tails of 'd's and 'g's within blue. We were certainly amongst the very last to have learned our times tables by rote. I can place the advent of the new, permissive regime into our lives at some time in the three years after 1979, because by the time my sister got to the same school in 1982, they had stopped correcting our work in any way that was recognisable to my parents.

*　·　·　✳　·　·　·*

'What's this?' said Mum, looking at an exercise book full of Emily's feeble scrawl. 'Why have they given this rubbish a tick?' My sister, busy building an Exocet missile out of stickle bricks, shrugged disinterestedly.

The next day, Mum asked the same question of the teacher after school, while we went cross-eyed behind her in an agony of boredom and embarrassment.

'Why have you ticked this?' she repeated, as Miss! went red and stammered.

'We ... we believe that telling them that they are wrong damages children's self-esteem,' she said bravely.

My mother looked up, down, round and to each side of her, as if searching for this strange beast, the Esteemed Self.

'I don't know who told you that nonsense,' she said. 'But from now on, you'll see someone corrects my kids' work, even if you won't correct the others'.'

'But their self-esteem ...' Miss! ventured once more.

Mum fixed her with a gimlet eye. 'They don't need self-esteem,' she said. 'They need to be able to spell.'

And she turned on her heel and left. We trotted silently after her and resigned ourselves to bookfuls of red crosses instead of green ticks and smiley faces. On the plus side, her intervention probably made us the last literate state school pupils of our time.

*　·　·　✳　·　·　·*

The rest of the day was taken up with the kind of obliquely educational activities that would be killed off by the installation of the National Curriculum in 1988 and the long, slow slide into the welter of league tables, standardised testing and key skills that the education system has now become. But not for us the frenzied hauling through SAT hoops and over key skills hurdles so that the school could be sure of its funding next year. These were still the halcyon days when teachers were trusted professionals and allowed to set their own lessons. We did things like colouring in digestive systems, drawing acorns, writing stories and making giant cardboard book covers with marbled endpapers to put them in.

Story time

And then, at 3 p.m., it was story time. Yes, that's how good primary school was. At 3 o'clock, you got to sit down while the teacher read you half an hour of *Tom's Midnight Garden* before you all went home. I tell you, compulsory institutionalisation doesn't get any better than that. Looking back, it's obvious that, just as assembly was a way of demarcating home from school, calming everyone down and preparing them mentally for the day's 'work' ahead, story time was a way of soothing kids after the rigours of the day, so that parents didn't have to shepherd home little hyperactive bundles who would bounce across busy roads like pinballs, flagrantly disregarding every rule of the Green Cross Code. But at the time it was another pleasant interlude, given over to more picking, licking, rolling, flicking and plaiting, but with the bonus of a further instalment of Tom's adventures (or those of *The Hundred and One Dalmatians*, back in the days when this was still a book and not a Disney merchandising opportunity or Glenn Close vehicle) instead of weird religious stuff. .

Do kids still have story time, or do they just plug in their iPods? Do girls still play with each other's hair or do they just text the person sitting nxt 2 thm? Or have teachers understandably decided that now that every other child has an ASBO, attention deficit disorder or some as yet unidentified allergy that means they behave like total shits, the parents deserve to suffer as much as they have all day and turf them out without half an hour's mollification beforehand?

What – as they used to say even in my day – ever. The lessons were merely backdrop to the real business of school: fomenting classroom crazes.

Crazes

For boys, crazes were simple obsessions, simply served. Top Trumps tournaments were held, and to the victor went the spoils. Likewise marbles and conkers – back in the days, of course, before the former were considered dangerous choking hazards and safety goggles had to be worn to play with the devil fruit of the horse chestnut tree. *Star Wars* figurine troops were amassed in preparation for war. Panini stickers were traded, albums were filled and the owner of the biggest number could go through life from then on secure in the knowledge that he was The Best. There are CEOs of international companies who can trace their multimillion dollar success stories directly back to the moment when they swapped eight Adrian Heaths for the elusive Kenny Dalglish and knew they would never cease from seeking such sweet victory again.

Girls did things a little differently. To the best of my knowledge, there have not yet been any studies made of the phenomenon, but as any woman knows, the love of stationery is deeply embedded in your heart from birth. Anyone with ovaries is in thrall to the stuff for a lifetime. Just as we will never understand the male love for *Battlestar Galactica* or for pissing all over the toilet seat, men will never understand the joy that comes from a new diary, an untouched snow-white pad, a shiny ring binder, a pristine packet of felt-tips or the fact that under certain circumstances the glitter pen can represent the pinnacle of human desire. The coveted writing paper may change over time from Victoria Plum to Basildon Bond to Smythson, according to age and disposable income, but coveted it will remain.

So in the classroom we concentrated our passions on and measured our social worth by three things: stickers, rubbers and pencil cases. There were occasional flirtations with pencil tops – I recall weeks here and there during which the classroom was a sea of titchy, fluorescent-haired, bobbing trolls, which must have made the teacher feel like she was on a bad LSD trip – but for some reason these never lasted like the others.

PENCIL CASES

Each school had a slightly different obsession, but they all had one. Did yours opt for the massed pursuit of the old-fashioned wooden box with sliding top that doubled as a ruler and whose top half swung out to reveal another compartment beneath? Or perhaps you all went for the novelty calculator-shaped one with a secret compartment in the corner? Or the denim one that looked like the back of a pair of jeans, with pockets where the – er – pockets would have been if they were real jeans? Or did you just prize pockets in any form? There was brief but glorious time when you could buy pencil cases that comprised about thirty press-studded pockets. You could get fuck all in them, but they were there.

RUBBERS

The US influence has such a firm hold over the hearts and minds of the young folk these days that teachers have to call them erasers unless they want to be put straight on the sex offenders' register, but in my day we could call them by the English name without sniggers or confusion.

Rubbers were a prime example of the female ability to become quite genuinely emotionally attached to inanimate objects. I know one thirty-five-year-old woman who has only just – and I mean in the last month or so – been able to bring herself to throw away the last crumb of her favourite rubber. Clearly, this is an extreme example and one that I suspect points to a number of unresolved psychological issues which I have neither time nor inclination to examine here, but nevertheless it is entirely true that every girl had her favourite rubber, one which was invested with talismanic properties and which no one else was allowed to touch without special permission and forms signed in triplicate to ensure safe return. When I became – briefly – a solicitor in the City, I drew up contracts between bankers and businessmen that had less complex conditions for asset transfer. My favourite rubber was a stone-coloured oval that Grandma had bought me in the local shop. It was weighty, it was smoothly curvaceous, it fitted exactly into the palm of my hand, it erased mistakes swiftly and thoroughly. It was admired by all. It was, in sum, a rubber you could trust. You think I'm about to tell you a tale now of a stolen rubber, an oval-shaped hole left in the owner's heart and bloody retribution exacted upon the thief, don't you? You misjudge me, my friends. No one was allowed to touch my rubber, and I used the secret compartment in my calculator pencil case to ensure that no one ever did. I hope that your own history is equally untouched by tragedy.

The craze for smelly rubbers was a different order of madness. For about a year we bought every pungent, chemically impregnated piece of indiarubber we could lay our hands on. When we opened our pencil cases the wave of synthetic scents – strawberry, banana, orange, melon – nearly knocked us out. It must have ruined our nasal passages for years, which at least would explain the passion for Body Shop Dewberry potions that would engulf us all a few years later.

STICKERS

I cannot emphasise enough how different a girl's sticker collection was from a boy's. His was a soulless collection of photographs, amassed with the sole aim of basking in the triumph of completing an album which would then be discarded without compunction.

A girl's stickers were her heart, her soul. You might as well ask her to cut out her entrails as throw a single one in the bin.

Oh, how I loved my sticker collection. Do you remember how they were sold on perforated rolls? You handed over an extortionate amount of pocket money and received a tiny section of pure happiness in return. The agony of choosing was exquisite – tiny, emerald-green frogs or glittery hologram hearts redder than sin? – the joy of acquisition unparalleled and the loveliness of the goods indescribable. And they are really hardly tainted at all now that I look back and see them for what they really were – a cunningly disguised initiation rite into consumer culture, the first deliberate creation of an appetite that could only be fed by the magic of Western capitalism. Still, if Western capitalism could produce something as gorgeous as my little silver hearts with metallic rainbow stripes arcing out of them – the closest, surely, that the adhesives industry has come to attaining the Platonic ideal of beauty – then let me sign up for life.

The only problem with this deep, passionate attachment to pieces of indiarubber and glittery adhesive pictures is that it is actually the first symptom of a pervasive female disease. It is an early sign of what will eventually turn into the grown woman's inability to distinguish sex from love and the tendency to fall in love with the kind of men that a rational soul would take one look at and dismiss as a stinking manbag of unreliability, infidelity and depredation upon your mental health and current account. Freud may have been right to say that sometimes a cigar is just a cigar. But a sticker is never just a sticker.

Interestingly, the more formal attempts of Western capitalism to stoke the fires of consumer lust amongst the younger demographic – I'm thinking of the 'official' crazes, like Care Bears, My Little Pony and Cabbage Patch Kids – rarely succeeded so well.

They had inbuilt limitations. Firstly, pester power hadn't yet grown to its full strength. There were still a number of parents out there who were quite prepared to say no to their daughters' demands for all things plush, pastel and overpriced.

Secondly, they weren't just overpriced, they were extortionate. Weight for weight, some My Little Pony accessories cost more than gold. Stickers (and rubbers and all other delightful forms of stationery) had the unassailable advantage of being purchasable without parental contribution or approval.

Thirdly, Cabbage Patch dolls were, to the more aesthetically sensitive sections of the target market, the ugliest things ever invented. They looked like they had a fatal syndrome of some kind. No wonder they were all up for adoption.

Fourthly, although the amount of love a girl has to give is vast and easily bestowed upon unsuitable objects, it is nevertheless a finite resource, and if most of it has already been allocated to stationery, then I'm afraid freakdolls and stupidly unsquashy ponies are going to be left out in the cold.

And finally, and most importantly, they were imposed on us from outside. While we could be blinded by advertising and temporarily bludgeoned by the hard sell into believing we wanted them, they never enjoyed the kind of grassroots popularity of stickers or the multi-pocketed pencil case. Oh, I suppose they must have succeeded for the manufacturers in financial terms (as if anyone cares about those!) because the price of one Care Bear or plastic pony would have bought several hundredweight of even the fanciest, glitteriest stickers, and the animals sold in their millions. But they failed in all the important ways. We never really loved them. You will rarely find a woman now who remembers her My Little Cabbage Patch Care Pony with any great fondness. But ask her about her favourite stickers and see her eyes light up.

Playground Pain

So far it's been all laughs, learning and looking at baby penises. But there comes a point in everyone's life when, alas, the laughter stops. For girls, that point comes at her first exposure to the playground.

Boys spend the first week's worth of playtimes fighting, wrecking their lunchboxes and throwing each other's Parkas up onto the toilet roof. Having established a basic hierarchy, they then settle down as one big group and – save for occasional fascinations with paper aeroplane competitions – get on with playing football across ninety per cent of the playground.

Squashed into the remaining ten per cent are the girls (a useful collective preparation, incidentally, for the years we subsequently spend crunched into slivers of seats on public transport, while the men on each side take the space necessary both to accommodate their mighty frames and avoid any suggestion that their genitalia are of dimensions that make it possible to close their legs. But that is by the by). In that remaining tenth of gum-scabbed tarmac, loyalties, alliances and friendships are formed and reformed a dozen times a day out of political expediency, desperation, occasionally genuine liking and more often genuine loathing for a third party. The speed of change is dizzying.

In 1893, folklorist Lady Alice Bertha Gomme said that she hoped her book *Traditional Games of England, Scotland and Ireland* would help preserve the games' 'civilising influence'. I regret to have to report here that it did not. As a result of the maelstrom of perverse and subtle machinations in which girls naturally operate, what looked to adult eyes like charming girlish games have in fact always been, and doubtless will always remain, nothing less than miniature war zones.

HOPSCOTCH

Parents and teachers love seeing hopscotch going on. It's fun, it's free, it's healthful exercise. What they fail to realise is that as a way of filtering out of the gang the fat, the clumsy and the slightly disabled, whose parents are insisting that they attend a mainstream school despite the fact that their daily lives are thereby rendered an utter misery, it has never been bettered. It is on the hopscotch grid that the most desperate insecurity that plagues all women is first stirred. It is from the thousand sniggers heard as one bends over to pick up the stone on square five that the question 'Does my bum look big in this?' is born.

It was a big day when we got a big, white hopscotch grid with blue numbers painted on the playground tarmac. Nowadays, playgrounds are covered not in simple hopscotch squares but snakes and ladders grids, checkerboards and running tracks. But nobody ever uses them. You can understand why. Enough feuds and tear-filled break times arise from the simple challenges presented by hopscotch. If we had exploited the possibilities for misunderstanding, injustice and nefarious tactics offered by complex games like snakes and ladders, we would all have been in a state of collapse by the end of lunchtime.

SKIPPING

The two girls holding the rope have all the power. If they take a dislike to the girl in the middle, they can casually increase the rate of turning beyond what they know she can cope with and bring her crashing down in more ways than one. The rope that eventually entangles the skipper's feet is a mirror of the creepers of humiliation that are choking her dreams of social acceptance to death.

Some schools have banned skipping ropes now, for fear of the boys using them to fight with. It's good to see that girls are still having to make accommodations for the cretinous behaviour of others from so early on. It's the kind of training that's got to be done early, otherwise they might start to object.

ELASTICS

Elastics is part skipping, part cat's cradle for the legs. Hence to the mental and social peril which, as I think by now we all appreciate, forms an intrinsic part of playground pastimes, is added physical danger. As I have legs slightly shorter than Coke cans and the stamina of a throw cushion, I never lasted at the game once the bands went past ankle-height. I would stumble and stagger away to the accompaniment of laughter and derision, but never ambulance sirens. Those of a more athletic bent could keep going until the bands went as high as the anchors' knees, but then when they made a mistake they would do so in spectacular fashion, usually bringing down the anchors with them in a flurry of pixie-booted limbs, swearing and spiral perms spontaneously straightening with the shock.

Nobody has ever investigated how many promising sporting careers were prematurely ended by elastics-related accidents, but I suspect it runs into thousands and could well be the unacknowledged cause of Britain's dearth of Olympic hopes in succeeding decades.

FORTUNE TELLERS

As already noted, boys are generally very keen on making paper aeroplanes. Like most of the things boys do, of course, this is very boring and offers no scope for exploiting that special gift for undetectable bullying that is so carefully nurtured by girls. So fortune tellers had to be invented.

Fortune tellers are those four-point tented things that you put your thumbs and forefingers into and pull together and apart in opposing pairs (it's very much easier to do than to describe) to the rhythm of a sinister ditty of your choice – 'Ip, dip, dog shit, you are not IT' being the original and best – or according to the number of letters in the colour of the flap first picked. I have, however, heard tell that, in Liverpool in the sixties at least, they were known as 'salt and peppers' because 'salt', 'mustard', 'vinegar' and 'pepper' were written on the first flaps instead of them being coloured in. Blimey, I know things are always grimmer up north, but I didn't know people couldn't afford colour until the seventies. You live and learn.

Anyway, you then invite your partner to open the chosen flap and reveal her fate. You can write anything you want on the underside of the flaps but tradition favours 'You are going to die at sixteen', 'Everybody secretly hates you', 'Everybody hates you and you are going to die at sixteen' and 'I hate you and wish you were dead'. It creates in many a psychical wound from which they never recover. On the other hand, they are usually the type who also believes in astrology, so we need not bother ourselves too much about what happens to them.

RHYMES

It is only when reflecting on them in adulthood that you appreciate how mental the average clapping rhyme is, but they made perfect sense at the time.

Take for example:

'Miss Mary Mack, Mack, Mack,
All dressed in black, black, black,
With silver buttons, buttons, buttons,
All down her back, back, back.'

She clearly can't decide between being a proto-goth or a fusilier. This does not augur well for Miss Mack's future.

'She asked her mother, mother, mother,
For fifty pence, pence, pence,
To watch the boys, boys, boys,
Jump over the fence, fence, fence.'

Things have gone from bad to worse for Mary, who has evidently been brainwashed into thinking you have to pay money to watch other children jump over common garden obstacles. So far, this rhyme is raising far more questions than it answers.

'They jumped so high, high, high,
Nearly reached the sky, sky, sky,'

Mary is so easily impressed by athletic prowess that one begins to suspect that she is simple and that her black and silver getup is the identifying uniform of the local private insane asylum.

'And they never came back, back, back,
Till the end of Juuuuuly.'

Yes, when Mary and her fifty pence pieces are tucked safely back into bed and behind bars.

Still, this is as nothing compared to the surreal madness into which a simple trip to a Chinese restaurant quickly dissolves.

'I went to a Chinese restaurant,'

Fine. So far, so good. Probably be banned in the playground these days for encouraging bad dietary habits and obesity, but carry on for now.

'To buy a loaf of bread, bread, bread.'

Eh? You went to a Chinese restaurant to buy bread? What is this place, the Kung Po Sainsbury's?

'I wrapped it up in a five pound note,'

You did what? You did what?! A loaf of bread only costs about 40p in the first place!

'And this is what they said, said, said,
"My name is Elvis Presley,
Girls are sexy,
Sitting in the back seat,
Drinking Pepsi."'

Not only have we spiralled into madness, but it seems to involve a paedophile restaurateur grooming his young customers by pretending to be a long-dead rock-and-roll icon. I think I need a lie-down.

The only one that stands up to any kind of scrutiny – and even then, not for long – is 'When Susie Was a Baby'.

'When Susie was a baby,
A baby Susie was,
She went wah wah wah wah.
When Susie was a toddler,
A toddler Susie was,
She went scribble, scribble, scribble, scribble.'

So far so good-ish: sound narrative structure, logical progression, albeit with a novel take on the actions that define toddlerhood.

'When Susie was a schoolgirl,
A schoolgirl Susie was,
She went, "Miss, Miss, I wanna go a piss,
I don't know where the toilet is."'

Alas, Susie has begun her journey into stroppy adolescence, which sadly continues in the next verse.

'When Susie was a teenager,
A teenager she was,
She went, "Oh, ah, I've lost my bra,
I've left my knickers in my boyfriend's car."'

After this, things go from bad to worse. During motherhood she is reduced to going 'bake, bake, bake' and as a grandma 'knit, knit, knit', before ending as a skeleton in a coffin doing not much at all, unless it is silently reflecting on how one can become trapped so easily in a brutally circumscribed life as the result of one youthful indiscretion and sending out her spirit to try to warn other girls of her fate through the medium of ill-scanning poetry. Poor Susie.

Since the seventeenth century, people have been worrying about the death of children's games and oral culture and traditions, fearing that everything from the coming of the railways to the advent of the gramophone, wireless and cinema would kill them off. Anthropologist and folklorist William Newell said in 1883 that the subject of his book *Games and Songs of American Children* was 'an expiring custom … perishing at the roots'. Our own experience, even after the coming of television (and indeed the video cassette recorder, which was beginning to make an appearance during my primary school years, in both its VHS and Betamax forms), of course tells us such fears were misplaced and even today it's not all about the whizzbangery of the interweb, iPodules and the rest. Girls still play skipping and hand-clapping games, although apparently they also rewrite pop songs in a big way. Nellie Furtado's 'I'm Like a Bird' becomes 'I'm like a turd, I only flush away' and Peter Andre's hit becomes 'Pooh, pooh, mysterious girl' – a slightly less clever reworking than 'I'm Like a Turd', but nevertheless still quantifiably more entertaining than the original.

Secondary school

Alas, fun can't last forever. Before you know it, you're eleven. In a very real sense, it's just one long slide into the grave from here on.

Victoria Wood once said, 'I went to a mixed school – all girls,' which is an unbeatably succinct way of making the vital point that if your parents decide to send you to a single-sex school, you should be very clear from the beginning that everyone therein is minutely graded, ranked and allotted a unique niche in the social hierarchy. It is a niche usually richly spiked with schoolgirl barbs to prevent even momentary relaxation, unless you are one of the handful of queen bees who come to rest in silk-lined alcoves which others visit only to pay obeisance and lay placatory flowers at your feet. Your shared gender will create no bonds, foster no sense of community, forge no immediate or instantaneous links between one girl and another. Secondary school is a brutal fight to the social death. But more of that anon, in the coming chapter about female friendships.

Apart from the abandonment of hopscotch and so on in favour of picking one's way over the social minefield and redrawing the friendship map every day, the biggest changes presented by secondary school are the sudden introduction of two things: school uniform and proper subjects – an hour of maths, followed by an hour of history, followed by an hour of geography … It's a hell of a change from weeks of bean-growing and marbling endpapers.

School uniform

You can wear the regulation skirt, shirt, jumper and tie if you are either a dull conformist (nothing wrong with that – you will earn twice as much as your peers for most of your life, at least until you have to take five years off work with post-natal depression after your first baby) or supremely confident that your good looks and vibrant personality will mark you out sufficiently from any crowd and secure you the attention and respect that is your due as a unique and exceptional individual. All those in between must customise whatever combination of navy gabardine, maroon serge or dark-green polyester pleats they labour under as quickly and as heavily as possible. Tried and tested ways include:

- *Shortening the skirt by rolling up the waistband or hacking six inches off at the hem. Your choice should depend on whether your mother has a propensity to treat irrevocably damaged clothes as a violation of her soul or whether she is so hammered by the time you get home from school that she wouldn't notice if you tattooed your thighs maroon in front of her and did without the skirt altogether.*

  And don't even think about lengthening your skirt in the winter. Protecting your flesh from the elements = instant ostracism. Remember: corned-beef legs are cool, blue legs are better, and if you can get gangrene to set in, your future as Miss Popularity is assured forever.

- *Shortening the tie or tying it so that the thin bit shows at the front instead of the fat bit. Any messing with the tie drives teachers nuts. They know it's wrong and you know it's wrong, but you are still in essence conforming in a big way by wearing this most distinctively uniform-y part of the kit, so unless they are very sure indeed that you are a teacher's pet whom they can panic with a look, they are in a quandary. Those to whom all students look the same don't want to rock the boat in case you are one of the girls that only comes to school when her foster mother has money for the bus fare, and insisting on strict tie policy will break the last fragile link you have with education and plunge you into the street-roaming netherworld forever. Those who have a greater grasp of who they are dealing with will engage in a brief internal struggle as to whether it is worth an argument with a lippy adolescent about the fact that school rules state only that you must wear a tie and not precisely how. All girls know instinctively which teachers can be embroiled in fine semantic distinctions and parsings of school constitutions and which will simply strangle you with the offending article. Ditto knotting belts instead of buckling them.*

❦ *Wearing jewellery. I greatly admire the story told to me about a girl – an admittedly mildly eccentric girl – who decided to test the limits of her school's policy on jewellery. Girls were allowed to wear earrings and 'religious symbols'. She began with one cross around her neck and one in each ear. She added another necklace and pair of earrings every day for a week until she looked like B. A. Baracus. The next week she started hanging rosary beads round her neck and massive crucifixes from her ears. When she was at last confronted by one of the teachers, she drew herself up to her full height, pointed a quivering finger at the hapless mistress and cried with a full Deep South preacher's vibrato, 'Ahh am an instrument of the Lahwd!' Legend has it that she was never bothered again. It is far more likely, of course, that she was sectioned.*

BRAS

The idea is to make the outline clearly visible under your blouse, so if you are white, wear a black bra under it and if you are black, wear a white one. Male teachers won't dare point it out because it would mean admitting that they have looked at your breasts, which was enough in my day to get them 'a reputation' and these days would doubtless get them hung, drawn and quartered by a local vigilante mob. Female teachers will assume you come from a motherless home and have no one to teach you the subtleties of outerwear–underwear coordination and be loathe to draw attention to your deprivation.

JUMPERS

Tie your jumper round your waist, round your bag strap, use it as a cushion, towel, pen wiper, hanky. Hell, unpick it and knit yourself some slippers. Just don't ever, ever wear it. Not even if your arms go as gangrenous as your unskirted legs and bits of them start dropping off in geography. Ditto coats. And blazers.

Alternatively, wear it all the time. At the height of summer, in stuffy classrooms, in the playground on days so hot that the tarmac is bubbling, in PE, on Sports Day. If they try to take it off you when you're unconscious from heat stroke and dehydration, wake up and fight. I don't know why. You just have to do it.

If any youngsters are reading this, I urge you not to take this as a definitive list of options. The possibilities are endless; use these more as a springboard than a blueprint. Just bear in mind that the aim at all times is to restore to your uniform the marker of individuality and the class, income and cool differentials that it is designed to obscure.

School subjects

HISTORY

I know someone who based her entire two years' worth of history coursework on what she had gleaned from *Blackadder*. She got a B. You have to fear for the country.

By contrast, the chances are that your parents, recipients of a better thought out and more rigorously instilled education, still have a working knowledge of the dates of England's kings and queens, major battles and revolutions, which hang together to give them a relatively coherent world view and a broad-brush understanding of how the world came to be as it is today.

I used to think this was the kind of knowledge that came upon you with age, was absorbed over the years through wide reading and the constant exercise of an enquiring mind. I now know that, in fact, it is the kind of knowledge that can only become lodged in a child's brain through constant repetition shored up by frequent applications of schoolmaster slipper to infant backside.

As a participant in the late-eighties GCSE curriculum, I got none of the corporal punishment (good) and none of the knowledge (bad). For our coursework and exams we did the history of medicine, from prehistoric times (Neanderthals banging holes in each other's heads to let malevolent spirits out) to the present day (riotous success except for antibiotic resistance and AIDS), and Britain 1815 to 1851 (rotten boroughs and the Great Reform Act). This gave me less than no idea of how my country came to be in the state it's in now, what powers and influences, chance circumstances or glorious leaders shaped the nation, but on the other hand, if you ever need someone who can trepan a Chartist, you know where to come.

SCIENCE

Here's what I remember from five years — that's half a decade — of science lessons: potassium is very reactive and turns purple if you mix it with something else; titration is a fancy word for dripping; the word 'pipette' is unaccountably funny and a crucible is a little pot that would look nicer on a bedroom shelf than on a tripod over a Bunsen burner.

HOME ECONOMICS

Home economics is the pedagogic equivalent of pompom-making. While we girls are fucking about with baking tins, boys are taking secret A-levels in the Arab–Israeli conflict and US politics. This is why when you're thirty and trying to have a civilised conversation round the dinner table, you suddenly realise that the men are no longer pretending to know four hundred times more about everything than you — they actually do. It's too late to catch up without help. John Craven needs to come out of retirement and start a Newsround for women. I can't fake much more general knowledge. The jig is just about up.

Nowadays, I believe the subject is more commonly called 'food science' and is all about nutrition. It has basically turned into an anti-anorexia class, in which girls are encouraged to make Nicole Richie models out of pastry and eat them.

10 Secret Exams Only Boys Sit

1. A-level Understanding the Middle East Crisis
2. GCSE Giving a mouse-sized shit about Star Wars beyond how they got Princess Leia's hair to do that circular thing
3. GCSEs in Understanding the inflation rate
4. GCSEs in What the FTSE and Dow Jones index is and why we care
5. GCSE Burping the Alphabet

6. NVQ in Doorslamming
7. City & Guilds in Having Attractive Forearms
8. Certificate in making that farting noise under your arm with your hand
9. Advanced certificate in real farting
10. Remedial diploma in wee-spraying

SPANISH

Hola. Me llamo Lucy Mangan. Tengo una hermana. Se llama Emily. No puedo remember any mas por que yo used to cheat on todos mis tests de vocabulario.

FRENCH

Et ici aussi.

ENGLISH

English lessons were an exercise in sustained aural torture, apparently specifically designed to kill any embryonic love of reading stone dead. What other reason could there be for condemning pupils to spend ninety paralysingly boring hours a week reading *Pride and Prejudice*, *Romeo and Juliet* and *The Importance of Being Earnest* out loud? The average schoolgirl is ten years too young to cope with iambic pentameter, appreciate a Wildean epigram or thrill to Austen's delicate dissections of ladies' emotional and financial torments in Regency England. She tends to switch off. When you also bear in mind that by the eighties education funding cuts meant that most schools had the kids sharing one book between three, it is an underreported miracle that anyone of that generation emerged literate at all.

Still, you can look back on them as halcyon days now. The current curriculum is so ridiculously overstuffed that English lessons now consist of the three fastest texters in the class gutting the prescribed books and sending edited versions to everyone's phones that they can read during food science. 'Wthrng Hghts — lds of ppl run rnd m0Ors in di@lct. Thnk they r mdly p@ssion8 bt really dull as fk. All Shkspre s@me bt usu@lly on bl@std hths. C u l8tr.'

MATHS

There has always been a distinction between 'masculine' and 'feminine' subjects. English comes top of the arty-farty feminine subject list and maths heads the other. There are studies galore on why this should be so — on whether the female brain is genuinely more predisposed towards success in arts and languages, while boys' are better designed to grapple with numbers or whether this is just an ingrained cultural divide born in the days when girls were believed to be frail and tender flowers who would be crushed under the remorseless wheels of mathematical logic and only needed to know how to read novels and noble tales of empire-building to keep them busy in between babies and fainting fits.

All I know is this: maths was by far the most loathed subject in my all-girls school, and I have never met a man who can get caught up in a novel or give une merde about mastering conversational French.

Personally, I parted ways with maths when Mrs Anderson tried to get me to calculate the area under a graph. I had had my doubts about her ever since she tried to insist that fractions could have different tops and bottoms and still mean the same amount and that X could equal Y in the right light. Calculating the area under a graph seemed to step over the line separating blind faith from utter madness and from that moment I embarked on an impressively consistent programme of passive resistance to all things arithmetical.

I know that maths, if you are good at it, has its own transcendent, timeless beauty and satisfactions. But for the rest of us it is a dispiriting affair involving much calculation of how many horseshoes can be made out of a length of iron and the like, which considering the parlous state of the native blacksmithing industry these days is of even less use than it was.

GEOGRAPHY

Glaciers, relief maps, latitude, longitude and the equator. At one point I think I could name all the countries on a map of Europe, but not now. And I don't know where China is, though I'm pretty sure it's different from Japan. I wish I were joking.

GAMES

PE in primary school was bad enough, and that was merely a matter of running round the school hall in vest and knickers, catching beanbags or following the mellifluously voiced Music and Movement man's instructions issuing forth from the tape recorder and pretending to be a tree blowing in the wind. 'Or if you are a deprived child who has never seen a tree, pretend you are a crisp packet floating and fluttering in the breeze.'

Games at secondary school were a whole different ball game.

Hockey meant tabards, freezing winds scything across the pitch, frostbitten fingers welded to the icy stick, perverts lining the periphery of the playing fields hoping to catch a fleeting glimpse of gym knickers under pleated games skirts and the ever-present threat of being trampled to death by an unstoppable forward line with a combined weight of fifty-eight stone.

Netball meant tabards, freezing winds scything across the court, frostbitten fingers welded to the icy ball, perverts lining the periphery of the playing fields hoping to catch a fleeting glimpse of gym knickers under pleated skirts, but an outside chance of surviving the match, as it was, theoretically at least, a non-contact sport and the ball was only hard enough to wind, not fracture.

School swimming was an unadulterated nightmare. Partly because, instead of the natural rock pools refilled every day by the ebb and flow of a crystalline sea that the girls in the *Malory Towers* books swam in gaily every day, lessons for the modern urban student took place in local municipal pools, refilled only when the water had taken on a saffron hue and — thanks to the unalterable drive of the human body to slough skin and plasters during exercise — the consistency of porridge. And partly because any kind of water-based exercise after the age of about four for women takes on its own special dreadfulness and becomes an exercise in despair and humiliation. You spend the ages five to twelve working out how you can get changed without showing your knickers and/or being molested by the gym teacher, twelve to eighteen pretending that you've got a six-year period and the rest of your life working out how you can get changed and go swimming without showing any flesh at all. And that is to say nothing of the delight attendant on the first time you haul yourself out of the local pool around the age of fourteen and realise — oh, the unending joys of womanhood! — that you appear to have pubic hair that reaches almost to your knees.

Of course, getting out of swimming lessons is a small subset of the principle held by all girls after the age of thirteen that all games are something to be avoided at all costs. They are no longer seen as a joyful escape from lessons and a chance to work off that pent-up youthful energy, but two-hour blocks of torture in which teachers who recently demobbed from the SAS devote themselves to making you get as hot, sweaty and unattractive as possible.

Tricks include:

- Faking a note from your mum, obviously. In ninety-nine per cent of cases this fails due to a superfluity of ambition. It is only natural to want to elaborate on the standard 'ill', 'sick' and 'flu' excuses, but equally naturally it is rarely possible for a thirteen-year-old to approximate the spelling of 'explosive diarrhoea', 'incapacitated by agoraphobia' or 'leprous and astigmatic' closely enough to fool even a games teacher, traditionally not the brightest of the breed.

- Falling down the nearest steps and claiming a twisted ankle

- Volunteering for a position on the wing and edging further and further out until eventually you are in a different postal district from the rest of the team and, if local geography is kind to you, sitting in your front room having a nice cup of tea while the other ten tabard-wearers stagger on till half three.

- Faking inside knowledge of a local crime syndicate and getting relocated under the witness protection programme.

There are exceptions to every rule, however, and every school harboured a handful of athletic girls who could not be dissuaded from excelling at and enjoying games. We had two or three in our year, but the interesting thing was that, perhaps for the first time ever, they had to stand up not just to peer pressure, but to wider anti-competitive feeling amongst the powers that be.

Sports Day

In the first half of the century, any such inter- or intra-school competition was a chance for the athletic girls to shine, to galvanise the rest, an opportunity for the best in the school to compete against each other and strive for an almost Olympian ideal in fulfilling their physical potential in the service of the school, God and country. Then came the sixties and everything turned to shit.

Since then, in the name of egalitarianism and empowerment, the best are no longer picked and there have to be enough races to include everyone. If there is a girl fortunate enough to have been gifted, by genetics or divine grace, the ability to outrun, outthrow or outjump her fellow students, she will not be lauded or held up to her friends as a shining example of human achievement. She will be kneecapped and tied to a tree trunk for the three-legged race as punishment for almost ruining the dream of equality.

Other factors too have altered the nature of Sports Day. There's the fact that there are no longer any playing fields, due to the great sell-off which started in the eighties. The ability to revel in students' physical prowess is necessarily muted when your environs limit you to arm-wrestling contests and seeing who can withstand the greatest bra-pinging.

Then there is the fact that most girls these days will only run if there's a recording contract or *Big Brother* application form at the end of the track. Without that it's 'Fuck off, Miss, and why are you pissing on about the honour of the school?'

So, if you are good at games, you will need to re-educate your teachers and governors about the concept of a meritocracy. You will be expelled, but take comfort in the fact that it will have been for a much better and more noble reason than the usual disembowelling-of-a-first-year-with-a-flick-knife.

The favourite after-school activities for girls were tap 'n' ballet classes and gymnastics club. I say gymnastics, I mean thirty pot-bellied nine-year-olds in green leotards, hurtling like little lumps of snot across lice-infested floor mats and throwing themselves off the wallbars, the air ringing with cries of pain and the unmistakable thuds of pre-adolescent bodies meeting the immoveable mass of the suede-topped horse. In our minds, though, we were the spitting image of Nadia Comaneci.

It was through tap 'n' ballet class, however, that I learned what it is to dread. The class took place in draughty church hall no. 8,056 and was run by a pile of tattered pink ribbons and chiffon scarves, somewhere deep within which lay the woman from whom instructions, clouds of Silk Cut smoke and gobbets of phlegm spasmodically issued. Did everyone in charge of children in the eighties smoke, or was it just a way of keeping warm in church halls? We may never know.

By the end of the first session, it was apparent that I had no grace, no poise and even less sense of rhythm. It was a shame because, aside from my stickers, my ballet shoes were the most beautiful things I had ever owned. Some girls – the more advanced ones – had dusky-pink leather shoes. But nobody wanted those and, for once, my mother's priorities and popular convention coincided. Pink, beribboned and satin shoes were the cheapest and most practical option for a beginner and I got them. In your face, Alice Bitchface-McFarthead. In. Your. Face.

CHAPTER 4

Friendship: the Power, the Pleasure, the Pain

Your eyes meet across a crowded playground and somehow you know. You just know. This is the girl for you, the girl you want to spend the rest of your life with. You have found your best friend.

What you have probably found, of course, is a manipulative, Machiavellian, two-faced, scheming USER who – after a brief and glorious period of sunlit happiness together, during which you unburden your every thought to her, unwrap every secret you have hidden in your soul, waiting for the day when someone would descend on your life like grace from heaven – will run off with some other pint-sized vessel of malice and betrayal.

She will listen gleefully as your former friend disgorges all your secrets in one great treacherous spew, the two of them glancing sideways at you – standing mere feet away across the tarmac, stunned, violated, paralysed with horror at the depthless chasm of treachery that has suddenly opened up beneath your feet – to make sure you are getting the message that you are Out and they are In.

So you – the innocent, desolate, broken-hearted victim – have three choices. You can march over, punch your hand through her chest, tear out her heart and hold the still-pulsing organ up before her appalled but rapidly dimming eyes. Or you can smile brightly, turn on your heel and vow to get your revenge by living well, which is less immediately satisfying but runs a smaller risk of attracting the negative attentions of the dinner lady corps. Or you can grab hold of the nearest schoolgirl, impose your best friendship immediately upon her and seal the deal by pouring out everything you know about your sworn enemy, with a few extra tales of bed-wetting and head lice thrown in for good measure.

Some wounds run deep.

In the meantime, boys are forming lifelong friendships based entirely on the ability to kick a ball the length of the playground or rescue it from the special needs annexe roof, into which no emotion or drama will ever intrude. Their bonding does not involve the sharing of secrets or the joint exploration of hopes and dreams, but begins and ends with the bestowing of nicknames. 'Nice one, Skid.' 'The F-Meister General strikes again!' They will probably die without ever knowing each other's real names.

But that's them and we're us. We are relational beings – we judge and value our friends in terms of the amount we can trust them, the emotional support they can give, the extent of the acceptance and the depth of understanding, validation and connection they can offer us and, crucially, vice versa. We know no other way. We base our friendships on things deeper than a shared interest in keepy-uppy. And if that means we are occasionally knifed in the guts by the abrupt end of a friendship, if it means we have to spend ninety per cent of our formative years running to the teacher crying, 'Miss! Miss! She's picking on me, Miss!' and the other ten per cent wandering around in a haze of tears, bewilderment and loneliness because we have recently been sold out by three best friends in quick succession, then so be it. Because when it works, there is simply nothing to beat it.

But it takes time to get there. The evolution of successful friendship amongst girls does not happen in a day. From the festering mass of hatreds, jealousies, tears, feuds and furies of the early years, through the festering mass of hatreds, jealousies, tears, feuds and furies occasionally interspersed with the discovery of a soul mate with whom to stand against the cliquey adolescent forces of darkness during the teenage years, to the relative peace and harmony of your twenty- and thirty-something friendships, onto whose soft sands you do, with any luck, eventually wash up with the grateful sigh of a long-battered mariner at last come home, accumulating a stock of good girlfriends is the work of decades.

Primary School

My first friendship was with Sarah Richards. It was more a test of endurance than anything else. She was an enormous child – about seventy-two feet tall, if memory serves – and took a liking to me that I could really do nothing about. She was particularly attracted to my portability. As I was about the size of a handbag throughout my primary school years, she used to like nothing better than to pick me up and carry me round the playground. All break time. Every break time.

I know now that it should only be people with whom you have a bond of mutual respect and affection that you dignify with the title of 'friend', but looking back I can see that I bestowed the title on Sarah because to make an enemy of anyone who could lob you over a wall at whim seemed a foolish choice. I did wonder why she took such pleasure in carting me about. Now I think it was either an early appearance of the innate female need to accessorise or the stirring of a kind of proto-maternal instinct. Then I just thought she was huge and bonkers and acquiesced accordingly.

Eventually, however, the relationship ended. It must have been a rare amicable separation because I don't remember much about it. Perhaps I just got too heavy to hoist and she lumbered off in search of smaller prey. Perhaps her mother bought her a real handbag. Or perhaps she left to go to a special school for giants.

It is truly incredible how complex the world of female-to-female relationships is from such a young age. By the end of the first day of school, a nexus of alliances, agreements, counter-agreements, political allegiances and personal loyalties has been established which only grows in intensity and impenetrability for the next six years. It's no wonder girls are better than boys at history – the multiple intrigues of ancient Florentine courts, the serpentine twists and turns of royal dynasties, the necessity of holding in one's head the multitudinous possible influences on the writer of a surviving text are as nothing compared to a day spent in the seething, frothing pit of pre-adolescent girls and their friendships.

My best friend: a cautionary tale

I had a best friend. We'll call her The Betrayer, or TB for short – which, incidentally but neatly, is the disease I hope she slowly dies of. We did everything together. We sat next to each other in class, swapped sandwiches at lunchtime and sweets at the weekend, shared custody of the lip gloss and, crucially, we went to dance classes together.

One day, the dance teacher, Miss Phlegmhocker, announced that there would be a contest to find who could put together the best two-minute dance on a chosen subject. I forget what it was. Autumn, probably, as that was her favourite season ('The beeyootiful colours, girls, the gra-a-ceful floating leaves') or maybe Marlboro Lights, her favourite cigarette ('Today, girls, we are going to do the dance of the emphysemic forty-something'). It doesn't matter. The point is that it was a competition, and each of us had to choreograph a little dance and try to win kudos and some dismal hand-scrawled certificate and a length of green ribbon. God, we were easily pleased.

Anyway, in this instance, my habitual sloth and disaffection when confronted with situations demanding effort and the competitive instinct failed to engage and I threw myself into inventing and honing my routine. I rehearsed at home and at school and frequently before the appreciative audience of my friend and her Sindy dolls, the former cajoling, encouraging and neglecting, as a good friend should, to mention the fact that then, as now, I danced like a tumour. So generous was she, so devoted a friend, that she never even asked me to watch her in my turn.

The day of the contest came. When Miss Phlegmhocker asked for a volunteer to go first, TB bravely agreed. We applauded, she stepped forth. And proceeded – you may, given the wisdom of age and the fact that I rather ruined the denouement with my none-too-gently allusive monicker for the childwitch, be ahead of my eight-year-old self here – to dance my dance before the assembled throng. I. Was. Poleaxed. When she sat down, she met my eye and nodded pleasantly, quite in the manner of someone who had not just revealed herself to be the distilled essence of evil. I hated her as I have never hated anyone before or since, and yet the purity of my hatred was diluted fleetingly by a sneaking sense of regard, an unwilling admiration for the thoroughness of her betrayal. It was so clean, so efficient, so ruthless. She was like one of those wicked half-sisters or nasty rich girls we read about in *Mandy* and *Bunty* stories, who schemed and plotted as naturally as they breathed and cared nothing as to how many innocent souls they trampled underfoot during their self-serving progress through life. What it would be, I marvelled briefly, to live like that, so atavistically, so pitilessly, with such a genius for exploitation of others' trust and naïveté! This feeling soon passed, however, and was replaced by an unyielding sense of loathing, which I find to my surprise as I type this has not lessened one iota over the years. I'd still push her under a bus as soon as look at her. So perish all traitors.

At this age, friends can be lost over just about anything. Failing to wait for a friend to finishing changing for gym or not saving a seat for her in assembly or in the dinner queue were particularly common causes of rupture because they all betrayed the main tenet of the friendship code: thou shalt not leave me alone at especially vulnerable points in the school day EVER. It was your friend's job not to leave you unprotected, and definitely not unprotected in your vest and knickers or in a crowded hall full of tiny, vicious hellhags just waiting to turn their backs on you and make you sit alone for no other reason than because they can.

The other great crimes against friendship – apart, obviously, from passing notes in class to another girl without including your acknowledged intimates – was failing to share. The main rules were:

1. *Choicer morsels of your packed lunch to be handed round with a smile on your face that belied the blackness of your Hula-Hoop-craving heart.*

2. *Girl's World heads to be loaned out at sufficiently frequent intervals to those not in possession of such bounty.*

3. *Minty lip balm/gloss must be available at all times to close friends. This was generally adhered to, as it then provided an easy and dramatic way of demonstrating that someone was suddenly outside the charmed circle. 'No, you can't borrow it' – the words would ring out with a sweet and dreadful*

clarity, a pause would follow to allow surrounding ears to
attune and heads to swivel in time to watch the moment the
verbal bullet went home – 'You've got the lurgy.' To revoke lip
gloss privileges was to revoke the friendship entire.

4 The possession of an item of true rarity and value – a kitten,
for example, or the very latest Sindy doll 'n' accessories – must
be made available, for a limited period at least, to everyone
not currently designated an actual foe. Even the most tenuous
claim to friendship may be invoked and must be honoured
when a go with a kitten or puppy is at stake.

5 Gossip about teachers must be shared with everyone. But this
is more of a pleasure than a chore.

A breach of any of these rules – and a thousand million more – a
misstep in the ever-thickening web of interconnections and misalliances
would result in a casting out from the group. It might be instantaneous,
resulting in a few playtimes as Norma No-Mates before your senses
rallied and you started searching for replacement comrades, but even
more painful in many ways was the tribunal alternative. Standing before
a panel of soon-to-be-ex pals, or more likely surrounded by them on
all sides like pumas round a limping gazelle, the questions would come
thick and fast.

'Do you like her more than me?'
'Do you think you're better than us?'
'Why did you say that Lady Diana was prettier than me?'
'Do you think you're prettier than me?'
'Who do you like best out of this group?'
'Who do you think likes you best out of this group?'

Sooner rather than later, the bites and gougings would take their toll
and the gazelle would collapse. Satisfied, the pumas would pad softly,

sleekly away. Probably to successful careers as lawyers or unblinking despots in tiny principalities in hidden corners of the globe, where they rule through fear and, hypocritical to the last, maintain total monopolies on the region's kitten and lip gloss supplies.

The feeling of being ostracised by people who previously welcomed you is one you never forget. It also gives rise to one of those mathematically impossible phenomena. Just as, later in life, everyone seems to feel they are the last one to get married in their circle, so everyone feels she was the one forever being excluded. There must have been some queen bees to whom it never happened, who were responsible for the giving and never the receiving of misery, but you never meet them. Perhaps they all die young. That would be great.

Most mothers, when confronted by daughters coming home from school in tears because they have been called names and unaccountably cast into the outer darkness by some fickle fiend, try to minimise the pain by insisting that it doesn't matter, that these moments and these people aren't important and that it's just something to be ignored. This is, of course, the wisdom born of hard experience, but the daughter simply gazes up at her mother's face and thinks, 'Why is this woman lying to me?'

Unless, of course, your mother is a psychologist. Then she will tell you that the alliances and betrayals that characterise younger friendships are caused by the fact that at that age we all have 'unstable senses of self' and have to keep looking around for new companions who appeal to our different shifts at different times. (This doesn't explain why boys seem to get along quite happily from birth to death with the same set of friends, whose bonds were formed by sitting next to each other on the first day at school. Are they born with 'stable senses of self'? How?) As we become older and our characters settle, we become better at picking suitable friends and the rapid turnover ceases and emotional turmoil subsides accordingly. Psychologists' daughters look up at them and think, as well they might, 'And how the blazes, woman, does this hopelessly objective and dispassionate take on the situation help me here and now? Thank you so very much for nothing.'

Much better, if you are or ever plan to be a mother of a tearful and betrayed daughter, to react as your most basic, primitive instincts surely demand. I intend to sit my (putative) daughter down and hash out a plan to bring her tormentors to their knees – a plan that involves kidnap, torture, arson, the murder of beloved family pets and calling on the gods of rancour to help me in my mission, a mission that will avenge not just her but me, and cause fear to be struck in the hearts of schoolgirl evildoers now and forevermore. After all, you know what they say – the family that plots bloody vengeance together stays together.

Nevertheless, psychologists are right in saying that things change as girls get older, although it's not quite for the reasons they think. It's not so much creeping maturity that causes girls to quit the field as creeping exhaustion. There is only so long you can live at such a hysterical pitch, only so much untrammelled affection, bubbling fervour and violent loathing you can produce before the wells of passion run dry, and only so much rejection, humiliation and mortification you can stand before your heart scabs over and becomes a wizened and cankered thing that you can only afford to offer up to people who stand a good chance of taking care of it instead of dropkicking it into the nearest ditch. Later still, of course, you will recognise a similar sensation in a slightly different context and it will dawn on you that this is what is meant by feeling ready for marriage.

In primary school, girl world is really only divided into two groups. Subdivisions and gradations of almost infinite subtlety will arrive in their millions later on, but for now the taxonomy is simple. The world cleaves neatly in twain: there are the cool and the uncool. Each is easy to spot.

COOL	UNCOOL
Pierced ears	Unpierced ears
Long hair	Short hair
Being thin	Being fat
Wearing barrettes	Wearing mittens on a string
Wearing short socks	Wearing long socks. Or tights that come up to your armpits
Strappy sandals you can't run in	Clarks shoes that are one pair of eyelets away from being orthopaedic boots
Sovereign rings	Wearing no jewellery because your mum thinks it's common and isn't about to shell out for bloody tat from Argos just because everyone else is doing it, blah, blah, blah.
Being pretty	Being ugly
Being tall	Being short
Pretending to have breasts	Pretending to have breasts if you aren't already cool
Passing notes	Being the one they're passing notes about

I don't really know why girls seem to be especially driven to observe whatever passes for orthodoxy in their various groups. There is still more admiration for a man who stands out from the crowd than for a woman, so I suppose we must imbibe the message early and this is one of the first manifestations of it. Or perhaps we are all just little control freaks from birth and cannot cope with the sight of other people doing things differently, and especially not if they seem to be having more fun in the process. Who's to say?

Whatever the reason, there's no question that an hour's professional observation of girls at work on each other at school should be a compulsory part of every psychologist's and management consultant's training. You want to know about group dynamics and shifting power relations? Watch the queen bee manipulate her subjects and deflect covert assaults on her position from her ambitious – but not quite as pretty – number two. You want to gain insight into mind control and mental torture? Watch the exquisite blend of perspicacity and psychological brutality that emanates only from the female brain and is deployed to punish those who have deliberately or inadvertently betrayed signs of individualism or independent thought. Marvel at the innate understanding and finely calibrated assessment of the renegade's strengths and weaknesses before her punishment is chosen: pitying comments on new shoes if she sets store by her appearance; ostentatious hand-holding and jointly turned backs at her approach if she is thick-skinned and requires a visual clue to discern her current standing; note-passing and mocking giggles from distant corners of the playground that will echo in her ears for eternity if she is the cerebral type who can imagine much worse things being said about her than the group could ever actually come up with. You want to know how to deal with non-team players? Take notes as the girls close ranks and begin an intensive retraining of their problem child that would do credit to the US Marine Corps, interspersing the chosen bespoke punishments with moments of kindness and the occasional friendly gesture, breaking her spirit without alienating her forever and slowly but surely, by fair means and foul, rebuilding her in their image.

Malicious geniuses all. But fascinating.

The Upside

I fear I may be at risk of suggesting that nothing good can ever come of allowing girls to mix unsupervised. This is, of course, not true and I myself can think of dozens – well, a dozen … okay, ten … a handful – of moments of fun and happiness with my peers in the playground, at parties and in therapists' waiting rooms. So, as I began this section with a tale of true evil, I feel I should end it with a suitably uplifting counterpoint, an encomium to Yasmin, the new girl who arrived in the last year of primary school and became a true and proper friend.

We lost touch in later years, but she lives on in memory, forever young, beautiful, bold and brilliant.

She scored points from the beginning for showing no inclination to treat me like a handbag or rip off my choreography. Instead, she appointed herself my friend and my protector. Up until this point, I had been accustomed to enduring any bullying by muttering dark imprecations and vowing to get my revenge one day by writing a book in which I could vent my spleen messily over several thousand words. Yasmin took a more direct route.

One day, I was queuing by the water fountains for my turn at a game of foursquares (you bounce a netball between four people standing in squares – it was a simpler time) when Shona Lewis elbowed me in the stomach and out of the way. Yasmin shot up the playground from, I think, Croydon, because she'd been nowhere in sight before then, and arrived in front of Shona before she had even had time to move into my place. 'Did you,' said Yasmin, all but paring her nails with a flick-knife as she spoke, 'just push in front of my friend?' Shona paled. 'N-n …' Yasmin held up a silencing hand. 'Did you,' she repeated, cracking her knuckles between syllables, 'just push in front of my friend?' Shona trembled. Yasmin bounced her head gently off the water fountain and replaced her at the back of the queue. She surveyed the scene for further potential lawbreakers, found none, nodded at me and ran off again, to fight crime and right wrongs in Metropolis, I imagined as I gazed after her in wonder and admiration.

It was my first experience of friendship, of sisterhood in the broader sense. Is it too much to say that this was when the first seeds of hope were sown within me that one day we girls would find a way to live together in peace and harmony? Maybe so. And they even found a way to germinate in the rocky soil of secondary school.

Secondary school

The basic cool/uncool divide gives way to a more detailed system of classification in secondary school. The basic cliques were:

Popular

Gilded youth: pretty, vivacious girls whose outward charms generally belied a core of steel and a heart of ice. They had all the latest stuff – clothes, shoes, records, make-up – and mainlined *Just Seventeen* and *More* magazines to make sure they never fell behind the curve. Their lives were generally mysteriously unblighted by the usual physical travails of adolescence, but on the infrequent occasions when one of them did get a spot, the group would huddle round her like professional mourners and sit sebaceous shivah until the blemish had disappeared.

They were usually the girls who had ruled the various fiefdoms in primary school, but age had mellowed them sufficiently that, encountered singly, a popular girl usually retained her human form. En masse, however, they were monstrous once again.

Unpopular

Anyone with short hair, braces, glasses, spots that merged into each other, who got breasts too early or too late, liked her parents, did her homework and didn't have an older brother. Whatever your grotesque physical deformities, a sibling who was a source of potential boyfriends automatically catapulted you into the premier league.

Cool

Tricky to define. It meant girls with an edge, girls who went to live gigs, smoked for real instead of gesturing ostentatiously with Consulate and drank spirits unmixed with Coke or orange, girls who were popular but looked like it was effortless and that they really didn't care.

Uncool

Everyone else. Especially goths. Because even other fourteen-year-olds can see that you're going to look back in a few years and really, really regret looking that stupid.

Slags

Anyone who wasn't popular or cool but went ahead and had sex anyway, even without peer pressure. It raised dark suspicions that she might be doing it because she enjoyed it, instead of for its intended purpose of accumulating social cachet.

Virgins

This was partly a term of abuse and partly just accurate labelling. Thanks to the average schoolgirl's propensity for sharing every thought and experience she has with fifty of her closest friends, everyone knows who's done it and who hasn't. Those who, thanks to a strict or religious upbringing, remain in the latter group until ridiculously advanced ages like sixteen and seventeen will be known as virgins till the end of their days, even if they spend – as many do – their university years taking on entire rugby teams every weekend. Late developers are prone to over-rebellion.

Hard, harder, hardest

I didn't know the term 'hard man' existed till I left school. At my single-sex school I only ever heard the word used to describe girls. 'She's well 'ard' was one of the great compliments, uttered with awe and carefully out of the hearing of the subject, just in case. It applied to all the girls who arrived at school every morning in rampant furies and spent their days throwing themselves round the classroom like trapped bluebottles and getting into screaming matches with as many teachers and pupils as possible before it was time to go home and do the same thing there.

Geeks, boffins and spods

Pallid, bespectacled creatures who scurried to and from the library, shrinking from daylight, getting all their homework done as soon as it was set and fretting about exams. What a waste of a life. I wish someone had told me.

Where you set the boffin bar depended on what kind of school you went to. At some, a moderate preference for reading rather than sniffing corrector fluid off your jumper sleeve was enough to get you marked out as a dangerous intellectual, and at others the ability to read without moving your lips made you indistinguishable from Gore Vidal. While I was at university, I learned that there are some places where you have to refuse to turn up to gymkhanas because you are in the middle of translating Tacitus into Old Church Slavonic before you qualify as a geek. Context is all.

Tomboys

These are brave and charismatic souls who decide that the whole fraught, girlish business is not for them and opt out entirely. One of my oldest and dearest friends was a tomboy and can recall her entire girlhood in perfect tranquillity. 'But what about the relentless feuding, the highs, the lows, the tears, the dramas, the early determinative experiences that made us all the ambulant bundles of neuroses you see before you today?' I protest. 'It was like eighteen episodes of *Falcon Crest* every lunchtime!' She shrugs and remembers nothing except running about in sensible shoes with her other tomboy pals and occasionally pestering her mother to buy her an Adidas sports bag. She is today a woman of imperturbable tranquillity and equilibrium. I hate her.

A girl's best friend

The members of a clique are, by definition, friends with each other, simply because they have too much in common with each other not to be. Often, for the word 'friendship' you can read 'slavish imitation of each other'. But gradually, a few faces begin to stand out in the crowd. You keep catching the same person's eye after a teacher's lame jokes or futile attempts to get down wid da kidz, and before you know it, you have got yourself your first real friend.

By real friend I mean someone you actually care about as an individual, and who concerns herself equally with your daily trials and tribulations. Someone you can trust, who can be counted on not to disseminate your innermost secrets across seventeen counties the moment she gets narked by a perceived slight. Your friendship revolves not around ballet classes, tea at each other's houses or any other recreational activity, but around talking and the minute analysis of everything.

It is so much better than actually doing anything. Do you remember the endless hours spent discussing what game to play and how to play it? International peace treaties are drawn up with less fuss. Mergers of billion-dollar companies are achieved with less consultation than a gang of six–year-olds will devote to the rival attractions of Doctors and Nurses versus Having a Tea Party. But by thirteen, it can truly be said that girlfriends have fully embraced the art of analysis. If, as Socrates said, the unexamined life is not worth living, yours is about to become the most richly rewarding existence in human history.

Every happening at home, at school, at the bus stop and the moments in between is dissected, examined from every angle, agonised over and put back together in the way that makes most sense to you and best suits the group's purposes. A boy yelled something at you in the street? He is, like, so childish. But if it was complimentary, his childishness is just a front to hide his incredible maturity and impeccable taste in women. If it was unflattering, he was just doing it to impress his mates. If he was alone, he was just jealous because he knows he could never go out with you. If you see him again, your friends will have furnished you with a dozen comebacks for every conceivable situation.

You are so sorted.

So you and your friend bellow at each other on the bus to school. You talk through roll call. During assembly, the entire female contingent is crushed into one back row, so that it can download its thoughts unseen by whichever teacher has the misfortune that day of trying to engage its attention with a moral lecture derived from last night's *EastEnders*. You talk on your way up the stairs to double maths. If the teacher is big enough and scary enough, you might tacitly withdraw into silence for the duration, otherwise, it's chat, chat, chat and to hell with simultaneous equations. The ingestion of food doesn't slow you down at lunchtime. You can talk on the in-breath, the out-breath and through gluey mouthfuls of Mighty White. By the afternoon, your mouth is like sandpaper, but you rehydrate with sneaky swigs of Coke under your desk in French and carry on. When you part ways after a quick recap of the day's events on the bus home, you rush straight in and call her on the phone. Your dad strides around wondering what on earth you can have to say to each other after spending the previous seven hours together. Ohmigod, it is like he just, you know, doesn't have a clue. It is like he is some kind of total mor-on! But you don't have to tell her that. She already knows and understands all. It is very lucky that your discovery of each other coincides with the moment that you and your friends each become the most genuinely, objectively fascinating and complex creatures ever to have walked the earth, otherwise the wealth of groundbreaking data that would have been lost does not bear thinking about.

What you are talking about at that age (Dad, for your infor*ma*tion, as you are so *in*terested) is everything and nothing. The words themselves and the information exchanged are frequently (alright, almost without exception) worthless. It is the verbal equivalent of monkeys grooming each other; it's there to forge bonds, reassure, support and consolidate the community. Every 'Oh God, I know exactly what you mean!' is a small infusion of confidence, something to salt away for the bleak, hormonal times you see ahead, during which you would otherwise come to believe that you are the only person who has ever thought, felt, dreamed, hoped, suffered in this, that or the other way. The passionate excesses of adolescence spill over everything.

. . . ✳ . ' .

My real best friend

I spotted her across a crowded classroom. It wasn't difficult, as she was thirteen feet tall even then, skinny as a rake and tended to buckle in a stiff breeze. She was living a relatively comfortable life on the periphery of the in-crowd, but I knew I could bring her over to my side and render her unfit for mainstream school society ever again. There was something in the way she went cross-eyed when the talk turned from Madonna to Wet Wet Wet that led me to hope that beneath that ordinary exterior beat the heart of a weirdo.

And so it turned out. It was Sally who tested the truth of the science teacher's assertion that peristalsis would ensure that drink went down your throat even if you consumed it upside down. She did a headstand in the cloakroom and directed us to pour Coke into her mouth until she nearly choked to death. It was Sally who deflected all attempts at bullying by claiming that she was seeing a psychiatrist because she thought she was a tap. Would-be tormentors backed off in confusion, never to return. It was Sally who, having no clue as to how to work out the correct answer, responded to a maths GCSE question about how many desks could be made out of a piece of chipboard with the words 'At least one, I should think. And I would make matching pencil cases out of the leftovers.'

Joined by Donna, Gillian and another Sally, we would sit in
the cloakroom on winter days, on playground benches in
the summer or, in our final year together, the sumptuously
appointed fifth-form common room (half a dozen stained and
erratically padded chairs, a fetid rug and a kettle in a disused
classroom) and laugh our lungs up every break time. I have
acquired some good and true friends since then, but the ability
to make me laugh for ninety minutes a day is a gift only Sally
has bestowed upon me.

Later on, she would report back on sex, drugs and music, so
that I didn't have to bother getting a life of my own. I have
always been more than happy to lead an essentially vicarious
existence. It's a damn sight cheaper for one thing.

A lot of teenage friendships fade over time, of course. If the swell of
adolescence temporarily obscures your fundamental differences, you
can be left standing on different shores once the waters recede. And
a lot of teenage friendships are ruptured by the advent of boyfriends,
because it takes time to learn that if you snog one that belongs to
a friend, it is you she won't forgive and take back, not him. As you
become more mature and aware of the importance of loyalty – and the
novelty of French kissing wears off – it becomes easier to privilege your
girl friendships above boys and prioritise your obligations towards the
former accordingly.

Some girls never make this leap, of course, and remain men's women
all their lives. You probably have at least one such person on the periphery
of your circle of friends. She is the one who seems perfectly normal,
perfectly absorbed in your conversation over lunch, and then, at the
approach of anything male – could be a waiter, could be a friend, could
be an XY chromosome in a matchbox – suddenly sprouts three inches of

visible cleavage and turns into a drawling, semi-liquid, shaggable heap of a woman, pouring herself seductively over half the table and your Caesar salad. There's no point getting angry at the interruption – just treat it as cabaret and enjoy. And, let's be honest, you didn't really want the Caesar salad anyway. You can reorder while you watch the act if you like.

But basically, your late teens and early twenties are (if you are reasonably lucky and reasonably able to refrain from sucking face with other people's paramours) the years in which you begin to accrue enduring friendships, perhaps because, for most people, it is the time when we are happiest, when we are most ourselves.

After that, things become trickier. Research shows that women do in fact experience a friendship slump in their late twenties. There are many reasons for this:

1. *Your true self is likely to find itself increasingly distorted by the need to act professionally here, be polite there, stop laughing inappropriately everywhere and by the soul-warping stresses of finding a job, paying the rent, being a girlfriend, wife and mother. This is good for forging bonds of comradeship in adversity, but these companions will never know or nourish you as well as those who met you in what I like to think of as the pre-buried-under-multiple-bucketfuls-of-crap years.*

2. *The said multiple bucketfuls of crap – aka the accumulating strains of adult life. To go from the ease of 'Hmm. I fancy a coffee. I wonder who's down the road/in the next room?' when you are renting back your bedroom from your parents/living with eighteen like-minded girls in a flatshare to 'Hmm. I fancy a coffee. Is there anyone around who keeps the same hours as me, lives anywhere that doesn't require three bus trips and a boat trip to get to, can leave their children, husband or ailing mother, still drinks coffee with enthusiasm instead*

of considering caffeine a convulsant and isn't consumed by
ten life crises that render her more of a drain on one's mental
resources than a restorative?' puts a damper on many a
friendly impulse.

3 *Marriage. Most of my closest friends turned out to be the*
early-marrying kind. If I'd known, I would have spread my
pal portfolio more widely, but it's not the kind of question
that crosses your mind when you hitch your wagon to a
companion's star at the tender age of eighteen or so, is it? If
you are still half a decade or more from even contemplating
a scintilla of a shred of a sliver of a possibility that marriage
might be a state you could ever enter, a friend's entry into it
can shut you out of her life pretty effectively. In fact, one of
the greatest benefits I discovered when I eventually embarked
on a long-term relationship was that it lets you back into the
lives of those who went maritally missing years before. Once
you become part of a 'solid' couple, the married ladies seem to
reach out once more. The traditional explanation for this is
that a ring on her finger causes any woman to conceive of all
single females as predatory devils and implode in a seething
mass of panic and hissing venom if one approaches. I do not
believe this is, in fact, the kind of behaviour which continues
much past the age of eighteen, unless the woman in question
is of the pathologically insecure variety, in which case she will
probably be surrounded by friends who are delighted to hand
over care of her to her husband and go off and find some less
exhausting individual to take her place.

I think the disappearance of married friends is more to do
with a failure of imagination. They discover that marriage is
not all sweetness and light and that it takes work, and rows,
and more work, and more rows to maintain the stretches
of happiness and equilibrium in between. And they assume

that until you have a husband or a long-term, co-habiting boyfriend of your own, you will not understand that they are not failures but victims of the simple fact that perfection does not exist for anyone.

When you are let into the married club as an honorary member, your pleasure at reconnecting with long-lost friends can be marred by the fact that they thought so little of your ability to make the necessary imaginative leap. 'Did they really think that I was so uninformed/ignorant/inexperienced that I couldn't understand that arguing with someone and getting fed up with them sometimes didn't mean that you didn't love them or were heading straight for the divorce courts before the first year was up?' you rage inwardly. 'Did they think I had never read a book, seen a film, met other couples or developed an ability to extrapolate from my own lesser experiences to a wider one? Could they not trust me to understand that living with someone might not be to experience a transcendental sense of bliss at every waking moment? Just how fucking dense do they think I am?'

Not that you ever said any of that, of course. They are your friends, after all.

☑ *Motherhood. More and more of your leisure time is taken up with supporting those of your friends who have decided to have babies. For a few years, your friendships become stuck in a loop, played out according the following script:*

Scene 1:
The telephone rings.
NEW MOTHER: I require the presence of another adult
    in the house before I tear my own eyes out.
OLD FRIEND: Don't you have health visitors for that
    kind of thing?

NM: They just sit there with their special judging heads and clipboards, waiting for you to drop the baby so that they can take it and sell it to rich couples who live on the internet.

OF (*sighing*): I'll be there as soon as you ring me back once you have remembered your new address. Why pregnant women always move house in their eighth month, I do not know. Does nobody tell you your brain is going to fall out and that you'd be better off staying somewhere that doesn't require the assimilation of new information for the next year?

NM: Who's talking, please?

OF eventually arrives at a suburban terraced house containing one semi-conscious mother – hair crusted with unidentified excretions, eyes rolling back in her head, one boob hanging out of her shirt, ricocheting round the house trying to remember where she left the kitchen – and a baby lying contentedly on the gin-soaked floor.

NM: Hello. Would you like some creamed peas?

OF: No thanks. Would you like me to make you a cup of tea?

NM: That would be great. Ooo, and could you make me a cup of tea?

OF: Of course. Do you want to put your boob back in your shirt?

NM: Oh God, yes, sorry. That's weird, because I put six bras on this morning. Some of them the right way round.

NM holds the baby up.

NM: Does he look OK to you?

OF: Well, I'm an amateur in the field, but yeah, he
   looks fine.
NM: I think he looks a bit green.
OF: Is that not just his cardigan?
NM: Oh yes. Would you like a cup of tea?
OF: I would. Shall I make it?
NM: That would be—
NM falls asleep. OF cannot rouse her with a Taser
gun. OF plays with the baby for two hours and
plugs it onto NM's boob when it starts to cry.
She sleeps through eight feeds. OF leaves five
hours later when the father comes home. When she
wakes on Thursday, NM rings to thank her OF.
Unfortunately, she is talking into the washing
machine, but OF intuits what has happened and
understands. This is what friendship means.

10 Favourite Topics Of Conversation For New Mums

1. Sleep
2. Blood
3. Shit
4. Sleep
5. Tears
6. Sleep
7. Vomit
8. Any story that starts, 'The doctor said he'd never seen anything like it ...'
9. Any story that ends, 'And then the rest just dropped out in my hand!'
10. Any story that contains the phrase, ' ... it was like a FIST ...'

5 *Money.* You might hope that nothing so superficial and vulgar
could come between you and your friends, but you would
be wrong. When you are still earning single-digit pounds
per hour as a temp instead of tens of thousands a year as a
lawyer, your relationships will change. Some of your friends
will simply become too expensive to see any more. I remember
meeting one friend I hadn't seen for months, since she started
some astonishing job in the city. I had had no qualms about
demanding that we met somewhere cheap (if you can't do
that, they really shouldn't be dignified with the title of friend
in the first place – you are, in fact, meeting an acquaintance
or paying a duty call of some kind) but then she started
talking about putting in a new kitchen. I was confused. The
last time I had seen her was at her housewarming party. I had
seen the kitchen and it was both very nice and brand new, put
in just before the previous owners had left. I said as much to
her and she replied airily, 'Oh yes, I know, but I've seen one I
like better and I don't like having so much money just sitting
in the bank, so I thought I'd get rid of it in Smallbone of
Devizes!' She laughed.

Oh, ha bloody ha, I thought. I knew then that we had
probably reached the end of the conversation and indeed the
road. This is the sloughing off of unrewarding friendships –
the adult equivalents of youth's 'users' and 'frenemies'. If you
are strong and gifted with preternatural insight into your
friendships, which enables you to diagnose the diseased parts
of your body of companions and cut them out, this will be a
clean and swift business. If you are like the rest of us, however,
you will employ the passive-aggressive method of ignoring
emails, screening calls and moving house to get free of them.
Or you can simply wait until you have naturally developed
such a cynical and selfish carapace over the years and become

so cankered of heart that the needy and manipulative will
find you completely useless for their purposes and take
themselves off elsewhere. The net effect is the same, and
equally welcome.

All this is in addition to the inevitable casualties of the years. Sometimes things just go wrong. Age lessens the chances, but you do still fall out with friends from time to time. Perhaps you or she blurts out a long-kept secret to a third party. Perhaps changed circumstances suddenly reveal an unexpected irreconcilability in your beliefs about childcare or estate cars. Perhaps you lose your usually firm grasp on friend etiquette and accidentally shag someone's husband in the broom closet (in which case, congratulations! And do try to make up with the family in time to shag her seventeen-year-old son in a few years' time).

Once you head into your thirties, however, the same research assures us that female friendships reassert themselves, which I can only assume is due to the dawning realisation that they can furnish something no doting husband, fulfilling career or adoring and adored child can. The Victorians were able to recognise this particular phenomenon better than we can, because they did not expect men and women to supply each other with everything. Husbands and wives were expected to be loyal to and support each other, but not to lead the same lives or share each other's interests and confidences. Nowadays, we are meant to be equal partners in marriage (and all preludes to it) and we have taken this to mean that you can talk to your bloke as you would to a girlfriend and get the same satisfactions from it. It doesn't, and you can't. So don't try.

Just as men still escape on stag weekends and to sports nights at the pub, we still need our girlfriends and nights of intense, overheated, forensically – and frequently pornographically – detailed conversation, punctuated by shrieking laughter, cathartic tears and professions of undying love, acceptance, adoration and validation. The friends you made in the playground, the girls you grew up with, the women you couldn't manage without at work, your former flatmates, the lazy-arsed cows from your student days, the women who have seen you through more bottles of gin than hot dinners and the one who is coming round to bitch about another one over coffee and chocolate cake in a minute are all of vital importance to one's health and merriment.

CHAPTER 5

Growing Up

Adolescence for girls is a series of letdowns, curtailments of freedom, physical upheaval and futile rebellions. How any of us survive it, I do not know.

Let's start where all the textbooks start, with what they call the maturing body and I call the series of revelations that your body is not a useful vehicle for your mind and spirit, but an agglomeration of horrors, betrayals and leaking orifices, a fleshly houseful of disappointments which will only increase in number and severity with age.

Skin

Did you know that your skin is your largest organ? All being well, it covers your entire body and has a surface area of around two square metres. Its thickness varies from an impossibly fragile-sounding 0.5mm on your eyelids to 4mm or more on the palms of your hands and the soles of your feet. In total, it accounts for around sixteen per cent of your body weight. But as an adolescent, you are concerned with only about twenty square inches of this amazing organ: the area covering your face and which your mother won't let you cover with a paper bag when you go out in public and which you therefore must expose to the unforgiving eyes and cruel laughter of post-adolescents who have achieved the one desire to which your teenage soul is strung – the matte face of the hormonally at peace.

From 1988 to 1992, my sebaceous glands pumped out more oil than the North Sea rigs. My hair was dark with grease and permanently plastered to my head. I didn't realise I was still blonde until I was twenty-two. When my mother wanted to take a photo of me to send to Grandma for her collection, she had to bring the camera into the bathroom and snap me as soon as I came out of the shower. If she waited for me to get dried, dressed and downstairs, I would once more be glistening with grease, creating both a formidable bounce-back effect with the flash and an instant recoil amongst any unlucky viewer. 'There were times,' my mother recalls, 'when we thought we could try to sell your skin to BP. I followed you round with a bucket on hot days, otherwise we'd have been hosing down seagulls 24–7.'

Spots were at first many and varied, but I came to specialise in whiteheads and blackheads. Once a set of the former had reached critical mass and was threatening to obscure my sight or breathing, my mother would put me in a half nelson and my sister would pop the pus-filled sacs, clad in a HAZMAT suit to guard against inevitable splatter. Of such shared moments is a family history built. Blackheads I took care of myself. I would excavate my pores with a teaspoon every morning and look like a doily till midday, and then the holes would start to fill up again. By 7 o'clock, my head would be three pounds heavier and I'd have to wear a neck brace till I went to bed.

Do you remember the Clearasil ads in those days? Two badly dubbed American teenagers passing bits of blue-stained cotton wool over their porcelain skins and then presenting to the camera the white fluff, which looked like it had been used to clean up an anthracite spill? That was the thing that first alerted me to the possibility that everything associated with the advertising industry might just be a total load of lying bollocks. A useful lesson, certainly, but I'd have traded it for skin that didn't make me look like I had a face full of buckshot if I'd had the choice.

10 Great Disappointments In Life

1. Adolescence
2. Bioré pore-cleansing strips
3. Sex
4. Work
5. Posh chocolates
6. Posh restaurants
7. Posh Spice
8. Boys
9. Men
10. Christmas pantomimes

Most people, if asked, will recall similar experiences with unsatisfactory epidermises. I do not know how this squares with the fact that a) not one of the friends you had during the teenage years, all of whose faces you scrutinised on a daily basis more closely than an *Antiques Roadshow* expert does a gem-encrusted heirloom, seemed to suffer one quarter of the eruptions, excretions and embarrassments that you did, and b) all the teenage girls you happen across daily – on the bus, in the shopping centre, or moving in a shrieking pack through the high street at the start of a forty-eight-hour weekend nightclub-and-drinking binge (as you wend your way home on Friday wondering if you have the energy to pierce the film lid on your microwave meal the requisite number of times before you fall asleep in front of *Coronation Street*) – have complexions like Dresden figurines.

These two samplings – one current, one vividly recalled from fifteen years ago – suggest that, in fact, in every teenage generation, eighty-seven per cent of girls have no trouble at all with their pores and glide through life not on a slick of oil, but a cloud of confidence born of the knowledge that they look like they have been carved from alabaster, lit from within by the glow of youth instead of rippling gently with the ebb and flow of excess sebum seeking violent release. Unfortunately, the remaining thirteen per cent produce enough to tar the entire population of adolescents with the same sticky brush.

Hair

Hair on women anywhere but their heads is, as we and the multimillion-pound depilatory industry all know, a Very Bad Thing, and one of the few unpleasant attributes of the human body for which even the most dedicated and inventive biologist has failed to produce convincing evidence of an evolutionary or current benefit.

I'd seen my mother naked on many occasions, so I knew it was coming, but it never occurred to me that something as ugly as pubic hair would arrive so soon. I thought it would be the last thing to be visited upon you, the final nail in the coffin of your childhood innocence, the very opposite, literally and metaphorically, of a crowning glory.

But no. That and hairy legs and hairy armpits descended in a rush, and I was horrified, especially as what was tactfully referred in books and magazines as the bikini area rapidly turned into more of an Edwardian-bathing-costume area.

As you get older, to this unholy trinity are added moustache problems and a liberal sprinkling of hairy moles. Oh, and nose hair. Nose hair! Yes, I'm sure that the culturally specific dislike of female body hair is the sign of a misogynistic, patriarchal society that still fundamentally oppresses its womenfolk, but at the same time, it is still quite possible that there is indeed something quite genuinely and non-culturally-specifically appalling about the fact that by the time you hit forty, you may well look like nothing more than a strategically shaven ape.

Fat

Sex education classes will tell you that the gathering hormones and the periods mean your body is ready to have a baby, and that your breasts ('milk-producing lobules covered in soft tissue' is a phrase that will be with me always) are growing so that you will be able to feed it. What they fail to tell you is that so dedicated to the task of baby-making is the female body, that it is prepared to commandeer large parts of your anatomy (and if they weren't large before, they certainly will be afterwards) as larders for future foetuses. Your bum, from now on, is the corporeal equivalent of a well-stocked Victorian pantry. Except that instead of big earthenware jars labelled 'Flour', 'Sugar' and 'As-yet-unnamed-spices-from-one-of-those-funny-foreign-places-we-keep-colonising', it comprises merely shelf after shelf of vast wooden barrels labelled 'Subcutaneous Fat'.

If you have always been a thin child, the panic and misery you feel when puberty bolts on to your frame a thick covering of fat to the rear and a large slab of the same to each thigh knows no bounds. My grandma referred to my own area of dimpled unpleasantness as my '*peau d'orange*' – orange-peel skin. 'Hmm,' said my sister. 'The man from Del Monte, he say no.' She fell to the floor laughing, overcome by the magnificence of her own wit. She stopped laughing three years later when it was her turn to be visited by the fat fairy. She went from child sizes to a size fourteen overnight. You could see her expanding before your very eyes, like one of those time-lapsed films in nature programmes. The entire family used to be invited round at weekends to gape at her stretch marks and take photos for *National Geographic*.

Breasts

In China, tiny, bound feet were once the most desired feminine feature. In fourteenth-century Europe, a rounded belly was revered. In Japan, the nape of a woman's neck is an erotically charged sight. But for the last three centuries or more, Western culture – Britain and America in particular – has become increasingly obsessed with breasts. You may, possibly, have noticed this if at any point in your life you have glanced at a magazine, billboard, pop video or advertisement for anything at all, in any medium. Teenage girls take this obsession and run with it.

Boobs are THE big prize in the teenage tombola. Everyone wants those soft-tissue-laced-with-milk-producing-lobules and they want them NOW!

What you get initially, however, is what my friend disgustingly refers to as 'knotty nipples' – hard little lumps under your childish nips that make you think you have got cancer, especially if one grows in before the other. What a beguiling introduction into the wonderful world of womanhood.

Once you have worked out that you are not malignant, an agony of waiting ensues. Will they grow big enough? Will they get too big? Will people notice? Worse, will people not notice?

Growing the right breasts is important – because, unlike pubes or periods, their development or lack thereof is visible to onlookers, most of whom will be young, male and generous with their opinions – and tricky. Too big and they hamper daily activities and draw the attention of perverts. Too small and you become the object of pity and derision.

And so begins the fascinating process of shaping your personality to fit your bust. The girl who, having led a hitherto quiet and unremarkable life, suddenly discovers that she has been harbouring the gene for 36DD bazonkas must decide whether to become the slapper that everyone now assumes her to be or spend the rest of her days battling exhaustingly against the assumption. Does she opt to devote her life to subverting expectations, fighting to be seen as something more than a great wobbling pile of mammary gland or does she give up and head for the slag heap (which, let's face it, is where most of the fun, albeit laced with chlamydia, for the next five years is going to be had)? Meanwhile, girls who had planned a life full of sexual adventurism and exotic adventure find themselves stymied by chests that stubbornly remain flatter than a Scrabble board and have to turn, with a sigh of frustration and bitterness, to a lifetime of book-learning and staying in instead.

In the absence of any recognised cultural or religious marker of adolescence to compare with the bat mitzvah or rumspringa, the ritual of the M&S training bra purchase evolved. This was a white nylon concoction, with dots printed on the upper halves of the slightly convex triangles that passed muster as cups.* At a conservative estimate, 99.9% of third years at school owned this hallowed strip of polyester and considered themselves the last word in mature sophistication.

Once Judy Blume's *Are You There God? It's Me, Margaret* entered the teenage consciousness, the bra-buying ritual was supplemented by mass enactments of 'I must, I must, I must increase my bust!' To this day, I still believe that if I'd just put that extra bit of effort in …

---

* I've still got mine. I can still fit into it. I still don't go out.

Periods

There have been many myths and special rites surrounding menstruation. Some say that they arose amongst primitive peoples to ward off the danger they felt must arise from the spontaneous and apparently purposeless bleeding that kept occurring amongst certain sections of the populace. Others say that inferring that women were unclean once a month was just another side effect of patriarchal cultures that were inherently suspicious of women and misogynistic to varying degrees. Myself, I think the women engineered it that way. Here, for example, is a description by the social anthropologist Jean La Fontaine in 1972 of the rules surrounding menstruating women in the East African Gisu tribe:

> [She] must keep herself from contact with many activities lest she spoil them: she may not brew beer nor pass by the homestead of a potter lest his pots crack during firing: she may not cook for her husband nor sleep with him lest she endanger both his virility and his general health. A menstruating woman endangers the success of rituals by her presence ... At first menstruation ... she must be secluded at once from normal contacts, particularly from contact with men of the village ... During the time that she is menstruating, she must not touch food with her hands: she eats with two sticks.'

Hmm. In other words, while she's got her period, the woman doesn't have to cook, shag, run about everywhere tending to men or domestic chores or attend boring social functions. Eating with sticks seems a small price to pay for securing that kind of time off every month, especially if you're eating on your own and no one's going to be checking if you've tucked away a spoon somewhere. Frankly, I think that by not preserving a choice ancient custom like that, the modern Western woman missed a valuable trick.

Whatever the reason, our grandmothers' and even mothers' generations remember a significant degree of shame and embarrassment attaching to 'the curse' or, if you prefer a slightly less loaded euphemism, 'courses', 'getting flowers', 'having a visit from Aunt Flo', 'having the decorators in' (the pre-war vagina must have been a crowded place), 'falling off the roof' or simply 'having your time of the month'.

Fortunately, by the time it was our turn, attitudes had improved. In an all-girls' school, getting your period was an eagerly anticipated event and news of an inaugural bleed was announced with fanfare and triumph. You can't have a minute's peace in any third-year classroom because someone is always bursting through the door yelling, 'I've got it! I've got it!'

Once you had 'started', it was incumbent upon you to devote most of your energies for the next year to trying to embarrass male teachers. 'Sir, sir, can I go to the toilet?' 'No, sit down.' A dramatic sigh. A pained look. A moment of vividly enacted hesitation for the benefit of those watching in the gallery and … 'But sir, I've got my —' The bleeding martyr to male insensitivity trails off with downcast eyes. Truly the English stage lost a superstar every time a teenage girl chose not to tread the boards. 'What? Oh. Oh. Alright then. Off you go.' 'Thank you, sir,' says the girl, quietly, bravely, rising gracefully from her chair and walking slowly and carefully to the door, like a soldier in a World War II film who has been mortally wounded but doesn't want anyone to know. If she is truly dedicated to her art, she will turn at the door and give him and the class one last small, courageous smile before dragging her poor, leaden-limbed body to the lavatory, where she will sit, smoke and add new graffiti to the cubicle walls until it is time for lunch.

The most memorable marking of menstruation was performed
by Donna Mansell. She tore the Tampax machine off the wall
of the school toilets, soaked the tampons in water, stood in
the playground and threw them at the roof and walls of the
school, where they dried rock-solid and remained for months.
We laughed for longer. When I relayed this story to one of
my sociology supervisors at university, she said it was Donna
symbolically rejecting the increasing constraints placed
upon the pubertal and post-pubertal female in a seemingly
immutably male-dominated society. But I have my doubts.
I think she was just an unexpectedly creative vandal. And if
we almost laughed our uteruses out when she did it, it was in
recognition of nothing more than the fact that vandalism, if
done correctly, can be very, very funny.

Hormones are responsible for your newly fatty, lumpy, malodorous,
greasy, hairy, bleeding body, of course, but let us not forget that they are
simultaneously wreaking far greater havoc on your mind, turning you
into a mental and emotional basket-case for at least half a decade.

Body image and eating disorders

Thin has been officially in since Twiggy took the fashion world by storm
in the sixties, although you hadn't been able to call chowing down on a
chicken leg a vital part of your beauty regime since Rubens. In the late
seventies and early eighties, the existence of eating disorders – mainly
anorexia nervosa – was just beginning to be recognised.

Since then, studies and statistics suggest that the phenomenon is creeping outwards – anorexia itself is more prevalent and has been joined by variant forms like bulimia and more mildly but still unnaturally and distressingly disordered relationships with food. You could argue, in fact, that all modern Western women can be located somewhere along the spectrum of eating disorders.

If you disagree, ask yourself this: do you ever feel smug, pleased or proud if for some reason you happen to miss a meal? You do? Wouldn't you say that is, if you stop to think about it, an irrational response? A somewhat perverted reaction to depriving your body of the food it needs to function? And it means that the vast majority of us (and I don't know where the minority are hiding, because I've never met anyone who, if she's being truly honest, feels differently) have unwittingly arrived at a point at which we feel happy about doing something as fundamentally unnatural and unhealthy as going hungry. We are weird.

But why are we so weird? And why – as the data suggesting that more and more girls at younger and younger ages are being affected accumulates – are we becoming weirder? I'm going to get myself a cake, or maybe a pie, while I think about this.

Size zero

Models have become skinnier and skinnier over the years. Twiggy, in pictures from the sixties begins to look pretty well padded to today's observers, used to the truly skeletal likes of Kate Moss, Lily Cole, Esther Cañadas or Luisel Ramos – the twenty-two-year-old Uruguayan model who died of a heart attack in 2006, after eating nothing but salad leaves and diet Coke for three months – or to Eva Herzigova, Jodie Kidd or Sophie Dahl during the lowest troughs of their fluctuating bodyweights.

The plummeting weight of the average model at least has a kind of logic to it – the logic of a madhouse, perhaps, but logic nevertheless. Models are there to show clothes off to their best advantage. If designers could animate sticks or build robots that could emulate human grace, they would happily use those in order not to distort the carefully worked lines of their beautiful creations. But they can't. So they still have to use models and as the industry has expanded and become ever more lucrative, the competition amongst models, and therefore the drive to become the thinnest, has become fiercer and fiercer.

Celebrities' weights have plummeted as well. Paris Hilton, Nicole Richie, Lindsay Lohan, Victoria Beckham and Keira Knightley collectively weigh less than the six raisins Elizabeth Hurley famously admitted she consumes as a between-meals snack (although as she also confessed to only eating one meal a day, I'm not quite sure how that works. Maybe she eats her sextet of shrivelled grapes at midnight). This too makes an insane kind of sense.

Again, it is partly competition for fame in an increasingly lucrative and crowded market. Everyone is trying to stand out, and if you are a pure celebrity (i.e. you are famous for being famous, frequently after failing to parlay a particularly meagre amount of talent into a viable career) the best way to do that is by using your body – which, if you have registered on the fame scale at all, is likely to be young and pretty – rather than your art (which is likely to be piss poor). Inches lost round the hips mean column inches gained.

For actresses, the cruel truth is that it is not enough to be amongst the most talented of your generation, you must also be amongst the most beautiful, which basically translates as 'amongst the most thin'. So Nicole Kidman transforms herself into a pipe cleaner, Renee Zellweger shrinks almost to nothingness, Aniston and Cox become slimmer with every series of *Friends* (while the boys gently swell with success) and so on and so on. It makes sound professional sense.

The media

I remember seeing a television programme demonstrating a new computer software which was used to doctor a particular advert at the time. I can't remember what it was selling, but the picture was of a woman lying on her side in a greenish, skintight catsuit and high-heeled boots at the end of impossibly long legs.

Well, they were indeed impossibly long. The designer showed us how they hadn't looked right in the original shot, so he had moved the mouse around the screen a bit, clicked here and there and slimmed them down, extended them by what would have equated in real life to a good six inches or so, made the boot heels higher while he was there, oh, and trimmed away the fold of skin (not fat – the woman is a model, remember. He is honing an already freakishly tall, thin frame, not carving away at a solid, great lump of ordinary woman) created by the slight bend at the waist as she propped herself up on her elbow. And he changed her eye colour to tone better with the catsuit, as an inspired afterthought.

That must have been at least twenty years ago. Since then, of course, the sophistication of such software and the readiness of fashion, magazine and ad agency photographers, designers and editors to refine, reduce and redraw their subjects has increased immeasurably. Retouched images are now so widely used that they have become wholly acceptable and go mostly unremarked

But here's the thing. Even though you know what goes on, when you see the pictures, you still don't dismiss them with an airy wave as impossible, nonsensical ideals, of no more interest or relevance than a picture of a Ewbank or a pickled pig. The mind is unfortunately not quicker than the eye. You see Jennifer Aniston's glinting upper arms and you don't think, 'Goodness, I wonder what digital trickery they deployed to heighten her certainly-impressive-but-probably-not-moulded-from-beaten-gold-as-it-appears-to-have-been-here musculature and achieve that highly unnatural effect?' You lower yourself immediately, hand over speedy hand, down the rope into a pit full of self-loathing and despair and think, 'I must go to the gym every day, start tanning, stop eating, give up carbs, give up chocolate and take up exfoliating. I can't bear to look like this any longer.'

And you're a sensible, rational woman with a mortgage and a godchild. What kind of state would you be in if these multitudinous images of perfection had been surrounding you continuously from the day you were born?

Naturally, young girls absorb these visual cues all the more uncritically. It's not that they are hopelessly naïve* or know nothing about how the world works or unquestioningly swallow everything we show or tell them. But they are, y'know, children and are more inexperienced, more impressionable and, like all of us, more instantly susceptible to visual stimulants and messages than rational, intellectual arguments, even if the latter were being made to them on a regular and persuasive basis, which of course they are not.

In short, I think what saved me and my friends from embracing eating disorders in the numbers girls seem to today was the fact that, in our day, although we may not have been encouraged to carry too much weight, we were allowed some and what we did have was still allowed to jiggle.

The Great Divide

The world cleaves in two at adolescence. The fault lines have been developing for years, but as the hormones begin to boil and bubble, the ground on which you stand suddenly begins to shake and finally

---

* Anyone out there who thinks they are should take a short bus ride at school chucking-out time and spend ten minutes eavesdropping on the conversations between teenage passengers. It's like listening to a coachload of mini Jenna Jamesons.

breaks in twain. A pretty much unbridgeable chasm opens up between the sunny pastures of the cool and the barren wastelands of the uncool, the golden beach and carnival-studded country of the popular and the rain-swept, boggy hinterlands of the unpopular. Where you are standing at the time is where you'll stand forever. A few – a very few – make the perilous leap from wastelands to lush pasture successfully. Many more die in the attempt. Most have enough sense to accept their teenage lot and use the time to lay grand plans for reinvention when they first start work or light out for university.

You could fill an eighteen-volume encyclopaedia set with details of what makes a girl socially acceptable or a pariah during the teenage years, but we shall limit ourselves here to the very basics. Do feel free to add more at your leisure, or – if you fell firmly on the right-hand side of the table below during what is called, with glorious understatement, 'that difficult age' – when your therapist decides it is time for you to begin to process some of those repressed memories which gnaw at your subconscious in the inky blackness of the night.

GOOD	WHY?	BAD	WHY?
Long hair	Sexy, feminine. You show the world that you prioritise correctly – grooming above all else. Also, you can flick it around endlessly, as a more than adequate substitute for conversation, words being, of course, hugely uncool.	Short hair	Because you look like a lesbian.

GOOD	WHY?	BAD	WHY?
Pierced ears	Sexy, feminine and a bit common, which is always cool.	Unpierced ears or other pierced body parts	You are not prepared to suffer for beauty or social acceptance and/or you are still doing what your mother tells you. A stud through the nose, tongue or eyebrow makes a statement. That statement is 'Fuck off,' which is only cool if said specifically to your parents, not indiscriminately to the world, especially when that world includes your peer group, whose benedictions you should be anxiously soliciting at every turn.
Convex chest	See section on breasts.	Concave chest	See section on breasts.
Smoking	Smoking is cool. Always has been, always will be. Blame Lauren Bacall in *The Big Sleep* and Sharon Stone in *Basic Instinct* or just blame the fact that there is something about sucking on a cigarette that the human brain is hardwired to find dirty, provocative and damnably sexy, but don't pretend there's anything you can do about it.	Not smoking	Anyone who privileges the Surgeon General's warnings over their friends' urgings deserves to be ostracised. Worrying about future cancer instead of immediate social gain is the surest possible sign of a total saddo.

GOOD	WHY?	BAD	WHY?
Drinking	See smoking. Has the additional advantage of carrying you over those awkward moments between meeting a boy and letting him stick his tongue so far down your throat that he can taste your pancreas.	Reading	Words again. What are you, some kind of, like, reader?
Drugs	See drinking, although with drugs you can consider the tongue–throat combination a mere prelude to far more invasive procedures that may involve surgical repair in later life.	Homework	Again, an implicit acknowledgement not only that the future exists, but that it might be affected by the present. Jesus, you need to be taken out to the bike sheds and beaten bloody.

Teenage passions

By the time the rest of my year were waking up to the existence of the opposite sex, I was covered in grease, cellulite-ridden, hairier than a goat and had a full set of orthodontic braces, complete with coloured wires and strung with rubber bands. It just didn't seem the time to be getting interested in boys. Of course, we are talking about pre-internet times. I presume if I were adolescing under such circumstances these days, I would simply set up my own website and service my own and others' sexual needs via the web cam at www.fangedbarelylegaloilydimpledgoatgirl.com. The wonders of the modern age.

From the end of primary school and through the first few years of secondary, we girls go about transforming our childish passions for stickers and pencil cases into more adult preoccupations: Elizabeth Duke gold jewellery from Argos, Silk Cut, shoplifting, getting fingered (I'll never forget the centre forward describing her experience of the phenomenon to an enthralled netball team during an otherwise lacklustre game. I knew about sex but never considered digital intervention as the remotest possibility, if only because, having no curiosity myself about what the inside of a vagina felt like, I couldn't imagine anyone else would either), moisturiser, make-up, Mad Dog 20/20 and Martini, Wonderbras and finding the best-paid Saturday job. Zodiac Toys only paid £1.72 an hour to under-sixteens, but WHSmith handed out a munificent £2.50 and it was a lot easier to steal stationery than Monopoly boards. A late developer in every field, I eventually got a job at Waitrose when I was fifteen, smashing all known pay records with £2.62 an hour and the chance to buy reduced cakes from the patisserie counter at the end of the day. All I had to do was be nice to customers and pretend to understand the endless salami and cream cheese jokes being made by the lads on the deli counter.

But once boys enter the collective consciousness, all other concerns and interests are forgotten, abandoned forlornly by the roadside as the girls scramble aboard the Hormone Express to Boytown.

The Three Stages Of Man

STAGE 1: POSTER BOYS

At first the focus was safely on unattainable males. Pretty, popular girls lined their walls, decorated their pencil cases and – in extreme cases – filled their scrapbooks with pictures of pretty, popular boys: New Kids on the Block, Face from *The A-Team*, Nick Kamen halfway out of his jeans, Rob Lowe and assorted fellow brat packers halfway to stardom, John Alford off *Grange Hill* halfway to

London's Burning and oblivion. For the slightly more sensitive and discerning there were John Cusack, Harrison Ford and River Phoenix. For the twisted Daddy's girls and those voted Most Likely To Be Having Affairs In Their Twenties With Older Married Men there were Tom Selleck, Pierce '*Remington Steele*' Brosnan, Robert Wagner and Bruce '*Moonlighting*' Willis. For the slightly more terrified of sex, the perennially unthreatening likes of Nick Heyward from Haircut 100, Matthew '*Ferris Bueller*' Broderick, Michael J. Fox and Phillip Schofield were ideal. For girls at the opposite end of the spectrum, those who would grow up to be the kind of woman who finds herself inexorably drawn to every bad boy in the locale like some kind of STD-seeking missile, the object of adoration was usually Judd Nelson in *The Breakfast Club* or Kiefer Sutherland in *The Lost Boys* (*Stand By Me* if you prefer your nascent puppy-killers with a slightly cleaner look).

I had crushes on Jack Lord from *Hawaii Five-O* and Aled Jones. It is a wonder to me that I wasn't simply taken out behind the school bins one day and killed.

STAGE 2: REAL MEN

Gradually, attention turns to real-life figures. The friend of an older brother, frequently, or a teacher. In our school, the lucky (or unlucky, depending on your point of view) recipient of our violently febrile teenage longings was Mr Allan, our only male teacher under 102.

One girl in my English class, called Claire, had a monumental crush on her best friend's older brother Steve. She was obsessed with him. She recounted his every facial expression, hand gesture and monosyllabic grunt in breathless detail, and the light of her love remained admirably undimmed through the years by the fact that he didn't know her name, who she was and never once glanced in her direction. My best friend Sally was fascinated by this groundless, boundless passion of Claire's and would demand a full account of her latest, one-sided dealings with him every lunchtime, punctuating the would-be lover's torrent of words every now and again with questions like 'And do you think you'll marry him? You know, when he knows who you are?' and 'Would you have his baby? You know, if he trips over you one day and accidentally has sex with you?' She insists to this day that her interest was genuine, but that doesn't quite square with the time she perched on the bench beside Claire and persuaded her to read out the song she had written to her unwitting inamorato – chorus: 'Steeevie, hold me/Steeevie, enfold me' – fell off backwards and was still laughing when they took her away on a stretcher.

Psychologists say that the crush is a natural and valuable part of growing up, that focusing your developing erotic impulses on a distant, unattainable, 'safe' object allows you to explore the strength and test the boundaries of those feelings without coming to harm. However, psychologists promulgating this belief would do well to ask themselves the following question: do you think the average male teacher, confronted with a lunging teenage female pupil eager to practise her clumsy but still somehow alluring feminine wiles, with skirt hitched up to her doodah and blouse carefully arranged to strain its buttons over the laciest half-cup bra in Topshop's Jailbait range, is most likely to say to himself:

a) 'I am both amused and, in an entirely adult, properly detached and academic way, flattered to find myself the object of this outpouring of pubescent erotomania. But I fully realise that X has subconsciously elected me so because she is not yet emotionally mature enough to embark upon a real relationship with a member of her peer group. I further realise, therefore, that it is my duty as a teacher, as an adult, as a sentient, well-intentioned human being more than twice her age and twenty-times better versed in the meaning of love, sex and the vagaries of the human heart to deflect these attentions gently but firmly, without humiliating her or otherwise exerting a damaging formative influence upon her, but also without admitting any room for doubt or misinterpretation,

or

b) 'Fantastic. I wonder if the gym cupboard's free?'

STAGE 3: SCALP-COLLECTING

Once the first, fearsome crush is out of the system, a girl can concentrate on racking up the snogs. What matters here is quantity, not quality.

During adolescence, girls' pursuit of boys is relentless and overpowering. Obviously, it is driven partly by simple curiosity and growing physical urges (although hearing boys talk at the time and about those years later on, it is hard not to conclude that whatever girls feel by way of sexual drive remains as nothing compared to the all-consuming fire that rages in male loins between the ages of thirteen and ... well, most of them seem still to be waiting for it to decline). But the main motivation is rampant ego.

Teachers and parents do what little they can to counter it, but whatever platitudes they spout about the importance of intellect, exams and being kind to animals and old people, and however high your mother had her consciousness raised back in the sixties, every girl knows by the age of twelve that the only currency that's worth anything is your attractiveness to boys. It follows, therefore, that your self-worth can be measured in the number of saliva samples swabbed from hapless males on sticky nightclub dance floors, school and youth club disco halls, bus stops and the last few desperate minutes of parties held in your parents' front room.

Again, there is a spot of social bifurcation. Some girls realise that all you have to do to succeed in this particular field is go to the right club, stand in the right spot with the right attitude and your top three buttons undone, dismiss all thoughts of taste and discernment from your mind and let the men and their eager tongues come to you. Others prefer to imagine that there is more of an art to the process, which is how girls' magazines were invented. Now sadly defunct, *Just Seventeen* (or *J17* as it became known in later years, when drastic abbreviation and random punctuation became de rigueur for any product aimed at pubescents) was launched in 1983 and we girls fell upon it like ravening beasts.

The editors of *Just Seventeen* (or *Mizz* or, later, *More*) filled their weekly or bi-monthly bibles with advice many consider invaluable to this day. 'Would I be the woman I am today without their 1985 piece about "the X factor"?' demands my friend Laura. 'Especially when you bear in mind that it included a detailed guide to pouting.' For Alice, who went on to work for the magazine, it offered even more illuminating counsel. 'I remember a long article about how to tell if a boy fancied you,' she says. Will she share this Holy Grail of romance with those of us who missed it the first time round? 'We all have invisible "love antennae" which send out signals if we fancy someone,' she explains. 'So, if you fancy a boy, it means you've picked up the signals he's sending out and he fancies you too. I honestly, really believed it then. I think part of me still subconsciously does.' Hmm. Personally, I've always found an unmistakable boner a more reliable indicator, but I can appreciate the attraction of something more subtle in the early days of courtship.

Still, at least the magazine bequeathed to us one sure-fire way to get a boy to speak to you. 'You catch his eye, smile, then look away – twice,' instructs the author Jenny Colgan with terrifyingly total recall, 'and then catch his eye a third time – and look sad. He will then rush up to find out what's wrong.'

And, having taught you to secure his attention, the valiant feature writers did not shirk from following things through to the thrilling climax, but furnished numerous detailed articles on how to kiss: 'Don't hold your breath and don't bite his tongue.' When my turn came, I remembered the vital edicts and the manoeuvre passed off successfully. And that is why I still go to bat against those who would claim that girls' magazines are nothing but a tool for the conditioning of females into passive clotheshorses who will trot gently into the nearest office job and then down the nearest aisle with the first young man who bobs his love antennae at them.

'At the time they were a really useful source of information and knowledge for me,' says Alice. 'And they made me want to write for magazines when I grew up. I don't remember the fashion aspects so much – I think there's far more interest in that nowadays – but the stuff about sex and boys was good.' And now that she's written for the magazine? 'Now I realise it's all written by some bitter, terminally single woman lying to teenage girls and wishing it was true.'

Still, it was all worth it to be able to come into school on Monday morning and report another double-figure score to be added to your running total of snoggees, with your cool rating adjusted accordingly (it was more finely calibrated than the FTSE).

Snogs had to be attested to by witnesses, of course – otherwise even people like me could have made up enough conquests to demand social recognition – which sometimes led to complications. Marie, Anne, Marie-Anne and Anne-Marie could have been out on the town happily together when Marie got off with a bloke Anne-Marie had had her eye on. If this happened, the offended Anne-Marie could avenge herself by withholding testimony on Monday morning, playing merry hell with the accuracy of the records and Marie's saliva league position. Moreover, Anne-Marie's best friend Marie-Anne could choose to support her and further enrage Marie (and Anne, Marie's best mate) or support Marie and saw Anne-Marie off at the knees, because, unbeknownst to Anne-Marie, Marie-Anne has her eye on someone she knows Anne-Marie likes and wants to not be friends with her for as long as it takes to add that particular scalp to her own belt. I had forgotten until now just how complicated life could be at fifteen.

The social divide

There are those in whom the sudden visitation of hormones and burgeoning bits and pieces induce a crippling self-consciousness. They make the occasional painful foray into the disco 'n' nightclub arena before deciding that the easiest and most sanity-saving option is to effect a complete withdrawal from the world until their spots and the situation at large improves. And then there are those in whom it precipitates entirely the opposite effect and who find themselves filled to the brim with self-confidence and lust for life and start straining at the parental leash and escaping through deadbolted bedroom windows every Friday night in order to drink deeply from life's suddenly bubbling well of pleasures.

Some people will tell you that every teenage girl is in fact plagued by self-doubt and insecurity, it's just that some hide it better than others behind bravado and posturing. B – if I may make so bold as to say – ollocks. This is one of the greatest lies ever told, propagated by the likes of psychologists and sociologists, all of whom spent their own youths firmly locked behind the steel gates of the crippling self-consciousness camp and had to believe that the gloriously hedonistic lifestyles being led by their self-assured peers were only desperate attempts to mask the dreadful pain within.

Some girls may have been masters of disguise, and I'm sure others successfully exaggerated the true level of devil-may-careness in their characters, but after five years of daily personal immersion in the field and years of reflection and hundreds of conversations about it since, I can safely say that most of the teen queens you knew then or have seen since, were and are as unshakably confident as you thought – obnoxious, awe-inspiring, uplifting and profoundly hateful all at the same time.

The girls you see confidently sashaying down the street, provoking admiring glances from younger girls, blisteringly lascivious ones from older men, filling the air with unrestrained shouting and screaming and flirting clumsily with anything with testosterone and a pulse, are not hiding any insecurities whatsoever. And why should they be? They are fabulous and they know it. They are good at this and this is their time. They are young, gorgeous, empty of care and full of exuberance, curiosity and promise. The vast majority of them will, like the rest of us, convert this over the years into apathy, cynicism and unwanted pregnancies, but the important thing is that they would not dream of letting that possibility spoil for them the glorious here and now.

Naturally, when you see them now, you have to choke down your bile and bitter resentment, rein in your bucking, retrospective jealousies and repress the memories of wasted years spent scurrying through the streets with your head down so as not to risk offending passersby with your Elephant Man face and substantial orthodontistry, lest you lose control of yourself momentarily, sprint forward and try to push the fearless, nubile mob under a bus.

At home

Whatever you are like in public or with your peers, at home it is your bounden duty as a teenager to be unrelentingly truculent and wholly unreasonable. It is a time for testing boundaries and carving out your independence, without, of course, taking on any of the responsibilities of adulthood or losing any of the privileges of childhood.

So you struggle valiantly for autonomy through carefully prepared and keenly honed argument ('But everyone else is gonna be staying till midnight. I'm gonna look like a total loser if I have to leave at half eleven!'), while still demanding your family's unwavering financial, emotional and practical support and taxi service. You fight nobly for the right to freedom of expression ('I am choosing to look like a whoregoth because That. Is. What. I. Believe. In!'), while reserving the right to dictate what your parents wear at public gatherings. You can say whatever you like, but can scream at your parents to shut up because whenever they open their mouths they do so with the sole purpose of embarrassing you beyond human endurance.

My mother insists that hormones didn't exist in her day – she thinks they were invented along with rock and roll and James Dean. Ever ready to defer to her greater knowledge and experience (or at least to stay crouching and silent while the larger waves of her madness roll over me) though I am, I believe she is probably wrong to deny the pre-war existence of the human maturation process. However, if we examine the sweeping statement, we find, as so often, a small kernel of truth lurking within it that bears further examination: namely, the underlying point that only in very recent years has it become possible for teenagers to exhibit their tantrums and emotional crises and to have them indulged or even taken seriously by the adults in their lives.

In times gone by, thirteen- to eighteen-year-olds would have their minds distracted from their misbehaving genitals and internal disquietude by the slightly more pressing need to work in order to eat, or fight wars in order to ensure the survival of a people or a country, or fight off cholera or bubonic plague in order not to become another lifeless body covered with limestone and flung into a giant charnel house. In which light, modern teenagers are an even more vile, spoiled and ungrateful lot than they first appear.

One final thought

The only comfort to be gleaned from the whole grotesque process is that boys have it so much worse. They have to talk with their broken voices, present their acne to the world without the benefit of make-up, are at the mercy of spontaneous and ill-timed erections and are deluged with testosterone, a hormone that turns them for more years than any of us care to contemplate into little more than rutting beasts in the field. True fact: columnist and writer Julie Burchill once wrote in an article that the average teenage boy was perpetually gagging for it to such a degree that he would happily have sex with mud if nothing else was on offer. She got a letter from a man a week later, saying that when he was fifteen he had done exactly that. And that, my friends, is very much all you need to know about why you should always stay as far away from fifteen-year-old boys as you possibly can.

What kind of teenager were you?

COMPLETE THE FOLLOWING SENTENCES:

SENTENCE 1

When I was thirteen, my sole aim in life was to:

a grow up
b stay a child
c leave home
d catch thrush

SENTENCE 2

My chosen method of parental persuasion was:

a reasoned argument
b a reasonable amount of shouting
c eye-rolling
d sighing
e all of the above. Except a. Like, duh.

SENTENCE 3

When I was fourteen, I wanted to stay:

a out late
b out of harm's way
c fourteen forever
d past closing time.

SENTENCE 4

When I was fifteen, I liked to:

a read and cry quietly
b slam doors
c ignore everyone
d give head

SENTENCE 5

I thought I was:

a gorgeous
b hideous
c immortal
d all of the above

SENTENCE 6

At sixteen, I used to make my mother:

a laugh
b cry
c drink heavily
d provide bail money

SENTENCE 7

When I was seventeen, I had:

a nine GCSEs
b a hangover
c thirteen STDs, six unknown to medical science
d twins

SENTENCE 8

When I was eighteen, I had:

a no regrets
b some regrets
c profound regrets
d no recollection of the previous five years

CHAPTER 6

Sex & Stuff

A true story. A few years ago, I was sitting in the kitchen having a cup of tea with two friends. We had all been without sex or relationships for a very long time and were feeling decidedly like spinsters-of-this-parish. So we fell to discussing whether the time might have come to purchase a vibrator (or rather, three. I'm very fond of both of my friends, but I'm an old-fashioned girl at heart and I draw the line at sharing sex toys). During the course of the conversation, which naturally enough broadened out into a general discussion about masturbation, it became apparent that one of my friends (whom we shall call Victoria, as this is emphatically not her name) was contributing little to the conversation. Upon further and closer questioning, it emerged that she very rarely indulged in the act under debate. 'I really try not to,' she said virtuously.

'Why?' we replied as one incredulous voice.

'I just think it's very narcissistic, very egocentric,' she said.

'Well, yes, I suppose doing something for yourself is always that, a bit,' agreed Jenny (names again have been changed to protect the not-very-innocent). 'But it's hardly the crime of the century.'

'And you're thinking about someone else, perhaps even several others, ideally in full dress uniforms and with eight hours to kill with you, who are, for some reason, dressed in an alluring mid-Victorian costume on a train steaming through the night,' I added. 'Aren't you?'

Silence.

'Well, aren't you?' I asked.

'Well … n-no, not really.'

'What are you thinking about then?'

'Just me.'

'What do you mean? Even if you're thinking about yourself pole dancing in a filthy nightclub, there must be notional people in the audience. Or perhaps a lascivious but darkly handsome club owner secretly watching you rehearse from the gallery.'

'No. I mean it's just me. I just sort of lie there and think about how marvellous I am.'

There are few times in my life that I have been reduced to wordless admiration, but this was one of them. The idea of being able to bring yourself to orgasm by lying back and thinking of your own fabulousness seemed to me to be a surpassingly rare and precious talent that it was a pity couldn't be brought to wider notice and adulation. Until, of course, now.

For the rest of us, however, less blessed with this happy combination of rampant egomania and hair-trigger orgasmic capability, our lives as we age become more and more firmly entwined with both sex, relationships and the almost limitless complications associated with both.

Let us look first at the joys – and frequent lack thereof – of sex.

The beginning

In the interests of creating a full appreciation of the subtle and beautiful evolution of a woman's sexual awakening, let us recap the preliminaries. After all, as our mothers always used to tell us, you can't get to anal sex without going through a few tongue sarnies first.

Kissing

A girl's first kiss was traditionally an important rite of passage because it was the furthest she was supposed to go without a ring on her finger, a date for the wedding and at least three preliminary dress fittings to her name.

But times change and a lady today can look back on her first kiss as an event of slightly less momentous import.* It tended to take place during parties geared to its mass orchestration. In other words, parties that were composed solely of games of Spin the Bottle and Postman's Knock, which went on and on, like some ancient medieval rite, until everyone, even the most charmless girl, had been kissed at least once, by even the most grotesque boy and the guests could gratefully depart for home. In even more recent times, however, the significance of the event is generally further obscured by the number of cigarettes smoked and alcopops consumed and later spewed into the gutter on the way home. It seems to be the consensus amongst the current crop of teenagers that if you can remember it, then you weren't there.

Boys rarely remember their first kiss, unless it was delivered unto them by their French teacher who looked like Charlotte Rampling and she then followed it up with a term-long initiation into the particular

---

* I think I received mine during a game which involved couples (chosen according to a system of coloured cards in hats, whose Byzantine complexities resist brief explanation) being locked in a dark cupboard together, but this may well just be me once again getting scenes from *Teen Wolf* mixed up with real life.

secret and mysterious arts of seduction that are written into the DNA of only Gallic women. This is because it is for them only a hurdle to be cleared in the only obstacle race in the world worth running: the one that hands to the winner at the end a giant key marked 'vaginal access'.

French kissing

The tongue is a strange organ. Used properly it can propel you to the very heights of ecstasy. Wielded by a fevered adolescent boy – usually in a determined counter-clockwise motion, like a saliva-soused windmill, or stuck so far down your throat that you have to hope he likes the taste of liver – it is an appalling instrument of torture. Magazines and books rarely prepare you for the horror of a bad French kiss.*

It's a good job young women are so full of vim and optimism that they remain largely undeterred by frequent oral trauma but plough gamely ahead in search of the next possible repository of pleasure, otherwise the human race would die out within six years.

So far, so gaily tripping through the rolling green pasturelands of tentative sexual sorties. But we now must move into wilder, more untamed land, where throbbing members, mucous membranes and other fearsome beasts lie waiting in the undergrowth. Readers of delicate constitution should skip ahead to Relationships. The word 'ejaculation' will be appearing shortly, and there's really nothing that can be done about it.

---

* Though I defy even the most comprehensive guidelines to prepare me for my worst. At sixteen, I locked lips and tongues with a boy from my English class and when we drew apart I had a massive bogey on my lip. It was his, and we had to go out with each other for six silent months after that, in case the other told anyone else about it.

Dry-humping

The arrival onto our shores of this useful expression from America means it is finally possible to give a name to what every teenager moves onto once they realise that tongue sarnies do not a full meal make. In case you are a) too terribly British to have come across the expression and/or b) too imaginatively stunted to discern its meaning for yourself, Wikipedia kindly supplies us with a working definition: 'two people engaging in clothed frottage in a manner that simulates intercourse'. To which you may or may not choose to add 'usually in a furtive and anxious manner due to the fact that it is taking place in a parental home to which the owners may return without warning at any time'.

It's not entirely accurately named, of course, because sooner or later – sooner for him, later for you – matters will end in an orgasm, which for fifty per cent of the parties involved will be a messy business. Dry-humping is one of the few times that, biologically speaking, the scales are tipped in favour of the female, who can enjoy herself, then rise, adjust her clothes daintily and betray no sign of recent exertions, save perhaps for a slightly bovine smile and unaccustomed air of serenity. He, on the other hand, has to go home and desplurge himself thoroughly before his parents (or, if the girl is ugly, his friends) find out.

I had an older boyfriend during my gap year and he was very keen on dry-humping (whether because he was terrified of getting me pregnant, seeing me naked or having to take his trousers off over his Doc Martens I do not know), which I found very dull until I discovered I could watch *Roseanne* over his shoulder if I got hold of the remote before he started. He was forever fiddling around with my front bottom. I didn't know what he was trying to do, but later learned that he should have been doing it about two inches further down.

Fingering

Some girls swore by it. One can only assume they had G-spots the size of Wisconsin or had taken as lovers award-winning gynaecologists who had, for reasons connected to a groundbreaking research programme into adolescent female sexual responsiveness, disguised themselves as a fourteen-year-old, acne-spattered scrote named Shane.

Everyone else just waited patiently until the boys had satisfied their curiosity about what the inside of a vagina felt like and then gladly went off to obey the strictures of the *Why Don't You?* gang and do something less boring instead.

Handjobs

Again, not the most fascinating or rewarding of pastimes for a girl (perhaps this is what French knitting was in fact in aid of?), but the boys loved 'em so the girls did 'em. If you were going out with a particularly highly juiced and demanding lad, you quickly developed forearms like Popeye. By GCSE time, there were girls who couldn't write an essay without crushing their pens to smithereens.

Blowjobs

When even the boys had tired of handjobs delivered by girlfriends, who by this stage had taken up one-handed macramé to relieve the boredom, the lockjaw-inducing alternative arose.

In our parents' day (and presumably for some time before that, at least until you go back to classical times, when everyone felt entirely free to partake of most pleasures currently frowned upon in polite society, if not necessarily on reality TV), fellatio was considered so outrageous, so perilously close to the edge of gross perversion that it was the preserve only of the marital bed (given a sufficiently broadminded wife) and the brothel (given a sufficiently well-remunerated prostitute). It was something you did after 'normal' sex had become an established part of your adult repertoire, not part of the adolescent prelude to penetration. I'm talking, of course, of the public conception of the blowjob. I daresay that, in private, people were, as ever, significantly less hidebound and were sucking away far more merrily than recorded mores would have us believe. Still, it's not unreasonable to assume that in a world where www.amputeedwarfleperbanging.com had yet to come into existence, the spectrum of deviance was calibrated differently and what we consider to be practices at the milder end of the scale attracted a larger measure of opprobrium.

For us, of course, if you cast your minds back, it had become exactly that, although it was still largely something you reserved for boyfriends – although at that age you can attach the title to anyone you snog and who doesn't actually gob on you in front of his mates in the street next time he sees you – rather than random strangers in pub or clubs.

Now, however, the emerging trend is for youngsters to engage in the practice simply to break up the monotony of the school day. No wonder literacy standards keep falling – one half of the student body spends most of the school day slumped in a post-orgasmic stupor and the other half can't answer the teacher's questions because they've got mouths full of boy gunk.

10 (More) Formative Sexual Experiences

1. Climbing the gym rope at school
2. Playing doctors and nurses with Stuart, the suggestible boy next door
3. The flasher in the park
4. Jilly Cooper's *Rivals*
5. Shirley Conran's *Lace*
6. Shirley Conran's *Lace II*
7. Another flasher in the park
8. Leaning forward in too-tight jeans
9. *More*'s Position of the Fortnight
10. Strange dreams about Face from *The A-Team* involving all of the above

Sex

And finally – the act itself. Perhaps nothing demonstrates the free-form nature of modern sexual rules and customs better than the fact that amongst my circle of friends and acquaintances, the age for losing one's virginity ranges from thirteen to thirty-one-and-still-waiting. I'm not going to tell you how long I waited to lose mine. Let's just say that I must be one of the few women in history to have had sex for the first time not at the insistence of a priapic teenager, but because of the remorseless ticking of her biological clock.

Why did I leave it so long? Because of two people. The first was my mother, who is a gynaecologist specialising in family planning and who took it upon herself to deliver impassioned and daily lectures (frequently involving slides and vividly coloured plates from 1950s medical textbooks) to her growing daughters which dispelled both ignorance and the possibility of any healthy future sex life with equal efficiency. There are very few aphrodisiacal qualities to being able to visualise one's fallopian tubes and chart the course of a virulent yeast infection from the age of four.

The second was Sally, my best friend. She first Did It at an entirely reasonable age, albeit one that I am not at liberty to divulge, as it is still five years before her mum thinks it happened, and it was from her that I got the most useful piece of information I think any curious teenager can receive. 'What does it feel like?' I asked her, the morning after the night before.

There was a pause.

'Imagine,' she said slowly, 'how you think it would feel …'

I concentrated. I nodded.

'It feels,' she said promptly, 'exactly like that.'

Ah, realistic expectations – nature's greatest prophylactic.

Maladies, morals and motherhood

You cannot open the papers these days without learning of some new and startling statistic about rates of sexual activity amongst young people, and all too quickly you become old enough to start being as appalled at them as your great-grandma was when girls started flashing their ankles at all and sundry and dropping their fans in front of complete strangers to effect an introduction without even ascertaining his annual income and family acreage.

But on the other hand, you could see it as a miracle that all teenagers are not now having all sorts of sex, all the time. For most of female history it has been fear of pregnancy, disease and social ostracism that has kept women from having sex, every point of which unholy trinity has now disappeared, or at least sunk to its lowest ever level of influence. For those who still insist on trying to scare girls into abstinence using any of these increasingly blunted weapons, I have this to say:

Maladies

We were the AIDS generation, the first people ever to be confronted by a sexually transmitted disease that had a one hundred per cent mortality rate, and even that didn't stop us. At the very height of the fear and panic, it may have ensured that a few more condoms were rolled on amongst those who could work out what all those advertisements with portentous music and shadowy icebergs floating across the screen meant, but that's about it.

Perhaps things were different in ye olden times, when people were forever dropping dead of plague, syphilis, TB and farthingale overdoses, but it is a truism now to say that young people think they are immortal. In fact, we were probably the last generation of girls even to entertain the notion of getting older, now that all our female celebrities, the only role models of note, seem to have arrested at the age of thirty-five. Nowadays, girls must assume that they are as invincible as Wonder

Woman. Not, of course, that they will know who she is. You and I, however, can truly comfort ourselves with the knowledge that Lynda Carter in real life still looks *fabulous*.

Morals

There has always been an insistence that sex, for girls, is hedged round with conflicting messages, guilt, shame and doubt. At least that's what grown-ups think. As ever, of course, their beliefs lag substantially behind the reality of the times. The truth was that, in my day at least, sex was a badge of honour; there were no mixed messages, no ambiguities. Having sex was, like smoking or drinking, straightforwardly cool. Yes, there were a few relics of an older tradition dotted about – religious girls usually, or those like me, being brought up in idiosyncratic households run by barking maternal despots – who were still crippled and confused by the whole impossibly freighted business, but, by and large, sex was socially very simple. You had it, and your stock went up.

A lot of the stories, of course, were bravado – not necessarily lies, but recountings with a spin – because the girls who were fooling around and having sex were aware that society at large did not approve and so the doubts and confusions engendered by their behaviour were quickly stripped out before they presented their tales of derring-do to an admiring public.

But I do still suspect that for a great many girls – and for even more today – sex was just not that much of an issue. The insults of 'slag' and 'slapper' were still drawn out and hurled when enmities arose, but they didn't carry any greater weight than others – it was just another form of invective to be used in the heat of battle, but it wasn't an accusation that persisted or even particularly stung. And, probably, the 'slag' was not actually guilty of or being condemned for sleeping around at all, but simply the target of bullies who, with those unerringly vicious female instincts, knew exactly which label would hurt her most.

They didn't like her and they knew how best to crush her – that's what ruined her efforts at integration, not her (probably non-existent) slaggery or anyone's real disapproval of it.

Motherhood

Sex was cool, contraception was not. But by some curious serpentine logic which exists only in the teenage girl's brain, the fact that it was available removed the fear of pregnancy, even when you weren't actually using it. It was as if its preventative effects could be absorbed by osmosis. By the fifth form, every tenth girl was in the labour ward.

There are more practical reasons why girls don't furnish themselves with a selection of the many contraceptive services available. The main one is the unwillingness of the powers that be to let them access such services. This septic isle has a long tradition of prudery and a marked distaste for talking about the pragmatics of sex, and has so far failed to embrace the model of more liberal countries like Holland and teach its children fully and frankly about sex and ways to protect themselves against its biological consequences. Any proposal to mitigate the effects of teenagers' tendency to Caligulan debauchery by making information or contraception more easily available to them generally gets shouted down by those who insist that 'it only encourages them'. They will persist in this line of non-reasoning, no matter how many studies you show them which demonstrate that the more informed girls are about carnal matters, the more pregnancy and STD rates fall, and no matter how long you spend explaining that sex is like any other taboo in the world: the more you acknowledge and demystify it, the less intriguing and attractive a prospect it becomes. Crazy, but universally true.

The hard fact is that girls today are prey to more and more powerful influences than even the most protective parents can deflect (and another hard fact is that a lot of parents aren't protective). They are growing up in a more heavily sexualised world than ever before. The time for idealistic whimperings about how children should be children and pointless moralistic assertions about how they shouldn't even be thinking about sex is long past.

Still, there remains nothing wrong with trying to scare the shit out of the randy little buggers. They may not buy the 'sex is wrong because God and I say so' argument anymore, but they are still susceptible to grotesque facts and stark truths, properly presented.

That is why, in an ideal world, sex education lessons would no longer be given by an embarrassed young teacher who throws delicate euphemisms like 'bodily changes' and 'odd sensations' into the air and hopes for the best, but by heavily muscled specialists who will drag the boys into one bright, white room with a picture of a vagina on the wall, point at it with trembling fingers and vomit copiously for an hour. Girls will be forced into a bright, white room with a picture of a penis on the wall. The professionals will point at it with trembling fingers and scream wordlessly for an hour. Then the boys and girls will be herded together into a room lined with pictures of the HIV virus, gonorrhoea and hepatitic livers and the two teachers will walk up and down the rows, shouting, 'Keep yer pants ON!' until it's time for home.

So much for sex. Let us turn from the merely mechanical and mucosal to the infinitely more complex world of relationships.

Relationships

Feminists may weep, but we must face facts: from the age of about eight onwards (later if you are posh and have ponies to obsess about instead and can sublimate your sexual urges into competing in gymkhanas), the race is on to get a boyfriend.

This doesn't have to mean much. To any suitably determined and self-confident prepubescent, any one of the following circumstances will entitle you to call an unsuspecting lad your boyfriend:

- ❧ *He spoke to you*
- ❧ *He looked at you*
- ❧ *He ignored you – but that's because he is shy and not because he is three years behind you in maturity and would only notice you if you were made entirely of footballs and sherbet fountains*
- ❧ *He was nice to you*
- ❧ *He was horrible to you – in a clever attempt to disguise the tender inclinations he harbours towards you*
- ❧ *The teacher made you partners with him for a broad bean-growing experiment and your romantic connection grows with every daily progress report you write together*
- ❧ *You bumped into him on the street outside of school hours and he recognised you*
- ❧ *You haven't left his side for nine days and in the absence of a judge's willingness to grant restraining orders to pre-teens, he must for the sake of his mental health and classroom reputation give a gloss of respectability to the situation by letting it be known that you are his girlfriend*
- ❧ *You just told everyone that he is your boyfriend and if he doesn't agree, well, it's twenty-eight against one, so there*

These early unilateral and often wholly imaginary relationships have much to recommend them. You dictate the terms and you can rewrite his crude or absent attempts at seduction to turn them into something more in keeping with your requirements. Best of all, you don't have to spend time with him when you would rather be doing other things with your friends or watching TV.

But like all the pleasures of youth, this too is fleeting. Before long, the childish egomania that protects you from psychical harm and renders the love-object an almost negligible part of the experience, subsides. Your confidence falters. Insecurities and hormones rush in and prime you for tears and paranoia. Congratulations. You are now ready for a proper relationship.

Before you can embark on one of these, however, you must engage in a wide-ranging sampling of the products on the market to find one that suits your requirements. This, I am sorry to have to tell you, means dating.

Dating

Many years of effort and billions of pounds have been wasted putting men on the moon, curing diseases and inventing turkey bacon, when what scientists should have been turning their minds and money to is finding a way of circumventing the need for dating, defined in the *Oxford English Dictionary* as a 'tortuous and inefficient method of trawling for potential mates, preceded by a mixture of optimism and nausea, characterised by rapidly decreasing optimism and increasing boredom and succeeded by sick apprehension that he won't (or will) call.' Dating may be the reason that we don't rule the world. Nothing saps a girl's will or zest for life like it.

Preparation

There are two ways to prepare for a date. One is the way the magazines recommend, which usually goes something like:

- *Stop eating and take eight days off work to start exfoliating. Use a belt sander on your feet, an oatmeal and lemon scrub on your elbows and a diamond-powder facial wash which should then be licked off by kittens.*

- *Every other day, have a light layer of tan sprayed on by fairies. Multiple layering is the key to a natural look. Do not apply it yourself unless you are going out with a Sheraton antiques expert and know he will find the sight of a woman who could double as a mahogany sideboard alluring.*

- *Shop until you find the perfect outfit and shoes and practise wearing it so that you don't feel awkward when you stand, sit or, given that you haven't eaten for over a week, fall down. Hang the outfit on the front of your wardrobe using a plumb line so that it doesn't get wrinkled and nail any pets you have to the cellar floor so they and their odour can't despoil it.*

- *Have cosmetic surgery to get rid of unsightly blemishes and noses.*

- *Spend the day of your date in a hot bath, being massaged with precious scented oils from Araby. Get servants to dry you with a big, white towel that has been hand-fluffed by recent graduates from the Massachusetts Institute of Towel Technology so that you remain tranquil and relaxed, and slide onto your buffed and perfumed skin your new outfit.*

- *Apply make-up with all the proper brushes, puffs, sponges and curlers. Choose your jewellery and handbag from the vast array of attractive accessories you have laid out on the bed beforehand and glide gracefully downstairs to the taxi you booked three days in advance. Don't forget to have a mint Tic Tac to ensure fresh breath and to take the edge off your hunger so that you don't elbow him out of the way and dive headfirst into the soup.*

The other way is that which we must, alas, term the realistic one.

- *Stop eating, because you are convulsed with nerves and your bowels have gone into meltdown. Keep going into the office, but concentrate on nothing and risk getting fired. Plan to exfoliate, meditate and relaxiate, but unfortunately get sidetracked by phone calls, TV and life.*

- *Two days before date, realise that your favourite outfit is still at the bottom of the laundry basket stinking of fags and spilt wine. Panic-buy something that makes you look like the sixth and saddest member of Girls Aloud and which you won't realise until far too late is tight enough to garrotte your crotch and induce a strain of thrush so far unknown to medical science.*

- *Spend the day of the date rushing round work in a state of gibbering frenzy, cursing yourself for not having the sense to arrange this ridiculous undertaking for a Saturday instead of a Friday, leave late, miss train, hurl yourself under a lukewarm shower because you forgot to switch the boiler on when you got in, shave the necessaries with such hasty slashing motions that it looks like you've got self-harming issues and get dressed while trying not to drip blood, tears or despair on vile new outfit.*

- *Call cab. Eat and drink everything in the house while waiting for cab and developing a tension headache that could power the national grid. Put make-up and wrong shoes on in the car that arrives forty minutes late, so that you arrive doing a passable impersonation of Coco the Mightily Drunken Clown and spend rest of night wishing you were dead.*

Execution

When it comes to first dates, time has stood still. The couple on a date in the third, nay even the fourth, millennium will cleave as tightly to their traditional roles as any mutton-chopped Victorian gentleman and lady friend who has spent the preceding six weeks cleaning her best crinoline and starching her most stay-thither corset. He speaks and she listens, occasionally interjecting a pertinent question to enable him to continue his monologue.

I have sat opposite men who have opened proceedings with a detailed history of:

- *Themselves*
- *Their previous girlfriends (either canonised saints who looked like Jessica Simpson, by the way, or the distilled essence of Beelzebub – although still, interestingly, incarnated in a Simpsonesque frame)*
- *Their mothers (saints or devil-women again, but – and let us be devoutly thankful for such small mercies as are granted to us – none this time a dead ringer for La Simpson)*
- *Intercontinental ambulance design (I wish I were making this up)*
- *Obscure terms in English grammar (do you know what a tmesis is? It's putting a word within another word, as in, to pick an example not entirely at random, 'This is unbe-fucking-lieveable')*
- *Medieval Florentine dialects (yes, really. It was at this point that I began to wonder if it wasn't them but me)*

Life plays many cruel tricks upon a girl and one of the cruellest is the fact that the worse a date goes, the more likely you are to go home and have sex (or, even worse, agree to another date) with the man involved. The catalyst for this illogical conversion is, of course, alcohol – you drink more in order to endure more and so end up embracing dreadful men more fulsomely than you would a nice one. I don't know what the answer to this is except to stay sober, and I hesitate to promote a course of action no one has yet succeeded in testing to the required EU standards.

Aftermath

Post-date behaviour is simple enough. You go about your business, adamantly refusing to fulfil the stereotype of sad single woman sitting at home waiting for the phone to ring and just as adamantly refusing to admit that however hard you try, however demanding your job or thrilling your social life may be, ten per cent of your brain will be tracking the silent minutes as they pass. For the first twenty-four hours, this will be accompanied by the ceaseless internal whispering, 'Is he going to call? Is he going to call?' For the second twenty-four hours, this is replaced by 'Why hasn't he called? Why hasn't he called?' After that, by way of light relief, you get to move on to 'What's wrong with me? What's wrong with me?'

Naturally, this applies when you like the bloke, but what is delightfully interesting and depressing is that it applies just as strongly when you barely got through the evening without stabbing him in the throat with a fish fork. After all, rejection by a tosspot is even more insulting than rejection by a sex god.

By the time he rings – which he does if a) you hated him or b) you liked him and sacrificed the correct animals to the correct gods while the planets were suitably aligned – you are a shadow of your former self and unable to muster a semblance of the vivacity with which you first charmed him. You agree bleakly to his proposal for another meal or trip to the cinema and start the whole exhausting cycle again.

Eventually, you meet someone with whom it is, if not quite a pleasure, then at least not a wholly unremitting nightmare to spend your time. He becomes your boyfriend, and even cognisant of the fact. You invest time, effort and, if you are really stupid, money in the relationship. He lasts about a month. He takes your PIN number with him when he goes.

You try again with someone else. It goes a little better this time. He lasts three months. The next one lasts six. Gradually, you are becoming more discerning, finding out what you are looking for in a boyfriend and learning to distinguish between must-have features (kindness, a sense of humour, no criminal record), preferred features (good looks, intelligence, rich and ailing parents) and deal-breakers (live-in ex-girlfriends, herpes, corpses under the patio).

The next one lasts a year. You realise that you can argue with each other without breaking up. You are indeed a proper couple.

In an ideal world, all this will take place just before you reach the age of twenty-five. Because it as at that age that things begin to take a darker turn.

Now, it is not fair, it is not just, it is certainly not fun and who knows why it happens, but the fact remains that once past the age of twenty-five, most women feel a tiny pulse start to beat at the back of their minds telling them that it is time to stop having a laugh and settle down. Don't look at me like that, I don't like it any more than you do, but it's true. I'm the most self-sufficient, misanthropic person I know and even I was found sobbing in the kitchen on my twenty-seventh birthday because another sodding wedding invitation had come through the door, which, if I held it up to the light, actually had the words 'There will be a special chair for you at the Desiccated Hags table' engraved on it.

Perhaps the over-twenty-fives among us should take a moment to do a little research on the subject. Would you say your mind started sabotaging your life with unwanted yearnings for cosy domesticity because:

a) *We are all programmed by God, evolution or the giant lizards that secretly rule the world to start hankering for a soulmate instead of a drinking partner and stability instead of variety, so that there's room for the next generation to have their fun and the globe doesn't become overrun with hedonistic geriatrics who drink and jackhammer themselves into oblivion every night and civilisation collapses into dust*

b) *We are all unwittingly primed during our formative years by fairytales and films to believe in the romantic notion of true love, lifelong ardour and two hearts that beat as one and start to get impatient for our turn to enter this promised land, or*

c) *There is some unfortunate kink in the brain that no one has yet come up with a way to correct, though we cleave to the hope that massive ingestion of Prozac might help?*

As a result, pre-twenty-five relationships are defined by a certain degree of happy fecklessness, a carefree ability to live in the moment, unperturbed by thoughts of the future because it stretches out smoothly before you and on out into infinity and the present is crammed with new jobs, new cities and new macchiato variations at Starbucks. Your worries are superficial, fleeting and discrete and can be banished by the purchase of a new handbag.

Post-twenty-five, your relationships are defined by unrelieved anxiety about the present – could he be The One? Could I make him into The One? Is it supposed to be this difficult? Should I feel better? Should I feel worse? Am I happy? Should I feel happier? Should I feel like babies yet? If he is The One, should I have all these questions? Where's my mother when I need her? Added to this list of delights are the questions about the future – If he's not the one, should we break up now, even though we're happy? Will a life of Bridget Jonesish desperation rush up to greet me if I do? How have I gone from considering her to be a whinging, spineless, useless affront to all of womankind to using her as an emotional yardstick? What if I'm doomed, whatever I do, to end up like my parents, staring at each other across the dining table and the yawning abyss worn by the ebb and flow of thirty years of festering resentments?

You can check the truth of this by casting your mind back over all the birthday parties you have ever attended.

First it's all fun and games, literally – pin the tail on the donkey, musical chairs, blind man's bluff and pass the parcel. We were even the first generation to get a sweetie in every layer of the parcel, which on the plus side ensured that nobody got to the end of the game without some little reward, but on the downside ensured that the game became utterly useless as a piece of social education. Instead of learning to cope with disappointment, we went out into life entirely unprepared for its manifest unfairness and ignorant of the immutable truth that not only are there few prizes out there, but in the end they are allocated entirely arbitrarily. It would have been a particularly useful preparation for relationships to have been taught as early as possible that no matter how many layers of rubbish you tear through with eager anticipation, the chances are you're going home empty-handed.

Then there are the first parent-free parties – sandwiches and soft drinks left in the kitchen and Mum and Dad sitting nervously upstairs, listening for sounds of damage or debauchery taking place, or off down the pub to drink themselves into a stupor without a second thought, depending on how cool they are. Boys and girls stay firmly on opposite sides of the room, the latter giggling, plotting and occasionally pouting and the former staring at them with the fixed and helpless look of a pack of spotty rabbits caught in headlights. There will, however, soon be enough illicit alcohol flowing to make sure that the initial awkwardness transforms into a mélange of face-sucking, bra-wrestling and wondering if that's a finger of fudge he's got in his pocket or if he's just pleased to see you.

From then on, the birthday party becomes an event ever more generously awash with alcohol and sexual opportunity, until the day you realise that, in fact, you have been here rather too many times before and would quite like to start going to and coming home from these things with the same person, and then stop going to them altogether so that you can spend more time on the sofa telling each other how wonderful you are.

The One

This point can be reached late, or by accident. But not if you're the particular breed of posh female, like my friend Charlotte, who has been brought up, even in this day and age, to consider marriage to a suitable partner your foremost goal in life. In which case Charlotte has come up with a set of rules of behaviour designed to maximise your chances of success. I set them out below for those of you who are keen to meet The One, but who habitually end up at the end of parties with the troglodytic dregs of humanity, or those who are simply keen to experience time travel without the inconvenience of having to learn astrophysics and build a Tardis.

1. Arrive early. This enables you to size everyone up as they come through the door and decide which are the ones worth pursuing.

   NOTE TO SELF: It is possible, of course, that any pre-emptive filtering advantage will be more than outweighed by the fact that, from the male point of view, they are being stalked by a stranger with scorecards who clearly has nothing better to do than turn up at parties three hours before the time generally considered socially acceptable.

I can only suggest that in my next life I make sure I am born to the kind of ancient lineage that makes such crippling self-consciousness a constitutional impossibility.

2. Don't talk to girls. It is a waste of time.

NOTE TO SELF: I believe Charlotte is wasted as a housewife when there are still thousands of small African principalities crying out for an unblinking despot.

3. Only talk to people you know if they are talking to someone to whom you would like to be introduced.

NOTE TO SELF: There are a number of implicit assumptions here, upon which we must pause for cogitation.

First, Charlotte assumes I am still sober and capable of rational thought/adhering to the masterplan by this stage of the party. Remember, I have arrived early and have worked up a thirst sorting the new arrivals by height, weight and eligibility.

She assumes that I know people.

She assumes that I will want to be introduced to new people, when in fact I have the social proclivities of an old sock.

4. If you are talking about plays or films, always say, 'Oh yes, I really want to see the new Tom Stoppard/reissued Ingmar Bergman/ *Puppetry of the Penis*.' When he says, 'Well, we should go and see it together,' you say, 'Oh, how wonderful. Will you arrange it or shall I?'

NOTE TO SELF: I love the 'when'. I also love the vision I have of him reeling backwards and heading to the nearest lawyer to enquire about the length of time it would take to procure a fake passport and a flight to Cuba.

⑤ Never leave a party without getting at least two invitations to
other events (and it must be a twofer minimum, as one is bound
to clash with an engagement already in your diary).

*NOTE TO SELF: I love the idea that I have a social life busy enough to
make a diary clash statistically possible. Almost as much as I love the
idea of having a diary.*

Never have I seen the gulf between impeccable vowel sounds, bone
structure and folk memory of the Raj and the rest of us open up so
sweetly. Still, this quintet of tips has secured Charlotte the love of a man
who makes Fitzwilliam Darcy look like a whinging milksop, with whom
she lives in connubial bliss, suffused with a lambent joy that sickens all
around them. So you may wish to tuck this modern day Debrett's guide
into your handbag just in case.

If you do have that voice in your head insisting on the manifold virtues
of settling down, you just have to keep on opening the next layer of
the relationship parcel and hoping that you don't get lumbered with
another penny shrimp. And it's odds on that one day you will find a
man with whom you wish to co-habit. In which case, I can only say
the very best of luck to you.

Co-habitation

Relationships are hard. Living with someone is so much harder. There
may be some of you out there who have not yet experienced this proto-
married state and still imagine it as some kind of cosy, blissful condition
involving a doubling of your happiness and a halving of your rent, roses
round the door and two bright, beaming faces gazing at each other with

the eye of love across a breakfast table laid with a gay gingham cloth and a matching milk jug, while a cat purrs contentedly at your feet.

I admire your optimism. I envy you your innocence. But it is my duty to disabuse you of this notion. So here's a bird's eye view of twenty-four hours of life as a co-habiting couple, to illustrate why, in fact, most women, despite fifty years of feminism, fulfilling careers, the wonders of modern technology, the ability to hire domestic help and the myriad other buffers modern life provides for them, still lead lives of quiet desperation. Interspersed with rather louder bursts of raging fury.

A day in the Life ...

6-7 A.M.

His snoring mutates slowly but unmistakably into coughing, snorting and spluttering. Quite why the phlegm mill chooses this early an hour to crank into wet and brutal motion, I do not know. I make a mental note to find out whether you can buy an adult-sized version of one of those suction things doctors use on newborn babies to clear their mouths and nasal passages.

I recall my days of singledom, when I was able to emerge in my own time from the depths of dreamless sleep and float gently into the shallows of pre-dawn slumbers before eventually opening my eyes and easing myself into the rigours of the day. Now I spend two hours lying in bed, eyes and ears tightly shut against the foul noises emanating from the mucus-filled lump beside me, wondering if I am ever to know the pleasure of a full and uninterrupted night's sleep again.

8 A.M.

Decide I can stand it no longer. Get up, make coffee, have breakfast. Pick up eighteen plates and mugs left on coffee table after his bedtime snack last night. Load dishwasher. Discover there is no dishwasher powder because he forgot to add it to the shopping list when he used the last of it. Make another mental note, this time to ask him which part of 'If you finish any commonly employed substance in this house or become aware of its absence, write it on the shopping list which I keep clearly affixed to the fridge door or inform me directly that we are now in need of it, otherwise it is possible that my psychic skills will fail and we will be without toothpaste/toilet paper/washing-up liquid etc. for longer than is practical or comfortable' he does not understand. Mental notebook already uncomfortably full. Make mental note to get a larger one.

Reflect fondly on the days of living with a female flatmate, when we would even inform each other when things were running low rather than out, because we did not need to be confronted with physical evidence that Essential Substance X no longer existed. Rather, we could contemplate a dwindling supply of Essential Substance X and envisage a time when it would finally disappear and its absence cause difficulty and discomfort. To avert this, we would buy more ESX before it happened, overlap supplies if you will, in order to maintain the smooth running of our home. It was a beautiful, happy time and it is now over.

Feed cats. Love cats. Pick cat up and gaze through window together at garden. Notice he has not done the one thing I asked him to do yesterday and the slippery, deathtrap leaves are still lining the path to the front door.

Vent anger in healthy, constructive manner by banging noisily into bedroom to wake him up. Somehow manage to pick socks and underpants off the floor loudly, fling them deafeningly into the washing basket and take it downstairs.

9.30 A.M.

Have shower and get dressed while he has breakfast so that I cannot see the mess he makes or hear the noise he makes when he chews. Return when most violent storm of mastication has passed. Decide time has come to try a spot of labour division. Ask him to sort the washing into dark, medium and white loads.

'Of course. Dark, medium and white. No problem.'

'Thank you.'

'So what's grey?'

'What do you mean, "What's grey?"'

'Which load should it go in? Grey's kind of everything, isn't it? A bit white, a bit dark, a bit medium.'

'If it's dark grey, put it in the dark pile. If it's light grey, put it in the medium pile. Never put it in the white pile.'

'I see.' Do you? Do you really? Maybe I should embark on an explanation of the underlying principles of the procedure in a desperate attempt to forestall innovative and/or ill-founded decisions when you are left alone to deal with the complexities of the tripartite washing system.

'You see, what we are trying to do is not only get the clothes clean, but also ensure that they remain roughly the same colour as when they went in. So the same sorts of colours need to go in together, so that the dark don't pollute the light, and the whites must stay together because any colour at all will taint them. I don't know if you remember Rachel's debacle with the red sock in *Friends*, *The One with the Laundry Detergent?*'

'I do.'

'Right. Off you go. Except—'

'Except what?'

Except that there are borderline cases. Except that sometimes unimportant mediums can go in with darks to make up a full load of the latter when needed. Except that there are a million other considerations that go into this and every other domestic chore I do every day that you won't be aware of, won't be able to factor in and which I cannot bring instantly to mind and tell you about. And if I did, you would just look at me as if I were mad instead of doing what you should do, which is gaze at me with reverent adoration as it gradually dawns on you how much thinking and planning goes into even the apparently most simple of tasks, and that will just make me more furious. And I've been angry for three hours already today (multiplied by two years) so I am very tired.

'Except that it's easier just to do it myself.'

'Now you're cross. Why are you cross with me? I'm quite happy to sort out the washing.'

'I know. I know you are. I'm not cross. It's just easier. It'll only take me five minutes. Why don't you go and have a shower?'

'I was going to have a bath.'

You didn't say you wanted a bath, so the heating hasn't been on long enough. If you have a bath, I'll have to hang around waiting for you and we won't get to the supermarket till an hour later, which will muck up my plans for the rest of the day. Half-formed plans, but plans nevertheless.

'You'll have to wait another half-hour for the hot water.'

'We should get a new boiler.'

It's nothing to do with the boiler, you Grade A twunt, it's to do with anticipating what you're going to need and when. But as there's no danger of you ever instigating a search for or installation of a new household accoutrement of any sort, I need not go into this now but will merely give a non-committal

'Mmm.'

11 A.M.

I have put the first washing on, read the paper, got my handbag, purse and shopping list together and am waiting in the sitting room for my lord and master. It dawns on me slowly that I cannot remember hearing the sound of running water, nor is there registering upon my now attuned ear evidence of vigorous ongoing ablutions. Suspicion mounts. Red mist hovers, waiting to descend

'Have you finished in the bathroom yet?'

'I've not run my bath yet. I'm on the internet.'

Of course you're on the fucking internet. This is what I get for not delineating clearly the need for a particular course of action, albeit one that I have outlined every other sodding Saturday since cohabitation time began and therefore rashly assumed needed no further reiteration. I seem to spend most of my life caught in endless loops of repeated explanations. You think I'm nagging. I think I'm trapped in a particularly hellish version of Groundhog Day.

'Can you stop being on the internet and get into the bath so that we don't have to go to the supermarket at exactly the same time as every other frigging person in the world and their screaming children?'

I'm standing at the foot of the stairs, looking like a female Cartman, eyes screwed up, tiny fists clenched, gesturing violently but impotently as I rage. And listen to this tone in my voice. Squawking harpy. This is not me. I am a laid-back, easygoing, kind person at heart. Or I used to be. He is destroying me.

'OK.'

Right. I'll just piss away another half-hour waiting for you then.

I'd go myself but we need to do a big shop and he's the only one who can drive. And as driving might be the only immediately quantifiable benefit he brings to this relationship, I am always eager to take advantage of it.

11.40 A.M.

'You're driving too close to the kerb.'

'No, I'm not.'

'Then why are you three feet further to the left than any of the cars in front of us?'

'Because they're all wrong. You're supposed to hug the kerb.'

'Hug it? You're lubing it up and buttfucking it. Why have you gone this way?'

'What way should I have gone, Geografina?'

'The other way, because of the roadworks.'

'What roadworks?'

What roadworks? Jesus Christ, not only can you not anticipate future consequences, you can't remember the past and factor it into the present. There are people with brain injuries and who have had strokes who get put in special homes for things like this, aren't there?

'The roadworks you must have passed fifty times on foot in the last fortnight. The roadworks! The roadworks!'

'Oh yes, now you've said it three times I remember and have reversed time so that I have now made the correct decision and gone the other way.'

'I hate you so much. I wish you would drive into that wall there and kill us both.'

12.30 P.M.

'Why have you put eighteen packets of sausages into the trolley?'

'I like them.'

'But I thought we agreed that we were trying to eat more healthily.'

'Sausages are healthy.'

'Do you really believe that or are you trying to force me to have a convulsion here in the meat and poultry aisle?'

'They're just meat.'

I look at him. A question that runs through my mind about 3,857 times a day takes another trip around my throbbing brain: does a thirty-three-year-old man really need [insert example of stupidity currently under scrutiny here] explaining to him? The answer is so frequently yes that I make a mental note to relabel the question rhetorical and stop asking myself it. Perhaps I will take up a soothing hobby or craft in the free time this will yield, which will help me knit back together my internally shredded self. In the meantime...

'They are not just meat,' I eventually choke out, between hefty belts of vodka from the now opened bottle from the trolley (this is why we needed the car — I get through eight bottles a day). 'They are fat, gristle, breadcrumbs, offal and any remaining scraps you can hose off a carcass after the prime cuts have been removed. And more fat. And some lard.'

'No, they're not.'

We are at an impasse. This happens quite a lot. He will never, ever believe that I know more about something than he does. Now, it is perfectly correct that he is far cleverer, better educated and more knowledgeable about the world than me. Only yesterday, he explained EU agricultural policy, the Treaty of Versailles and a joke about Senator John McCain on *The Daily Show* to me and I accepted each of the three on trust, with gratitude and in their entirety, because I know I am pig ignorant in matters of politics, history and current affairs. One of the many things I do not understand, however, is why this phenomenon does not occur in reverse. Why, when I assert something about an issue that belongs firmly in the domestic sphere, about an issue such as sausages (to take an example far from at random), to the superior comprehension of which no possible honour or glory attaches, but which, simply by virtue of it being simple, mundane and at least in part the result of applied commonsense rather than yer book-larnin', I am likely to know far more about than he does, he cannot simply accept what I say and move on. Ideally to something more interesting than sausages.

So now, somehow, I am in the position of having to justify what I consider to be the God-given truth, that sausages are not top of everyone's list of slimming aids. Socrates would weep to see the dismal ends to which his methods are bent, but here goes.

'What do you think of as an unquestionably healthy food?'

'Salad.'

'Is a sausage a salad?'

'No.'

'Is it perhaps as unlike a salad as it is possible for another foodstuff to be?'

'Yes. But that doesn't make them unhealthy, that just makes them not salad.'

'OK. When you grill sausages at home, what happens?'

'Stuff comes out.'

'And it runs into the grill pan and solidifies into what?'

'Fat.'

'Would you spoon that fat into your mouth?'

'No.'

'Why not?'

'Because it would be bad for me. Ahhh.'

'Excellent. Now, as to composition: are sausages one whole piece of meat like, for example, a steak or a chop?'

'No.'

'No. What are they?'

'They're sort of bits all mashed up in a casing.'

'Right. So far we are in perfect agreement, yes?' I should just let this go. At one level, it is, after all, only a minor disagreement about sausages. And yet, at another, it is so much more.

'Yes.'

'So. Would you agree that, given the final appearance of the stuffing in the casing, it is difficult, if not impossible, to ascertain its actual provenance? You cannot, for example, pick out a morsel, hold it up to the light and tell me it came from the belly of a pig, or the hindquarters of a cow?'

'I agree.'

'Would you also agree that if you were a meat-producing corporation that had as one of its product lines a foodstuff that lent itself to deployment as a receptacle for the offcuts of meat, fat and gristle too meagre and/or unappetising to be sold in their own right, you might use it as a lucrative way of pressing these scraps into profitable service?'

'Yes.'

'OK. Stay with me, we're coming up to the home stretch now. What do I read?'

'Books, newspapers, magazines, websites.'

'Right. And which ones in particular? What do they all have in common?'

'You read books I don't read, the bits of the paper that I ignore, magazines I never realised existed and websites that I find so boring I start to fall into a vegetative state when I just read your Favourites listing.'

'Correct. Would you say, therefore, that there is a possibility that I have read articles which you have not about the recovery of meat, the formation of sausages, the workings of the meat-packing industry?'

'Yes.'

'So when I say that sausages are rarely formed of minced prime rib, will you accept that I make this statement not through some mad hope of self-aggrandisement or spontaneous desire to thwart your sausage-eating plans, but because I am more fully aware of the sausages' likely origins, history and constitution?'

'Yes.'

'Can you please put the sausages back on the shelf and bring me a packet of chicken breasts instead?'

'Yes.'

'Thank you.'

1.30 P.M.

We unpack the shopping. He drops the apples into the fruit bowl from a height of about three feet.

'Don't do that!'

'Why not?'

'Whaddya mean, "Why not?" How can you not know that apples bruise? Something in my head just burst. I suppose you don't know the number for an ambulance either? Would you mind finishing the unpacking while I go upstairs for a little sleep and a cry?'

'No, go ahead. I'm going to have a chicken breast for lunch. I might roll it into the shape of a sausage, for old times' sake.'

Do what you want. Shove it up your arse for all I care. This, an old, frail part of my brain murmurs before it is finally choked off by the creeping tendrils of bitterness and cynicism which have overgrown the bulk, is not the default reaction I should have towards my beloved. I take the vodka with me. Better soon.

2.15 P.M.

I am awoken by the sound of him smashing a mug. This means he's made tea. This means there are brown drips across three surfaces and down the vertical face of at least one counter, all of which he will deny making. I close my eyes again and try to resurrect the dream I was having about George Clooney. It wasn't sexual. I was just living in his eighteen-bedroom mansion, watching the servants clean, cook and shop, while he was off shooting another intelligent film with a liberal bias that we could both be proud of. He is guaranteed to be away for at least six months.

I drift off again, my face wreathed in smiles.

2.45 P.M.

I am awoken by his inability to raise the toilet seat quietly. He smashes it back as if the cistern is his personal nemesis. 'Don't forget to piss all over the rim,' I almost shout, but George has just sent a telegram saying that filming has been delayed and I will be living alone in his clean and silent house for another three months, so I slip happily back into sleep.

3.05 P.M.

From the door-slamming that has been going on for the past ten minutes, I deduce that he has now found his wallet, keys and jacket and has gone out for a walk. I must remember to ask him which has done him more wrong over the years, the toilet or the door frame?

4.20 P.M.

I am staring into the fridge when he returns.

'Why are you staring into the fridge? Are you too hot?'

'No. I am, in fact, staring at the leftover chicken breast from your lunch.'

'I know,' he says proudly, puffing up like, well, a chicken is the image which springs, understandably, to mind. 'I put it in the fridge.'

'Yes. Yes you did. But — and here's the thing — you didn't put it on a plate first. You didn't put it in a Tupperware box. You didn't wrap it in clingfilm or a piece of foil. You just took a piece of meat and put it on the refrigerator shelf.'

'So?'

How can you explain to someone how wrong this is if they cannot see how wrong this is?

'How is this an action that roars across the line separating tolerable irritations from molten imbecility?'

Perhaps I should not embark on another pointless diatribe, another futile attempt at education and enlightenment and instead mould this moment into the beginnings of an epistemological debate. How does one person know that leftover chicken goes into a container before it goes into the fridge, and how does another person of the same age, nationality and background have not a single, tiny inkling about the existence of such a practice? Or even any comprehension of the principles of hygiene and preservation that might encourage him to initiate it without such prior knowledge? I wonder if this could form the basis for a series of scientific experiments to contribute to the ongoing nature versus nurture debate. Is leftover-wrapping an inborn skill found only amongst females or purely a matter of cultural conditioning? If the former, can it be taught to males and if the latter, why are they so fucking stupid that they never pick it up?

Thirty-five per cent of people are expected to be living solo by 2021. I suspect that is a significant underestimate, and I hope with all my rage-blistered heart that I am one of them. Oh well, here goes nothing ...

'Do you agree that this piece of poultry smells, has marked the shelf and is now drier than it would have been if you had placed it in some kind of non-porous container or form of wrapping?'

5.40 P.M.

'And we keep the Tupperware in that drawer there. I see. That's that sorted. Now, what are we doing tonight?'

'I am going out with Sally because otherwise I fear that the sensation of being immured in a living hell, tormented by the thought that I am doomed to spend eternity in a crude facsimile of a particularly unkind sociological experiment, whereby one independent adult is forced to do the entirety of another (allegedly sentient) being's thinking for him, while scientists see how long it takes her to work out whether this is due to his genuine and all-encompassing cluelessness or a chosen adherence to a particularly thorough version of learned helplessness, will mean that I start self-harming. You must go out with your friends.'

'I think I'll just stay in.'

'No, you have to go out. Otherwise, I will spend the entire evening worrying about how many broken mugs, dirty plates and scorch marks on the carpet I've got to come home to. And you have to go out first, so that I can get ready in peace.'

6.30 P.M.

He goes out. I change into my pyjamas and dressing gown, curl up in front of the TV with a delicious ready meal and relax for five blissful hours. One of the cats pads in. 'Would you like to sit up here with me? It's entirely up to you. I have spent the last ten hours micromanaging the life of another, I will not do it with you. We are both free to spend the evening in whichever way we like best. You're going to stretch and roll for a bit? What a good idea, so will I.'

11.30 P.M.

I am in bed. The door slams, the toilet seat reverberates, a teapot breaks. Another door drops off its hinges. He blunders into the bedroom, belching loudly, sweating and farting. I wouldn't mind, but he's not drunk.

He redecorates the bathroom in spit and toothpaste as he cleans his teeth. He drops his clothes on the floor because he knows nothing gets a woman in the mood for bedtime manoeuvres like the sight of dirty underpants coiled on the carpet like buffalo crap. He gets in. He reaches over.

'Don't even think about it,' I snarl.

He lies back down. The coughing, snorting and spluttering mutates slowly into snoring. With any luck I will die in the night.

If you live together for long enough, things will get better. Slightly. This is largely because your spirit gets broken and your happier former existence, when your home was a haven, a place of peace in which you worked, read books, entertained friends and generally lived a life of boundless ease and serenity, recedes so far into the past that it seems to belong to someone else. You almost forget what it was like to have the freedom to wander round, to stand and stare without being asked what you're looking for, to be able to go out without explaining why or for how long, to have the right to read undisturbed for vast tracts of time and, above all, you forget what it was like to be without the constant voice in your head factoring in his presence and his requirements to every decision, large, small, life-changing or toilet-roll-changing, that you make, which pollutes your train of thought and ruins your concentration. It is quite possible that you are actually suffering from a kind of marital Stockholm Syndrome and that this may be the key to all flourishing male–female partnerships. But it must also be said that your serotonin levels will improve because over a period of time he will master the art of Tupperware, learn how to load the dishwasher (not well, not efficiently, not quietly, but it does – after a fashion – get done) and may well reveal an entirely unsuspected ability to change a tyre.

For those who survive, and even enjoy, the cohabitation experience, the next step is, of course, deciding whether you can also survive, and even enjoy, being legally and divinely bound to your beloved for the rest of your life. In other words, do you want to get married?

We are pretty much the first generation to be able to ask ourselves that question in any meaningful or widespread way. For our grandmothers, it was the only way to have sex without fear of censure or producing illegitimate children who would have to be passed off as nieces and nephews come to stay, which is a lot more of a strain on the nerves than Catherine Cookson novels make it look. Even for our mothers, the expectation that they would get married (and have children) was so strong that it amounted almost to a mandate.

But it seems that increasingly the answer is yes, we do want to get married. After a good few decades of declining popularity, the state of matrimony is on the upturn again.

Not only that, but people are lavishing more money on it than ever before. The average cost for a wedding in the US is now over $20,000 and in the UK a traditional church wedding costs around £11,000. Either budget can double without very much effort at all if you live in an expensive region or have a thoughtlessly large family or want to decorate the church with real flowers instead of newspaper cutouts.

So why are people still doing it? Well, there are probably as many reasons for getting married as there are people getting hitched – everyone makes the decision based on their own personal blend of circumstances and beliefs – but here are some of the best and the worst.

Five good reasons to get married

1. You are pregnant and your parents are Catholic

Just do it. Don't try to argue with them, just get married. It will save you years of futile arguments and Christmasses spent breasting constant waves of disapproval, meeting stony glares and ignoring broken-hearted sighs. Also, it might mean you don't go to hell. You never know.

2. Egomania

One of my best friends was in a bridal shop trying to choose various fripperies and furbelows. 'What,' asked the assistant trying to help her choose from the array on offer, 'is the theme of your wedding?' Emma looked at her in astonishment. It had never occurred to her that such a question should need to be asked. 'The theme of my wedding,' she said in tones that brooked no possibility of error, 'is ME.'

I admire this approach very much. Every human being is fundamentally a rapacious limelight hunter. Alas, once you are an adult, there are precious few socially sanctioned means of ensuring that you are the focus of everyone's attention for an entire day (and at least one of them requires that you be lying in a coffin, which rather takes the edge off). So, if you hunger for the spotlight but prefer to be alive under it, yet can't be arsed to queue for *Pop Idol* or fill in all the forms for *Big Brother*, if you have unfulfilled theatrical desires and a longing to walk just once through a crowd of people who are required by law and the fact that you are about to pay for a lukewarm chicken dinner for them all to look at you with love, respect and awe, then you need a wedding.

(N.B. If this is your motivation, then you will undoubtedly become, in the preparation of the event, the beast known as Bridezilla, causing all your friends and family to run hither and yon in mounting panic as they struggle to follow your increasingly hysterical and outlandish orders, until they collapse with exhaustion or you trample them, unheeding, underfoot. You should be aware that although they will still turn up on the day, it is the pride of creation that draws them there. Your friendships are effectively at an end.)

3. The groom is very rich

You may be earning a decent salary yourself. You may take pride in being an economically independent woman, and so you should. But that's no excuse for not availing yourself of the chance to lay your hands on some free money. Nobody but a damn fool does that. Marriage means that if he dies, you get his share of the house and all sorts of pensions and health care stuff, depending on how financially prepared you made sure he was before he popped his clogs. If you divorce for reasons that can be laid entirely at his door (and let's face it, the chances are that you will and they can be), then you can take him for as much as you can carry. Or you can walk nobly away with your head held high. The important thing is to have the money. I'm sorry, I mean the choice.

Also, if you live in a big city, the chances are you cannot buy property on a single income that doesn't come with mildew and coprophagic sitting tenants. It is tempting to marry someone for their loft conversion, or at least for their usefulness when it comes to getting that coveted dual income mortgage multiplier, and – delightfully – this is one of the few instances in which giving in to temptation makes sound financial sense, as it is both cheaper and more profitable to keep getting married and divorced than to keep renting.

4. The frock

There isn't enough silk, satin or tulle in modern life. There just isn't. I went to my babysitter's wedding when I was seven and sat on her lap afterwards. The cold, heavy, impossibly smooth white folds of her dress were the most beautiful things I'd ever seen or felt. I'm afraid you can't undo that kind of formative sense memory, and I wouldn't try. You just have to give in and recreate it at some point in your life.

And sometimes a girl just hankers after a bit of corsetry. Unless you are part of the 0.0000001% of the population still going to balls, this is the only chance you're going to get to inject some of it into your own life. I myself have a secret yearning to yomp up the aisle in a dress that involves thirty pounds of brocaded whalebone up top and a satin covered farthingale below. I may look like the bastard offspring of a sofa and a Pavlova pudding, but at least I will be able to look back and know that I exploited my sartorial opportunity to the full. Especially as Sally wants to be my bridesmaid and has demanded that we do the whole thing on rollerskates.

5. The presents

Ask any of your friends what they remember best about their wedding. They won't say, 'I remember my heart bursting with the knowledge that we were now bound together unto death by the laws of both God and man' or 'Realising that in plighting my troth to this man I had at once subsumed my own identity within his and yet in so doing becoming so much more myself than I ever dreamed I could be' or 'Looking round to see the faces of all the people I love gathered in the one place and shining with happiness, radiant with joy, to witness the sacred blessing of our union.' No. They will say, 'Coming back from honeymoon to find eighteen boxes of presents waiting for us in the living room.'

Also, there comes a point when you really do deserve restitution for the time, money and effort you have spent on everybody else's matrimonials. When the connubial carousel begins, the sight of the first few cards through your letterbox is delightful and the

> *consequent ceremonies are beautiful, beguiling and gilded with*
> *the charm of novelty. Three years and thirty-six of the buggers*
> *later, and you are ruthlessly applying the following formula to the*
> *invitation to work out whether you have to go at all:*
>
> *Time off work x (cost of present + distance to travel + price of*
> *accommodation + how much you like whichever of the bride or*
> *groom is your friend + amount of interest in pulling eligible man*
> *at party + likelihood of doing so). Minus (pressure of shopping for*
> *new outfit + how much you dislike whichever of the bride and*
> *groom is not your friend).*

When it comes to your own wedding presents, just make sure you register. Really takes the fun out of a marriage if you find that all you get out of it are seventy-two toasters and a photo album.

Five bad reasons to get married

1. It's romantic

The prime purpose of marriage was, for generations, to ensure the safe passage of property. Bewhiskered Daddy picks out a suitable wife, Less Bewhiskered Son marries her and inherits land which is then passed on to his children when LBS has grown enough whiskers and/or dies. No splitting of estates amongst competing bastards' claims or wily peasantry getting in on the act. But that is a bit brutal, so they had to start dressing it up and feeding the notion to malleable childish minds that it was actually all to do with love and clouds and pretty dresses and the fulfilment of a beautiful destiny.

If you reach the age of thirty still believing in this, I am torn between admiration for your ability to remain untouched by every facet, every feature, every message and every influence of the modern age and horror at the thought of what is about to befall your naïve and tender soul.

2. Peer pressure

Another one of those mathematical impossibilities is thrown up by the fact that everyone is always the last person they know to get married. So you watch all your friends pair off and disappear into Wedded World and before you know it, you feel eight years old again, alone in the playground, bored and dragging your toes in the dust of single life.

Being fed up and lonely is a good reason for buying new shoes or going on holiday. It is rarely a good reason for legally binding yourself to someone for life.

3. Immigration laws

You will be found out and arrested. It will not be at all like Gerard Depardieu and Andie MacDowell in *Green Card*. It will be a giant and sprawling mistake.

4. To lose your virginity

Honestly, you really should have a crack at it before then. Otherwise it's ten to one that you will be lying there in your white silk nightie and he will come out of the bathroom with a set of iron manacles, a double-ended dildo and a gleeful expression on his face that all together will give rise to a profound suspicion that you may not be the two most sexually compatible people ever joined together in holy matrimony.

Or, if he's virgin territory too, you will spend your entire holiday trying to get it in (and then trying to stop it popping out), which is an exhausting way to spend a fortnight in Fiji.

5. One of you is dying

The stress will just speed up the process. Do you really want to spend all that money just to usher the Grim Reaper more rapidly in? Have some sense, do.

Charlotte should have the final word. 'Do not compromise AT ALL when choosing a husband,' she said firmly to me at the end of her Five Simple Rules. 'But compromise a little every day with him after that.'

If you can remember these words every time you are confronted by yet more evidence of your husband's molten imbecility, you may just make it to an anniversary.

10 Secrets To A Long Lasting Relationship

1. Separate interests
2. Separate workplaces
3. Separate televisions
4. Separate beds
5. Separate meals
6. Separate houses
7. Separate friends
8. Separate holidays
9. Separate Chrismasses
10. Separate bank accounts

CHAPTER 7

Working Girl

Once upon a time, careers advice for girls meant looking at her parents and knowing whether she was destined to be a scullery maid with impetigo, a governess with ambitions to be a lady novelist or a wife with an errant husband and secret laudanum habit. Then the Industrial Revolution happened and women got the chance to work in factories, spinning, weaving and losing fingers in giant looms for employers rather than for their families. By the beginning of the twentieth century, women were making forays into nursing, teaching and secretarial duties – anything that was remarkably similar to the domestic work that had once made families so self-sufficient but could now be traded on the open market for low pay and free husbands so that male employees could go off and do something more interesting instead.

By the fifties, career horizons had expanded wildly. Girls could now become nurses, teachers and secretaries, at least until they married, and if they were very determined and/or ugly they could even, technically, become doctors and lawyers.

I remember my mother telling me, as we walked to the shops one day, that it used to be possible to walk out of one job and into another the day after. I remember it because she told me this in 1984, when the idea of a world where there were more jobs than people chasing them seemed like the ramblings of a madwoman. We were coming to maturity at a time when the old notions of a job-for-life have been sluiced from the national psyche by the flood of new technologies and changing working practices and people were only just learning to scramble for annual contracts and freelance fragments in the way that seems second nature to us now, but was frightening the bejasus out of workers at the time.

By the time my generation was turning its thoughts to the subject of gainful employment, things were slightly less scary. Of course, this was partly because the kind of jobs we were aiming for remained relatively unaffected by social and economic upheaval. The school and local library were still full of books trilling away about the glamorous lives of air hostesses and hotel receptionists ('Or, if you love ponies even more than you love smiling, why not be a vet? Only joking! Why not marry a man who owns a lot of ponies?'). It had been long understood that to leave school at sixteen meant you were going to work as a hairdresser, in a shop or maybe, if you knew you looked particularly good in navy polyester, a bank. Those who were persuaded by the teachers to stay on and do A-levels or shorthand and typing courses would become nurses, primary school teachers or secretaries. And anyone who went on to university was going to become a secondary school teacher if they could spell and a doctor if they could not.

Few girls' teachers thought to laud the careers of astronauts, barristers, particle physicists, bankers or stockbrokers. This was partly ingrained sexism and partly the result of teachers being generally an irredeemably idealistic bunch of pedagogues. Those dispensing careers advice laid great store by something called 'job satisfaction', doing something you could be proud of and giving something back to the community. Presumably, it was this kind of hippy shit that kept them there, trying day after day to cram knowledge into the hardened skulls and softened brains of 600 recalcitrant teenaged girls in grimly depressing municipal buildings.

As with their attempts at sex education, they had left things a little too late. By fifteen, most of us were long past the stage of nurturing a sense of civic responsibility. We had Saturday jobs and were thoroughly addicted to the sweet, sweet jingle of cash in our pockets – our own cash, herald of freedom, adulthood and consumer durables. On £2.74 an hour, it was possible to take home £93 a month, which when you factor in the absence of rent, food and utility bills and the fact that Sunday trading had yet to be introduced so there was never any chance to spend it, means that you'll never be richer than you were at fifteen.

When I joined a new sixth form for my A-levels, in a richer borough, full of kids who got fistfuls of twenties every week as 'clothing allowances', I was the only student who had a Saturday job. A snotty teacher came up to me and told me I would have to give it up.

'Why?' I asked, with honest interest.

'Because you cannot do justice to your syllabi [syllabi! I should have beaten her to death right there and then] if you are working at weekends.'

'But if I give up my job,' I replied with ineffable logic,
'I won't have any money.'

'But you will have your A-levels.'

'But I would rather have my money. I love my money.
I do not love my A-levels.'

'Don't be ridiculous.'

'One of my A-levels is general studies. I think two years' deli
earnings will amply repay me for anything I miss in the way of
being bored out of my mind while learning about the nation's
various infrastructures and institutions.'

'Now you are being even more ridiculous.'

'And you are totally getting on my tits. Good day to you,
madam.'

I didn't say the last bit. But I kept my job and gave up general
studies, and so far I have suffered no ill effects beyond being
forever slightly unsure about quite what the House of Lords does.
But I'm told that this is an uncertainty common to most people,
up to and very much including those actually in the House of
Lords, so I have decided not to concern myself with it overmuch.

These days, girls aren't champing at the bit to leave school and start
work because they know that, without further qualifications, wherever
they start on their first day is exactly where they will stay until they
die. They know that any promotions will be taken by the individual
with the foresight to have accumulated the necessary pieces of paper
and they will have to spend their entire working lives getting cups of

coffee for increasingly youthful and ungrateful bosses whose jobs they are not allowed to apply for.

But they are all fibrillating with indecision because they don't want to go to university and accumulate mountains of debt either. So, if you are one of the unfortunate staff who didn't dive out of the window in time when the head came prowling through the staffroom looking for volunteers to coax petrified students into filling in their UCAS forms, you have to come up with a sound fiscal rationale. If you can convince them about how much more they can earn over a lifetime as a graduate trainee, how little £20,000 in fees is compared to that, the reduced-interest loans they can get, the array of fascinating temping jobs they can do in the holidays, the bar work in the evenings, and teach them how not to think of debt as a black hole into which they can sink forever but as a catapult into which they should gladly strap themselves and allow to be drawn further and further back, so that it may one day be released and ultimately launch them further forward into the land of plentiful salary than they could otherwise get, then they might just sign up for the three-year gig. You must avoid giving any sign at all that their lives will from hereon out be governed and ruined by the following equation:

Going to university = average £13,000 debt on graduation. Call this X.

First job = average starting salary of £13,000. Call this Y.

Cost of smallest, dampest flat just near enough your first job for you not to have to leave for the office before you get home in the evening in order to get there on time in the morning = £150,000. Call this A.

Deposit for (A) = £15,000. Call this B.

Monthly mortgage payment, food, travel, utilities and the occasional pint to cry into about your imminent council tax bill,

the cost of TV licences and boiler repairs and the price of
nooses = £16,000 per annum. Call this C.

To solve the equation Y-X-B-C = A, you will be living in your
childhood bedroom at your parents' house until you are
thirty-seven.

Or, of course, you might only get halfway through your lecture before
you become so overwhelmed by the relentlessly practical, joyless and
depressingly money-obsessed nature of it that you morph into one of the
teachers of old. Visions of the friends you lost over the years – chewed
up in the City meat-grinder or broken on the rack of lawyerdom – start
to swim so thickly before your eyes that you eventually fall to your knees
and implore the girls to throw away their calculators and go with their
idealistic, hippy shit instincts. 'If we don't have you providing a tiny
injection of hope and optimism every year, society will shrivel and die!
Just die!' you shriek before the head hauls you away and throws you
back into the staffroom in disgust.

Workin' it: temping

Temping can provide much in the way of valuable insight into the
workings of various types of company, office and industry, and you can
accumulate vital skills, make useful contacts for the future, consolidate
your commercial knowledge, increase your competence and extend
your proficiency in a variety of professional arenas as you learn to
incorporate yourself seamlessly into one corporate behemoth after
another, adding to your own expertise even as you yourself add to
theirs, a walking, filing, typing tribute to the fact that the mutually
beneficial, symbiotic relationship between employee and employer is
not an idle, beautiful dream but a noble and achievable goal.

That, roughly, is what the temping agencies will tell you, as you haul your ass before them in an increasingly dispirited fashion. They are not being entirely honest with you. The average temp's day can go one of two ways:

Good day

9 A.M.

Start work.

9.30 A.M.

Everyone else starts work. They take a few minutes out of their busy schedules to ignore you every time you ask where anything is.

10 A.M.–1 P.M.

Photocopy the quarter's financial statistics and address thirty-two internal mail envelopes in which to distribute them (flaps, your 'supervisor' tells you thirty-one envelopes into it, not to be stuck down but tucked neatly inside). Distribute envelopes superefficiently and go to lunch.

1–2 P.M.

Sit alone in cafeteria chewing a sandwich that seems to be committing suicide in your mouth. Scald mouth on coffee dispensed directly from the sun. Smile nervously at permanent employees, who look at you with what it would be a woeful understatement to call contempt as they pass by. Feel mildly grateful when no one actually pisses on you as they go.

2–2.30 P.M.

Return to desk to find supervisor spitting blood because the superefficiently delivered financial statistics were technically embargoed till tomorrow, even though you could sieve the entire office through the smallest mesh and still not find any particle of a person who cares about this fact. Bite tongue. Do not point out that if supervisor had in any way — gosh, what is the word? Oh yes, supervised — what you were doing, neither of you would have to be going through this ritual of caring that a mistake has been made. Apologise and vow inwardly to slash her tyres at first available opportunity.

2.30–5.30 P.M.

Search through six foot tall pile of computer printouts to find out how many times the cryptic annotation DVA appears on them. This is so that your supervisor knows how many times the cryptic annotation DVA appears on the average six foot tall pile of computer printouts and can rest easy in her mind once more.

Go home. Repeat for next six weeks.

Bad day

This is when the temp is assumed to have a working knowledge of, or, worse, *interest* in, the employment sector to which the office is devoted – for example, law.

9 A.M.

Start work. A lawyer of indeterminate sex barks at you to research whether s.21(2) of the Landlord & Tenants (Covenants) Act 1995 means that it was implied into every post-1995 partial covenant against alterations of a further covenant that the landlord's consent to such alterations would not be unreasonably withheld. Instead of asking him/her/it to explain every word that he/she/it has just used, you — fool — give a watermelon smile, nod vigorously and trip off to the library with all the joy of a Von Trapp infant skipping towards the Austro-Swiss border, giving him/her/it to understand that you are both enthused by the project and overwhelmingly confident of its success.

5 P.M.

The lawyer finds you sitting on the library floor in the middle of a pile of Halsbury's law books, looseleaf supplements and draft suicide notes. You say that you should have the answer in no more than three to six years, or however long it takes you to get a law degree and decipher what he/she/it said. He/she/it says it doesn't matter any more because he/she/it had a look around the back of his/her/its enormous brain, lifted up a few folds of cerebellum and found the answer just sitting there. But you're still sacked.

The best thing that can be said about temping is that it exposes you to a wide variety of people and teaches you to keep a straight face throughout, which, if nothing else, comes in very handy when you realise that the only way you can bring your earnings up to living wage standard is to supplement them with poker or prostitution, in both of which situations an air of implacable unshockability can be a great asset to a lady. And some of the people you meet can provide you with the kind of life lessons you just don't get anywhere else.

The parable of The Shell-Shocked Divorcée

The only constant amongst all the places you can temp is the number of middle-aged women there will be who are in the process of getting divorced.

Some of these middle-aged divorcées (or MADwomen, if you will) wander about the office with unseeing eyes, filing everything in the bin and being covered for by sympathetic colleagues because they are still trying to get used to the fact that their husband of twenty-five years has run off with his secretary/the au pair/their daughter's friend/ some other equally nubile and unimaginative option from page ninety-six of the midlife crisis catalogue. They can at least function as proof to your foolish and naïve young self that even the most apparently stolid and trustworthy man can turn into a total shit if the timing and circumstances are right, and you can adjust your relationship gyroscopes accordingly. And your finances.

If your placement lasts long enough to let you see these women emerge from the initial shock of revelation and pain of separation, you will soon see their equilibrium shot to hell once more with the news that the house and car were in his name and he's selling them both to keep Little Miss Newtits in the style to which she would like to become accustomed. He's also cleaned out the joint bank account and she soon learns that her married woman's pension contributions will not even be enough to pay the rent on the one-room flat she will be forced into unless one of her children has done well enough for itself to convert its loft for her.

On the other hand, the jubilatory MADwoman is an equally common sight. She is the one whizzing about the office, doing the work of ten people with a smile on her lips and a song in her heart because she has finally succeeded in ridding herself of what one of them once vividly described to me as 'fifteen fucking stone of manflap apparently welded to my sofa'. Usually the change is precipitated by the children leaving home and the MADwoman suddenly becoming conscious of a void not just in the home but in her heart, and the prospect of a house whose silence is broken only by the internal screams from thirty years of accumulated frustration and her husband's stertorous breathing becomes unendurable. Either that, or early menopause gives her an unexpected sense of how brief and easily inglorious a span it is we have on this earth and she vows not to waste another moment of it listening to him eating soup, softly scratching his genitals every morning or telling his dinner party story about bumping into Jack Nicklaus in his conference hotel while guests faint with boredom. Again, this woman is a useful corrective to any fanciful notions you might be entertaining about the possibility that love, marriage and cosy domesticity a) exists and b) lasts. Not coincidentally, the only things these happy MADwomen have in common are separate bank accounts and their names on the house deeds, so think on.

The S&M practitioner

Never judge a working drone by her neat, grey-suited cover. I have lost count of the number of swingers, S&M practitioners and women running mail-order businesses selling their dirty knickers from the front room I have come across in various offices, all of whom proved themselves unexpectedly eager to share the intimate details of their lives with the stranger sent to cover Marie's maternity leave.

Thanks to the unrivalled generosity of such women, you will learn the pros and cons of most forms of lubricant (purpose-bought and improvised), how you might fit eighteen links of steel chain up your bottom (though not, precisely, why) and how to install a sturdy hook to your upper landing ceiling in such a way that it will take the weight of a fully grown man who wishes to be hung from his feet while being gently flogged with a Laura Ashley tasselled curtain tie-back.

These Jekyll and Hyde characters are most prevalent in suburban offices, though this may have changed now that Starbucks has penetrated the furthest reaches of most concrete wastelands and a woman's lust for novelty and stimulation can be sublimated into the purchase of ever more esoteric variations on a milky coffee. But they provide a salutary lesson in the truth of the adage that truth is stranger than fiction, and often involves a lot more in the way of deviant usages of soft furnishings.

The hidden talent

The more family-friendly version of the above rule about not judging a person on first appearances is that you will frequently find, especially amongst the women, that they are nursing some amazing hidden talents: the woman who can add up entire columns of figures pages long in her head, the one who has total recall and can remember every financial and personal detail of the 800 people whose records she deals with in the HR department of a big company and, of course, the one who can always, always unblock the three-hole punch when everyone else has declared it beyond the wit of humanity to fix it.

* * * ✳ * * *

I also worked for a company who had an accounts administrator who was five feet two and who kept her files on the top shelf of the office, very impractically, I thought, until I saw her come in, jump six feet in the air from a standing start and get one down with no more thought or effort than I would put into popping open a can of Coke. It was the most amazing physical feat I have ever seen. I turned round to look at the rest of the girls in the office and they all grinned in recognition. 'I know,' said one of them. 'But don't tell her. We worry that one day she'll realise and get embarrassed and stop. Then we'll all have to leave. We only stay to watch her.'

* * * ✳ * * *

The heinous bitch

Temping will also prepare you for the existence of real ruthless depravity in the world. They can be any age, rank, shape or size, but there is always one total and utter dead-eyed, backstabbing, muck-spreading, canker-hearted bitch in the office. If she's the boss and you're the temp, just leave. She makes enough people's lives a misery on a daily basis without adding yours to her villainous store. If she is a co-worker, however, I would advise you to stay and examine her machinations closely. Even if you harbour no ambitions to become a cold-blooded bitch from hell yourself, it is always worth learning from the enemy in order to arm yourself against their assaults in the future. Watch how she divides the workforce, sets colleague against colleague, flirts with the men who can let her go home early, craps on those who can't, avoids work, sidesteps extra responsibility and yet manages to claim everybody else's ideas and efforts as her own, with a word dropped in the right ear here, a modest glance in the right direction there and the occasional bald-faced lie whenever she thinks no one important is around to hear it.

Much of this will, of course, already be familiar to you from the playground, but there is something darkly fascinating about seeing it played out in the adult sphere. And, of course, if you can catch her out, if you can bring her down, if you can leave her standing in the middle of the boardroom exposed as the ruthless, manipulative witch she is, like the final scenes of a particularly satisfying chickflick, possibly starring Cameron Diaz or Sandra Bullock, then you will find many of your childhood demons have been laid to rest. Much cheaper than therapy.

Sexual harassment

Most women quite enjoy their first experiences of sexual harassment. Getting your bum pinched by a seventeen-year-old shop assistant when you are a sixteen-year-old shop assistant is more of an initiation ceremony into the joys of adolescence than a moral outrage and can be squealed at and shrugged off accordingly. Or, occasionally, it can be converted into a valuable business arrangement. When I worked in our local bakery, for example, I used to let the owner's toothless son rub up against me on condition that I got first pick of the leftover cream fancies and coconut whirls. Everybody was happy, except perhaps the more hygiene-conscious of our customers.

As you get older, however, your definition of sexually validating gestures becomes narrower. One becomes more discerning in one's choice of groper, preferring to permit advances only by those who have gone to the trouble of introducing themselves and taking you out to dinner, instead of just bumping slowly into you in the stockroom with their flies at half-mast.

In addition, for every year older you get, you become prey to another half-decade's worth of men, so by the time you are thirty, you are safe from neither the new teaboy nor the seventy-year-old senior partner who has to ask you to put his papery, palsied hands down your blouse yourself because he can no longer manage buttons.

It is as well, then, to protect your aesthetic sensibilities from the approach of lascivious septuagenarians as well as for any wider moral and feminist principle, to learn as early as possible in your career how best to dissuade the buggers.

RULE 1

If you are being harassed by someone younger than you, just tell them off. Not in a schoolteacherish way – with at least half of them this will just get you into more trouble than you were in before – but in a sick-to-the-back-teeth-of-this-kind-of-behaviour-now-go-to-your-room-and-stay-there-until-I-say-otherwise, Mumsy kind of way. If he continues, allow yourself to become embroiled in some kind of semi-naked situation with him, look down at his genitals in consternation and say, 'Oh my God ... I'm so sorry ... I didn't know ... Don't worry, I won't tell anyone.' Continue to gaze at him with a kind of horrified pity as you back away towards the door insisting that his tragic secret is safe with you. Not only will he not trouble you again, but you will probably also get his job after he fails to turn up for a month because he is spending every waking moment studying his penis with angled mirrors and a microscope trying to find out what's wrong.

RULE 2

If your cretinous pursuer is your age and/or roughly your seniority in the company – in other words, he holds no real power over you – you say, simply, loudly and in front of as many sympathetic witnesses as possible, 'Why are you such a fucking dick?' They rarely come back with a cogent and persuasive argument, particularly when said sympathetic witnesses start clapping admiringly as you continue gracefully about your day.

RULE 3

So your harasser is older and more senior than you. The wise thing to do is to keep a written record of the incidents and the names of any witnesses to them, accumulate, if possible, evidence of other offences perpetrated against your female colleagues, lodge complaints with all the right people, go through all the right channels up to and including an employment tribunal and, with any luck, metaphorically saw his legs off before a panel of judges and stride on to your next job with a nice wedge of compensation in one pocket and a glowing reference in the other.

The normal thing to do is to put up with it for as long as you can and get another job somewhere else without mentioning anything to anybody.

But there are other options:

- Ring his wife and tell her what's going on. Or send a letter. That way they get to read it at the breakfast table together before he goes to work to spend another day waving his Magic Marker at you from across the room.

- Go with it. Write him a four-page memo setting out the terms on which you are willing to service him on a regular basis. Don't forget to include a flat in Chelsea and ample employee pension provision.

- 'Accidentally' forward a dirty email he sent you to the entire department.

- Or, for a less technologically advanced solution, knee him in the crotch. It is amazing what a physical threat to the nether regions will do to a man's bullying tendencies. It also curiously heightens their reference-writing skills, should you decide that your talents would be better appreciated elsewhere.

There is no apology to be made for men who grope, lech after or make their female employees feel unhappy and uncomfortable in any of the million more subtle ways the committed lothario finds to express his dispiriting urges. There is no excuse to be made for men so stupid that they cannot remember that just because an employee has breasts and is junior to them, this does not automatically give them the right to have sex with her.

That said, I have on occasion watched and felt just a little sorry for men in the office who are confronted with women who do themselves seem to have confused the workplace with a sixteenth-century French brothel and habitually turn up sporting four inches of glitter-dusted cleavage and skirts split up to the hootenanny. There comes a point at which you have to take responsibility for what is bound to ensue.

I cannot put it better than to describe the exchange which took place between a young(ish – they are all born thirty-five years old) Glaswegian barrister and a (definitely) young secretary when I was temping in chambers. He was new to the place and she had been there a while. She went about her work with a sashay in her step that caused paper to peel from the walls, and most of the clerks and lawyers had learned to close their doors as she went past, in order not to be distracted from deadlines by her heaving bosom, at least three-fifths of which was gloriously on display at all times. Richard, however, had not. One day, she marched up to him in front of his various bosses and said indignantly, 'Stop staring at my tits!'

'What the f—!?' he exploded. 'They're staring at me!'

She was mortified, and he found a case of whisky from the bosses on his desk when he got back from court that night. And I think that's probably fair enough.

Workin' it: job interviews

Once you have had enough of temping (or rather get tired of playing the will-I-won't-I-make-rent-this-month game) and start hankering after a regular salary and, if you are very lucky, the kind of job that will enable you to qualify for a mortgage on a condemned broom cupboard a mere six-hundred-mile commute from the office, it is time to get to grips with the formal job interview. It's not like temp agency interviews. They have a variety of 'opportunities' on offer, so they just look you up and down, grade your accent and stick you in the next slot appropriate to your level of personal grooming, proximity to Received Pronunciation and willingness to act as coffee-brewing monkey for an ungrateful corporate department.

Once you start applying for jobs you actually want and would like, if at all possible, to follow as a career, everything becomes a lot more serious. As with all important events, proper preparation is the key.

1. Be born naturally confident and witty. This is particularly necessary for girls, as they do not receive as consistently as boys do the message from wider society that everything they say and do is automatically of importance and value, and so need to be innately sure of it themselves.

2. If you have not been born naturally confident and witty, pop into the loo when you arrive and take small nips of vodka from a purse-flask until you are.

3. Buy a suit. If you are being interviewed for anything your parents would consider a 'proper job'* remember that you cannot dress too conservatively. To us, it is the year 2007 and trousers are neither a personal or political statement. To the averagely antediluvian male interview panel, they are at best a reminder of 1940s land girls and munitions workers who first made people realise that women could do things other than breastfeed and wear red lipstick and who upset the whole bally employment applecart, and at worst a clear signal that you are one of those Lesbians they keep reading about who is going to reach into their

---

* That's anything they remember from their own youth that still brings in a regular wage. They don't care whether you are a hairdresser, flintknapper, miner, ballerina, nurse, lawyer, hatbox seller or croupier, as long as they know what you are going to be earning each month and how. If you do anything connected with the internet they will simply tell people that you are still unemployed.

trousers and pull their scrotums up over their heads as soon as you get a chance.

And, of course, if this is what mere trousers can do to them, do remember to take out any visible piercings, cover tattoos and don't chew gum. They will probably draw out a blunderbuss and shoot you.

4. Take six extra pairs of tights with you. This is the one thing that happens both in films and real life. You will ladder a pair on the way. You will ladder a pair trying to get through the revolving door that the receptionist has sabotaged for her own amusement because she knows that forty nervous applicants will be turning up that day, unable to cope with their own limbs, never mind a misbehaving entrance. Two more pairs will ladder spontaneously as you just sit quietly in the waiting room, because God hates you. You will ladder three more trying to put them on in the lobby lavatory. So actually you need eight. And two more just in case.

5. Don't wear a thong. It is a known fact that it is impossible to give a successful interview when your underwear is garrotting your rectum.

6. Assemble a good CV. It helps if you thought far enough ahead to have made your parents send you to the kind of school that runs the Duke of Edinburgh's Award Scheme and has after-school music and athletics clubs. If, however, you went to a normal school – and particularly if you went to one during the eighties, when the teachers' strikes and disappearing government funding was such that you were faintly surprised when you turned up in the morning and found that the front doors were open and a couple of people were still expressing themselves willing to try to lob a bit of English and maths in your direction – you will have had none of that. Nor, if you absorbed Mrs Thatcher's wider messages during that glorious decade, will you have any voluntary

or good works from later years with which to pad out your skeleton document.

When it comes to outlining the professional skills you have gained from previous employment, you will need to get creative. On some occasions, very creative. And on others you will need to bound energetically over the line that separates 'creative' from 'pathological lying' and start building some towering but necessary edifices of untruth.

How to write a good CV

Pour yourself a large whisky. Drink it. Drink another. Repeat until you are feeling no shame. Look back on your working life, from stacking shelves in your first Saturday job to whatever the current position is from which you are plotting to escape. Now dredge your memory for any smidgen of a scintilla of a speck of a scrap of useful knowledge, experience or learning you managed to accumulate over all those years you spent trying to do as little work and leave as early as possible. And now, ladies, it is time to put those embroidery skills to work.

You think …

> *When I worked in Threshers, I suggested that the woman still trying to hide her thirteen-bottle-a-day vodka habit from her husband could switch to a more economical half pint of meths.*

You write …

SKILLED AT IDENTIFYING AND FACILITATING FULFILMENT OF CUSTOMER NEEDS.

You think ...

> *While temping at Nameless Corporation, I spent hours listening to my freakish colleagues talk about fashioning gimp masks out of old PVC jackets and selling tea-stained underwear to Japanese businessmen without letting my eyes pop out of my skull or suing for sexual harassment.*

You write ...

> EXCELLENT INTERPERSONAL SKILLS AND AN ABILITY TO ADAPT TO ANY WORKING ENVIRONMENT.

You think ...

> *I spent a year slicing cold meats at the supermarket deli counter.*

You write ...

> ALTHOUGH MY FORMAL QUALIFICATIONS ARE LARGELY IN THE ARTS AND HUMANITIES, I AM ALSO WELL-VERSED IN NEW TECHNOLOGY. I HAVE PRACTICAL EXPERIENCE OF MANY OPERATING SYSTEMS, INCLUDING MICROSOFT OFFICE AND THE PORKO200 SALAMIGUARD.

Workin' it: gainful employment

If you survive the interview and get the job, congratulations! All you have to do now is survive your first day. And week. And the endless years of drudgery after that.

Probably the first thing you will have to do is go on a load of training and orientation courses. You should go on as many of these as you can because they always provide free coffee and sandwiches and, unless you are the kind of weirdo who always remembers to pack her homemade lunch the night before, this will save you about £800 a day in lunch money. They also provide you with a useful opportunity to swap gossip about the firm and catch up on some sleep at the back of the room during presentations. What they don't do is provide you with anything at all in the way of genuinely useful training and orientation.

What women really need to succeed in the workplace is a compulsory set of courses entitled:

* *How to get through your annual evaluation without crying*
* *How to get a pay rise without crying*
* *How to prepare and deliver a presentation without crying*
* *How to save money when you're getting through ten pairs of tights a day and your daily £4.50 lunchtime chicken and avocado wrap is the only bright spot in your otherwise bleak and futile 9 to 5 existence*
* *How to take people who take themselves seriously at conferences seriously*

To Sob Or Not To Sob?

I would like to address the problem of crying more closely, if I may, as I think it may be an overlooked factor in women's failure so far to colonise all sectors of the working world as fully as men have done.

I know plenty of men who actively look forward to their annual evaluations as a chance to tell their superiors what they have been up to, hear some constructive criticism on how they could do better next year and forge some mutually beneficial plans for the future. I don't know a single woman – including myself – who can get through the ordeal without dissolving into tears. It is so annoying. You don't want to cry. You don't intend to cry. Your rational mind knows that constructive, professional criticism is necessary, helpful, well-intentioned and not to be taken personally. Your rational mind, however, has precisely sod-all control over whatever other part it is that is intent on letting you turn into a soggy, quivering lump of snot and tears.

Much the same happens if you try to summon up the courage to ask for a pay rise. The thought process of a man goes something like: 'Hmm. Want more money. Am worth more money. Will ask for more money. How much more money? X pounds. Ask for 2 × X pounds. Then bound to get at least X pounds.' And, nine times out of ten, that is exactly what happens. If it doesn't, he thinks, 'Worth a try. No harm done. Bossman thinks I am Man of Courage and Conviction for asking. Triumph.'

A woman's thought process goes something like this: 'Hmm. Want more money. Need more money. But if I ask for more money they will think me rapacious, greedy, grasping bitch who would kick her own mother's face off for an extra farthing when simply not true. But have massive amount of anecdotal and documented proof that I am worst paid member of office. And am only one forced to drink out of toilet. Still. They probably have a good reason for paying me less. It would be embarrassing to ask them what it is. It is probably because I am crap and they are only keeping me on out of the kindness of their hearts. Best not put my head above the parapet. Is quite possible they have forgotten about me completely and my monthly pay-packet is terrible oversight of accounts department. If I mention anything I will be sacked and required to pay back last three years' salary. Perhaps if I offered to take on extra work and fellate my line manager every Saturday they would let me stay? Yes, that's what I'll do.' Before you know it, she has dragged herself into the boss's office and spent twenty minutes sobbing and berating her work before sacking herself and committing hara-kiri in front of him.

This at least partly explains why women still frequently earn less than men for doing the same job* – on average twenty-nine per cent less. Or, to put it another way, for every pound your exact but male counterpart earns, you earn 71p. Between ourselves, ladies, this will not do. Money is important, both as a means of, y'know, buying stuff and as a mark of respect and a sign that the work you do is appreciated and valued appropriately. You are not there to be exploited, you are there to do a fair day's work for a fair day's pay, and nobody's going to think you are insanely avaricious for making sure that this is so. We must rid ourselves of these crippling insecurities and self-doubts. They make no sense, they have no root in fact and they do nothing but damage our prospects and our bank accounts.

Motherhood

So you eventually find your feet at work, start to make friends, ratchet up a few promotions, maybe even a pay rise or two. You are crying no more than two or three times a week, tops, and generally beginning to feel that you are successfully establishing yourself in your chosen career.

Then you start wanting a baby.

It doesn't matter what kind of job you are in, having children will fuck it up in some way for you. If you have a 'high-flying', full-time, working-all-the-hours-God-sends-and-then-some kind of job, your diary will look like this:

---

* The other main reason is that a far higher proportion of women work in low-pay and/or part-time jobs. This in its turn is partly because the jobs women have traditionally done – cleaning, caring for the old, the young, the sick or disadvantaged in some way etc. – are underpaid and employers tend to rely on casual labour that does not accrue rights to expensive benefits and so on, and partly because women still take greater responsibility for childcare than men and so more frequently have to go part-time or do shiftwork.

27 JAN

11.55 p.m. — Close multi-million-dollar merger between Omnicorp and Megaomnicorp.

11.56 p.m. — Have sex with husband

11.58 p.m. — Start work on management buyout of UberCo by Gigajumbo Ltd. Book caesarean for lunch hour on 27 October.

27 OCTOBER

1 p.m. — Have baby

1.03 p.m. — Introduce baby to cleaners, au pair, wet nurse, reserve wet nurse, nanny and back-up nanny while being stitched up.

1.07 p.m. — Have sandwich

1.10 p.m. — Back to office. Hope someone has not poached job during extended absence. Will sue for sex discrimination if so.

1.15 p.m. — Drain boobs into paper shredder. Arrange for photographer to take picture of me every Friday to send to baby so it knows what I look like. Remember to ask nanny what sex it is. Will need to tell secretary so she can send correct presents on birthdays.

And the high-flyers are the lucky ones. The rest of us will be unable to throw nearly enough money at all the problems that bedevil the working woman.

Problem page

Dear Deirdre,

I need to go back to work because our monthly bills come to £500 a month, my husband earns £600 a month before tax and I was lying about the £500. I think it's actually closer to £90 billion once you factor in the mortgage and electricity. But the local nursery charges £150 a month and most of the kids I see in there are heavily bruised and scratching a lot. What should I do?

Penurious of Penwortham

Dear Penurious,

You are asking me to solve a massive structural problem in our society, namely the absence of state provision of childcare. Politicians promise much and deliver little. This is either because they themselves are protected by the amulet of money and privilege, which prevents them from truly understanding or giving a monkeys about the plight of ordinary parents, or because they still secretly think that women should be at home looking after their children instead of going out to work. On the other hand, they did set the minimum wage at such a level that it would barely support one adult living alone who wanted to eat more than rice and mince, so perhaps they do want everyone working all the time. It is very confusing and as I am not a mindreader, I do not know what the reason behind it all is.

None of which is of any concern to you, because of course all you are asking for is a simple answer to your current crisis. So here, as I see them, are your options:

1. Become Prime Minister. Tax rich people more. Use the money to build a network of publicly funded nurseries that pay their staff enough so that they don't have to recruit people with criminal

records who will use the younger children as footballs and the older ones as drug mules.

2. You could chain your children to the bedroom radiator before you leave for work each day. However, modern opinion has it that this is detrimental to a child's mental and physical wellbeing. So, buy one of those mesh bags you hang from the ceiling to keep toys off the floor and put your children in there every morning with a few banana sandwiches. Less burning, less risk of chafing and it will nurture a love of tidiness which will be a great advantage to both you and them in later life.

3. Sell one of your children and use the proceeds to pay for childcare for the other.

Good luck!

Deirdre

Dear Deirdre,

I am just about to go on maternity leave. Everyone at work is treating me like crap because they think I am leaving them in the lurch to bugger off on some kind of holiday. I'd like to know what kind of holiday involves pushing a nine-pound baby through an orifice normally the size of a 10p piece, then spending twelve hours a day poking your cracked nipples into it at one end and shovelling the results up at the other, but perhaps I am being unreasonable?

Confused of Kidderminster

Dear Confused,

It would be very nice if we as human beings were gifted with the kind of broad perspective on the world and generous temperament that would enable us to look at the gravid form of a heavily pregnant woman and think, 'My goodness! What it must be to contribute to the perpetuation of the species, to the renewal and reinvigoration of society! Though I may not be embarking yet or ever on such an awe-inspiring undertaking, I am glad to be able to support her in her endeavour by waving her happily off into the statutory maternity leave sunset and shouldering the minor inconveniences caused by her absence and the need to show whoever comes in to cover where we keep the good biscuits and the spare water cooler bottles. Without women like her, after all, there would be no life, no water cooler and certainly no biscuits at all.'

But we are not. Instead, the sight of a pregnant woman packing up her hole punch and swanning off for a year is guaranteed to raise feelings of anger and resentment amongst colleagues who see those weeks stretching grey and featureless before them and would gladly put up with a few hours of childbirth and the need to pop a boob out now and again for the chance to lounge around at home for three months receiving the occasional solicitous visitor armed with gin and baby gifts. And all your boss cares about is the amount you cost him to train and the price of your temporary replacement. When he watches you leave, all he sees is a woman-shaped pile of cash giving him the finger and walking out the door.

So tell them about the impending agony, the cracked nipples, the shit-shovelling, the vomit-splattered clothing, the sleepless nights, the coming years of ceaseless anxiety and nervous exhaustion, grief and fear. Suddenly, explaining the photocopier PIN number system to the temp won't seem so onerous after all.

And look on the bright side – if everyone is hating you for leaving, at least it means no one is after your job. And at least you're in the minority that gets maternity leave. If you were one of the millions of women in casual work, unprotected by any fancy legislation, you would be totally shafted, wouldn't you?

Good luck!

Deirdre

Dear Deirdre,

I have recently gone back to work after having a baby. I asked my manager if I could work flexible hours so that I could still see her occasionally. He nearly laughed his leg off. My friend at another firm arranged it quite easily, so why can't I?

Knackered of Nottingham

Dear Knackered,

Because your friend obviously works for Hemp, Sandal, Hippy, Dippy, Alfalfa & Co. I bet they have an apple press in the office instead of a water cooler. And a muesli dispenser where a fax machine ought to be.

In most companies, asking for flexible hours is career suicide. You say: 'Please may I work exactly the same number of hours as I was before and as everyone else does, but in a slightly different format, so that I may obtain some of this much-vaunted work–life balance that the company's advertising and marketing literature keeps going on about and thereby protect my own mental health, provide a loving and energetic maternal presence for my child and still remain an economically productive member of society so that I do not deprecate upon taxpayer resources or damage company turnover by turning up so worried and distracted by the multiple and confounding demands on my time that I accidentally file the entire office in the sea?'

They hear: 'I am stupid enough to believe all that crap you spout when trying to lure in new employees and clients. Please may I therefore have the entire company rearranged around my desire to be close to my child. Yes, just as you always suspected, motherhood turns even those few women who manage to pretend for a few years that they are committed, focused professionals into drippy, mush-brained milch cows who would rather raise a child than sacrifice their lives to the holy work of increasing shareholder profits. I understand for the first time that there is something bigger than the quarterly report. Now that I have given birth, I am deeply, primaevally connected to the underlying ebb and flow of life that unites us all in some indistinct but primordial manner. As a result, I am now fit for nothing. If you agree to my request to come in at eight and leave at four, I promise I will interpret this as carte blanche to come in for forty minutes a day, file my nails, drop breast pads all over the computers and fall asleep in the boardroom. That is what we do.'

So, what is the answer? You could try to reassure your managers that none of the panicked thoughts currently jostling for space in their tiny brains is true. But this would take time that you can ill afford.

Fortunately, there is another way. The very definition of a manager is someone who is out most of the day and is rarely seen by his subordinates unless his hangover has crippled him so badly that he needs to stay in the office for twenty-four hours with the blinds down. If this is the case, might I suggest that you don't bloody bother asking for flexible hours, but simply work them regardless? You need to make sure that your computer or IT department keeps a record of the times you log on and that your colleagues always return from their lunch hours to find on their desks memos, photocopies, completed forms, accounts or any other form of irrefutable physical evidence that you have worked through yours. Leave, unobtrusively but unapologetically, at four.

If your managers ever challenge you, bring out of your desk drawer a list of all the working hours pissed away by male colleagues gathered round the nearest plasma screen during the weeks of the FA Cup, World Cup and Ashes series.

None of this, of course, will help solve the wider issue of how to persuade the powers that be that 'thou shalt work only between the hours of nine and five' is not, in fact, one of the ten commandments but an outmoded tradition which could be safely adapted to allow almost infinite variations without too much damage to life, liberty and the pursuit of the bottom line, but then I am an aunt who can only seek to alleviate individual agony, not systemic stupidity. I hope you understand.

Good luck!

Deirdre

Dear Deirdre,

I get the children up. I get their breakfasts, I get them to school with lunch money, gym kits and notes explaining that they can't go swimming because they are now ninety per cent verruca. I then go and do an eight-hour shift changing beds, cooking meals and cleaning bums at the old people's home. I get home and put a wash on. I do another round of cooking, cleaning, ironing, vacuuming, packed-lunch-for-school-sodding-trips-

making, send off cheques to pay bills, hang the washing up, arrange for a man to come and look at the roof, the damp and the wonky wall, eat my dinner and go to bed. My husband expects a gold medal and a Horse Guards parade for remembering to take the bread out of the freezer this morning.

Where have I gone wrong?

Frustrated of Filey

Dear Frustrated,

We have all gone wrong in thinking that our embrace of the world of work would be matched by our menfolk embracing the world of domestic chores. With hindsight, it was obvious that any gender which had managed to avoid scrubbing lavatories for hundreds of generations would not suddenly rush to take up the practice. So we have ended up doing everything.

If your legs are not too tired by the end of the day, there is nothing wrong in giving your husband a good kick up the arse every evening. It will make you feel better and it might even have some effect on him.

Good luck!

Deirdre

CHAPTER 8

Body = Temple

It is right and proper to pursue health and fitness, to respect and try to maintain the only bodies we will ever have in order to encourage them to carry us through to a great and still sentient old age in which our bones don't crumble under their own weight and our joints don't give out dry puffs of dust whenever we try to bend them in order to take our heart, bowel and liver medications.

It is wrong to do what we all, in fact, do in real life – pursue health and fitness only as a means to a thinner end, but, baby, I'm afraid that's exactly what's going to happen until the day Jennifer Aniston or Elizabeth Hurley cracks and starts stuffing her face with complex carbs and roast suckling pig in the middle of a live Oprah interview.

To most women, the body is not an instrument of pleasure or a mere house of flesh in which to shelter a vibrant life of the mind. It is a battleground. We are at war with it, and in an attempt to wrestle it into submission, we deploy two forces in a pincer movement – diet and exercise. And they are in a pincer movement so that they can periodically grab hold of the flab roll that is hanging over our collective jeans and see what kind of success we are making of the fight.

History of dieting

Until the 1800s, the concept of dieting did not really exist, since the vast majority of people were concerned with getting enough food to fill their bellies, not with looking for ways to avoid it. Before that, the Ancient Greeks and early European sages had preached the value of moderating one's consumption of food and drink, but as a means of maintaining a well-balanced moral character rather than losing weight. Although, as these were usually men preaching to other men (the only gender whose moral fibre was really considered to be either present or worth honing), you have to hope that women of the time took the opportunity to fall face-first into stuffed oxen as often as possible and eat their delicious fill.

So, until then, to be over- rather than underweight was desirable and attractive. We look at the well-padded women in Rubens' paintings now and think they should be rolled gently into the nearest detox facility, but they were the supermodels and sex symbols of his day. He wouldn't have known what to do with Kate Moss or Keira Knightley, except perhaps use them as paintbrushes, an image I find quite disproportionately pleasing.

But by the1800s, the Industrial Revolution had ensured two things. One, the transformation of agriculture, farming and the importation business so that there was now a surplus of food and money in the country, at least amongst certain classes of society and two, that some people had therefore developed very big bellies indeed. Excess weight became a sign of affluence and prosperity – for the Victorian bourgeoisie, a stomach you could barely stretch your fob chain across and a generously proportioned wife on your arm was a big, fat sign of the big, fat success you had made of yourself.

The diet book

Halfway through the century, the first diet book was published. William Banting approached his doctor one day with a problem. He was so fat that he could no longer tie his shoes or go downstairs while facing forward and was rapidly reaching a point of total immobility. What was to be done? This being 1850, the doctor was unable to give him Channel Five's number and recommend that he offer himself as a subject in the string of documentaries being made for their new Point and Laugh season, so he put him on a restricted diet – 'avoiding all starch and saccharine matter'. Banting was so impressed with the results that, with all the reformatory and entrepreneurial zeal of his age, he quickly published a tome entitled *Letter on Corpulence Addressed to the Public*, Victorio-speak for *Fatbuster: I Lost Nineteen Stone in Three Months – See How You Can Too!*

But Banting and his book were primarily concerned with lessening the physical difficulties caused by what I suppose we would now classify as morbid obesity, not with attaining health, thinness or improving one's character. By the late 1800s, however, things were changing. Health concerns were mounting and the Victorian obsession with moral rectitude had started to infect what had hitherto been a relatively simple and unproblematic relationship with food. And just as their rules, regulations and pervasive guilt-trips concerning sexual matters had a particular impact on women, so did the new strictures surrounding food. If a sexual appetite was unfeminine, so was any other kind. Amongst the daughters of the rich, the first recorded cases of anorexia emerged.

You are what you eat

From then on, the story has been largely one of increasing female obsession with dieting in order to lose weight. In the early 1900s, women were ingesting various herbal remedies, injecting themselves with thyroid extracts from dead animals and swallowing the fabulous new amphetamine drugs that had just been invented and which burned calories in a trice. In the 1920s, the calorie-counting diet was invented by US doctor Lulu Hunt Peters, which would, as anyone who has been born female since will know, become the most insidious form of dieting throughout the Western world (for which, I am sure you will join me in saying, many fucking thanks, Dr Lulu). Then the flapper girl and her unnaturally boyish shape arrived on the scene and the passion for dieting to get rid of those exasperating curves that wouldn't let a dress hang straight took on a new intensity. The most truly dedicated ended up swallowing tapeworms. No, seriously. It is perhaps at this point that we must begin to think that the relationship between women and food cannot end well.

In the 1930s, a new influence was added to the dietary mix by the rising popularity of the movie theatre and its stars. For the first time, women (and men) had icons and aspirational figures who existed in real life instead of in religious tracts and were under pressure to emulate the secular stars' physicality, instead of the righteous, spiritual lives of saints and moral crusaders. This is when the first 'official' diets emerged. The Hay Diet was one of the first to promote food-combining as a way of losing weight. It divides the nutritional bounty of the natural world into three groups: alkaline (that's carbohydrate-rich, starchy foods like rice and potatoes), acidic (protein-heavy foods like meat and fish) and neutral (everything else). All over Britain and the US, women cleave to his strictures and stop eating starches with protein or sugars with certain fruits and leave four-hour interludes between the ingestion of acidic and alkaline food groups, despite the overwhelming evidence – in the form of humanity's continued existence and proliferation across the planet – that the culinary union of meat and potatoes or rice and fish over the preceding hundreds of thousands of years had not done any notable damage to our ancestors' health, wellbeing, bums or tums.

Ladies who felt that their lives were complicated enough without the addition of a tripartite eating system could opt for the Hollywood, or

Grapefruit, Diet. This involved eating half a grapefruit with each meal because the enzymes contained therein helped you burn calories faster. Or, just possibly, because eating half a big, low-calorie fruit encouraged you to poke less of your normal meal down your throat and so you lost weight by taking in fewer calories in the first place. Who's to say?

In the second half of the twentieth century, such fad diets have proliferated, as our willingness to embrace lunatic methods of losing weight has been matched only by entrepreneurs' willingness to invent them.

Large numbers of women have, for example, spent years replacing solid meals with 'nutritional shakes' or cabbage soup. As a child, you could spot the mothers who were on a liquid- or Brassica-based regime by the fact that they stood limply at the school gates gazing covetously at your Monster Munch and drowning out the sound of playground yelling with the noise of gurgling bellies and exhausted weeping. They stuck to it, however, because such diets promised 10lb off in the first week – a promise that was actually frequently fulfilled, but usually by women lightheaded from self-starvation who fell under buses and had limbs amputated as a result of injury.

At least they were there to pick their kids up. Women on the High-fibre Diet couldn't leave the house until they had chewed through that day's allowance of rope pieces and coconut matting. Opinion was divided as to whether the High-fibre Diet really worked or whether it was simply the effort of masticating three bales of Bran Flakes a day – roughly equivalent to running a half-marathon every mealtime – that formed an effective route to substantial fat-shedding. Either way, how they would have envied future generations and their access to Atkins, the only diet in history to allow – nay, require – dieters to eat all the bacon, steak, butter, cheese and cream they wanted, as long as they treated bread, potatoes and pasta as if they were radioactive cyanide capsules in a prussic acid coulis. And what's the possibility that it would give rise to bad breath, constipation, insomnia and create a generation of women who can still barely look at a sandwich without hyperventilating compared to the fact that it was the only diet in history to let you shovel a fried breakfast into your mouth every morning and pretend that it was doing you good?

* * * ✷ * * *

Many women, of course, are sensible enough never to have followed any of the fashionable fad diets that abound, but stick firmly to the traditional weight-loss regimes that have been tried and tested by figure-conscious ladies for generations:

- The getting-drunk-too-quickly-to-bother-with-food diet

- The getting-up-too-late-to-have-breakfast-and-then-working-through-lunch diet

- The food-eaten-with-the-intention-of-going-to-the-gym-afterwards-has-no-calories diet

- The food-eaten-while-walking-has-no-calories-either diet

- The nor-do-broken-biscuits-or-squashed-chocolates-even-when-you've-broken-or-squashed-them-yourself diet

- The steely-resolve-required-to-eat-just-half-a-KitKat-burns-off-the-calories-ingested-and-makes-it-OK-to-eat-the-remainder-twenty-minutes-later diet

Though I must, in the interests of public health, point out that these diets are not foolproof. I know this because I recently attended a session with a fitness trainer who was armed with a special set of diagnostic scales which told me that I was underhydrated, unfit and had a body-fat percentage of thirty per cent. Yes, I am almost one-third lard. In addition, my vital statistics measured 27, 37 and 41.5 inches, which either makes me a comical minor Dickens character or a bean-bag chair.

* * * ✷ * * *

There is probably more pressure on women and girls to be thin now than there has ever been. And what constitutes thin is now more extreme than ever. Marilyn Monroe, the nonpareil of female beauty throughout the fifties, was a size sixteen. That's eight 2006 Lindsay Lohans or forty-two Nicole Richies. They are held up as the ideal (despite whatever lip service magazines pay with their occasional, 'Oh, Lordy, put on some weight, lass, so that we don't have to print pictures of you looking bony on a beach as we are currently being forced – oh yes, at gunpoint – to do!') at a time when more and more people of all ages are struggling with genuine weight problems and obesity. As food has become cheaper and more heavily processed and our time-pressed, sedentary lifestyles and broken families mean we have all turned away from the leisurely, home-cooked meal after a hard day's graft in the fields in favour of lowering trays of microwaved lumps of aspartame and trans-fats down our throats in empty rooms enlivened only by the flickering images from the forty-two-inch plasma-screen telly, the weight of the average Westerner is on as steep an upward curve as the Victorian bourgeois belly once was.

So we are now in a situation where:

- The diet industry is worth around £2 billion per year in the UK and $50 billion in the US

- Globally, obesity is known as the trillion-dollar disease

- Thirty-four million Britons a year are trying to lose weight. 57.5% of the women in the UK have been on at least one diet in the past year, and almost 25% have been on two or more, twice the percentage of men on diets

- About 46% of men in England and 32% of women are overweight and an additional 17% of men and 21% of women are obese

- Around twelve million people are in a slimming club or on a diet in the UK at any one time

- 90% of people who diet end up putting the weight back on

- The average model is six inches taller and 23% lighter than the average woman. Twenty years ago, she was just 8% lighter

- Four out of five US women say they are dissatisfied with the way they look

- 50% of nine- and ten-year-old girls in the US say that being on a diet makes them feel better about themselves. 35% of six- to twelve-year-old girls have been on at least one diet

- 10% of British women are permanently on a diet

- 20% would like to lose more than two stone

- 21% say they believe they will be dieting into their eighties

- A survey for *Glamour* magazine found that nearly 50% of women would rather lose 10lb than achieve a career ambition or meet the love of their life

The first point to note from this is that dieting does not seem to be a terribly effective way of losing weight. An industry does not grow into a £2 billion or $50 billion monster by permanently solving the problem it is designed to address. Ninety-five per cent of dieters put the weight they lose back on within a year. A 1992 conference at the National Institute of Health Technology suggested that:

> In evaluating a weight loss method or program, one should not be distracted by anecdotal 'success stories' or by advertising campaigns. The information that should be obtained about the program includes:
>
> - the percentage of all participants who complete it

🌿   *the percentage of those completing participants who achieve various degrees of weight loss*

🌿   *the proportion of that weight loss that is maintained at 1, 3 and 5 years*

🌿   *the number of participants who experienced negative medical effects as well as their kind and severity*

In 1997, a conference of scientists and public health officials and representatives of the weight-loss industry found that the long-term success rates of the diets promoted were 'terrible', that consumers were not told the usual outcomes of the programmes and that the best the representatives could come up with in their defence was that giving out the latter information would discourage customers and 'take away the dream'.

It is hard not to avoid the conclusion that the question you should ask yourself whenever you see a tempting offer at the back of a magazine or alluring range of low-fat/low-carb, high-cost, multi-vitamin, multi-promising dietary foods, aids and supplements at the supermarket should be the same one that springs to mind whenever you see a politician speaking on the radio or get trapped in the bank with a man trying to sell you eight sorts of 'vital' insurance to accompany your lifestyle. And that question is, of course, why is this bastard lying to me?

The second point to note is that we are not getting any better at resisting the pressure to slim. If anything, we are getting worse and falling victim to it at a younger and younger age. I suppose the earlier onset of weight concerns is understandable. After all, our generation can vividly remember doing everything we could with fingerless lace gloves and fishnet tights in order to be Madonna. If your role models were now the Lohans and the Richies would you be any less unthinking in your mad rush to emulate their defining features, even if they were visible ribs and collarbones instead of customised accessories?*

There are lots of reasons put forward as to why women are more susceptible to the pressure to be slim (it's true that men are starting to take more of an interest in their personal appearance and hygiene – for which let us, overall, be devoutly thankful – and are even starting to make a showing on the various anorexia and eating disorders statistics – for which let us not be so thankful – but it is equally true that they are still vastly outnumbered by the number of hungry women out there). Some say it is because women are still judged far more than men on the way they look, and that society still places a far higher premium on youth (and a correspondingly lithe and lissome figure) for women than it does on men. Others point to a longstanding tradition of women being expected to be more restrained, self-controlled, conformist and better at denying appetites of all kinds than their male counterparts and

---

* We did also have Sindy dolls and Barbies, of course, and there were occasional minor outcries at these unhealthy role models from concerned feminists and parents. And perhaps not unjustifiably – a computer simulation of a Barbie doll scaled up to real-woman size revealed that her back would be too weak to support her upper body and her body would be too narrow to contain more than half a liver and a few centimetres of bowel. Dedicated Barbie fans should look away now: in reality, Barbie would have led a life dominated by chronic diarrhoea before collapsing into an early grave due to malnutrition.

  Still, I do feel our generation was at least somewhat distanced and protected from the unhealthy body messages sent out by the fact that Sindy and Barbie were made of extruded plastic. Girls are quite bright. Most of them understand at some level that there is a degree of slippage between the real world and Dollyland. But I suspect that our daughters will rightly have more difficulty understanding why they should not aim to look like the living, breathing celebrities they idolise. We will just have to spend three hours a day shouting at them the terrifying facts that the stars occasionally let slip. 'Elizabeth Hurley calls six raisins a snack!' 'Beyoncé just eats cucumber!' 'Renee Zellweger … fuck knows. I think she has her whole body siphoned out and put into a secret cell compressor in Geneva three hours before every premiere and party. And Nicole Kidman is entirely made of stiff twine.'

that this bleeds, into the arena of food consumption. Still others – in order to explain why such extreme thinness is currently the ideal – point to the fact that it is human nature to value what is scarce or difficult to attain. Now that, for the first time in history, large parts of the world enjoy a staggering surplus of food, rejecting it, and having a body that shows you reject it, is the desirable, admirable thing to do.

Most women have a mixture of all these reasons running through their subconscious whenever they look in the mirror or at a Twix. If you stopped to examine your motives for skipping a meal or dragging your flobbery arse to WeightWatchers, they would look something like this:

- BLIND FAITH. My life will be better without cellulite. It just will. You know it, I know it, and – for all their valiant championing of magic knickers and A-line skirts, Trinny and Susannah know it too. I truly believe that thighs without *peau d'orange* will transform my existence. I will become sexually magnetic, full of self-confidence and altogether captivating. I will also be able to play the piano and paint. Yes, I will.

- SARTORIAL LIBERATION. No unsightly bulges = the freedom to wear what you like. I know this is wrong. I know you should be able to go out in a thong and flippy summer dress, even if you look like the bastard offspring of Moby Dick and a giant carrier bag full of yoghurt, if that is what your taste and the weather demand. But we do not live in such a world and so I consign piece after piece of an already not overstocked wardrobe to the charity shop as yet another area of my lacklustre body becomes unfit for public display. By the time I am thirty-three I should be rolling down the street in a securely fastened bin bag.

- SELF-LOATHING. If you are overweight, whether by a few pounds or to a knocking-down-side-walls-of-your-house-to-get-you-into-the-reinforced-ambulance degree, it is for one simple reason. You eat too much. When you are full, you do not say, 'I am full up, replete, satisfied, sated. Lucky me. I shall stop now.' You say, 'I am full up. But I still want those six Cherry Bakewells because they are there and they taste nice.' And then you eat them. So you hate the extra weight you carry because you do not like having your weakness written on your body, making you aware of your failings at every waking moment and broadcasting unstoppably to passersby whenever you set foot outside the door the fact that you are a person who is basically greedy and undisciplined.

Most recently, there has been a push towards leaving fad diets behind and concentrating on educating people about healthy eating instead. The problem with healthy eating, of course, is that it is expensive, boring and requires extensive mental readjustments after a lifetime of thoughtless self-indulgence. You may be one of the lucky people who genuinely grows with age to like salad, couscous and steamed fish. But you ain't related to me, or anyone normal.

Basically, you have three options when it comes to dieting.

1. *Ignore the fact that all fad diets are fancy ways to trick you into cutting out entire food groups, causing your body to go into metabolic shock and quickly thereafter into starvation mode, thus hanging onto your fat reserves like a* Celebrity Big Brother *contestant to a shred of dignity, and follow each of them in turn, emptying your bank account but never letting the hope die.*

2. *Rise above our culture's body fascism. Eat, drink and be merry, for tomorrow we may die. Remember that if you commit to the first part of the sentence overenthusiastically, the second may come to fruition rather sooner than you were hoping. On the other hand, even if brief, it will still be an infinitely more rewarding and joyful life than any which is too heavily strewn with quinoa.*

3. *Stop pushing things down your fat frigging throat.*

A history of exercise

As with dieting, for the vastly greater part of recorded time the question of exercise simply did not arise. Cavewomen felt they got all they needed in terms of strenuous work-outs during their ceaseless hikings over wild terrain to collect roots and berries, interspersed with sprinting away from woolly mammoths, sabre-toothed tigers and pterodactyls.* And I imagine all that scraping off the fat from hides with a sharpened flint took care of their upper-arm development too and gave them a nice set of abs if they remembered to pull their tummy muscles taut as they worked.

And, of course, for many generations to come, the mere struggle for survival would ensure that the gym and leisure centre remained low on the list of things that needed inventing. Poor women got their share of cardiovascular training whether they worked their twelve hours in the fields or down mines or stayed at home spinning (wool, not in twenty-second bursts on yellow bicycles), churning butter, washing clothes with a big stick and no Ariel, and alternately thrashing their eighty-two surviving children and digging graves for the ones who felt it incumbent upon themselves to keep the local child mortality rate up.

Richer women got theirs by carting around ever-increasing weights of corsets, farthingales, brocade, steel-hooped skirts, crinolines and privilege. They were thought to have an innately more delicate physiology than their lower-class counterparts, and were encouraged to maintain their healthful glow with the occasional game of croquet, seawater bathing session or turn about the grounds. Eventually, those who didn't mind being thought of as a bit of a lesbian were allowed to don bloomers and

---

* My summary of the threats facing the cavewomen may not be entirely accurate. My knowledge of prehistoric timelines is largely based on an idiosyncratic conflation of *One Million Years BC* starring Raquel Welch, Ross's scenes in the museum in *Friends* and partial viewings of *Jurassic Park 1* and *2*.

go bicycling. By the early 1900s, lawn tennis was added to this select list of appropriate pastimes for genteel ladies, but it was nothing like today's game. It was played only by the very rich, in their gardens and country clubs, by women holding a tennis racquet in one hand and a vial of sal volatile in the other. They stood there in full, long-skirted, corseted dress while people carried balls on cushions over to them and enquired whether they would like to hit them over the net. If a lady got overenthusiastic and reached too dramatically for a wide shot, everybody screamed, 'Mind your womb, Emmeline!' which must have been quite disconcerting, especially if your name wasn't Emmeline.

So, for most of our days gone by, exercise and a toned body has been either a by-product of lifestyle or a sign of poverty. To anyone born before our delightfully mechanised age, the idea of needing to pursue it deliberately, make time for it consciously and build commercial centres dedicated to it would have seemed a form of barking madness.

But, as our lives have become increasingly cosseted and sedentary, this is exactly what has happened. It is no coincidence that the great eighties fitness boom coincided with the most affluent and desk-bound era of British and US history. As female obsessions go, 'feeling the burn' is a relatively harmless one. It is much harder to develop a disordered relationship with the treadmill than it is with food, if only because you tend not to keep ten types of delicious treadmill at home in the fridge.*

The leisure industry has never really looked back since the eighties. Gyms remain irrationally popular as we keep paying through the nose to do in an indoor, sweat-scented, air-conditioned environment what we could be doing for free outside. We are forever chasing the dream of

---

* But not, as the recent identification of the phenomenon of exercise addiction has shown, impossible. Still, exercise addicts are probably only about half a rung higher than sex addicts on the averagely compassionate person's list of Disadvantaged Groups With Whose So-Called Problems I Am Rapidly Losing Patience, so let us not dwell on them any longer.

a perfectly pert bottom, heedless of the irony of doing so on a stationary bike, and in every sense getting nowhere.

However, although it is still slightly galling to think that there is yet another swathe of business folk out there successfully exploiting our insecurities and gullibility and persuading us to part with large wodges of cash for the privilege of having fresh towels and water on – er – tap, at least exercising is an inherently healthy activity that the body welcomes and to which it is superbly adapted and responsive (compared to, you know, starving yourself).

It is unutterably boring though. The best part is going shopping beforehand for the gear you will need in order to embark on your chosen exercise programme, but even this is a muted pleasure. Searching for the right sportswear is shopping of a perverted and joyless kind.

Sports bras

Even if you are small-breasted, an ordinary bra will not do. A normal 32A bra is basically just a bit of ribbon you tie on every morning to help make you look grown-up. However, you will discover when you get on a treadmill for the first time and start running that even tiny boobs are essentially loosely attached pieces of flesh that do not respond well to being thrown about.

If you have big boobs and try to run in an ordinary bra, you are likely to concuss yourself and in extreme cases the person to your left. Then right. Then left again.

So you need a sports bra. This is tricky if you are a little lady, because all sports bras are made of the same strength elastic, no matter what the size of the boob they are hoping to restrain. So if you are not careful when trying them on, you can end up with eight broken ribs and a concave chest.

If you are the proud possessor of an über-bosom, you will find yourself having to buy the kind of bra that you have to be cut out of at the end of every session by a fireman. If you are a daily exerciser, it might be quicker and easier to have a breast reduction. You could always sell the excess to the wheezing midget on the next mat who looks like she's got a vet's tourniquet wrapped round her chest. Everyone's a winner.

Trainers

You do not need to spend a fortune. Leave that kind of thing to adolescent boys who believe that the right kind of tread on your air-filled soles will vouchsafe you beautiful women and a penis that takes a day and a half to unfurl.

The truth of the matter is that you are not going to be running far or for long. Let's face it, for all our good intentions, ninety-eight per cent of us could dig out our old, tissue-thin Dunlop Green Flashes or those black elasticated things from Mothercare that curled up and tried to bite your hand off when you removed them and still be in no danger of doing ourselves an impact injury.

Just buy ones that look nice, and make sure you scuff them up a bit before you wear them to a class. Your novice status is going to become clear soon enough. No need to tip off the sneerers before you've even started cramping.

Everything else

If you are an exercise novice and any of your formative years overlapped with the *Fame*-loving, *Footloose*d, Green Goddessed, Jane Fonda-worshipping, burn-feeling, getting physical, Mad Lizziefied, Olivia Newton John-stained decade, you need to exercise, before anything else, a little caution. You will be saved from the worst possible effects of indulging your instincts by the fact that it is now impossible to find neon legwarmers outside of certain highly specialised fetish shops. But you will also naturally be drawn to brightly coloured, complex outfits made of elasticated man-made fibres which do still festoon the shops despite repeated attempts to pass pan-European legislation outlawing their production and sale.

Have a care. If you find yourself stroking anything that could have been worn in a pop or exercise video from your youth, take eight paces backwards and remind yourself of the following:

1. *They looked ridiculous then.*

2. *They look ridiculous now.*

3. *They looked ridiculous on women like Fonda and Olivia Newton John: women who had already won the jackpot in the genetic lottery and then devoted their lives to burnishing the bounty yet further, until their naked bodies looked like sculpted marble.*

4. *Imagine how they are going to look on you, whose naked body looks like a dead seal.*

5. *Most of the women you saw jumping around in leotards, bodystockings and footless tights were feeling the burn in a highly localised area, from the kind of virulent yeast infection that only comes from having three layers of Lycra wrapped round your crotch on a regular basis. A cotton gusset on your knickers is not going to protect you in that kind of situation.*

Buy shorts if you are the kind of woman who keeps her upper and lower legs waxed at all times instead of just gesturing at her shins feebly with a disposable razor every now and again, trousers if not.

Buy a baggy T-shirt, or be honest and dig out one of the many you have got lurking at the back of the wardrobe. It will hide a multitude of sins. You have no idea which bits of you will start to jiggle once you embark on a period of unaccustomed vigorous movement.

The venue

Depending on how much you have spent on the above, you may wish to save yourself some money by eschewing the private gyms and heading down to your local leisure centre. You may want to apprise yourself of the relative merits of each before you make your final decision.

PRIVATE GYM	LEISURE CENTRE
Clean changing rooms	Changing rooms crawling with unidentified creatures which skitter off down the sewers at your approach
Full of beautiful people	Full of people with mental disorders looking for somewhere warm to sit
Fitness trainers who won't leave you alone but keep pushing you harder and harder until you go puce and fall over	Fitness trainers who couldn't give a shit if you fell over and died on the cross-trainer, as long as you don't interrupt their MTV viewing
Fresh towels	Dirty sanitary towels poking out of every brimming lavatory bin
Eighty-page questionnaires to discover your fitness levels, goals, strengths and weaknesses and design an appropriate personalised exercise plan for you	One hungover teenager at reception casting a glazed eye over you to check you have at least two functioning limbs and a head before he jerks his thumb over his shoulder to illustrate where he thinks you might find the collection of machines and fitness facilities you seek
Cripplingly, ruinously, eye-wateringly, thigh-gougingly expensive. They charge the kind of monthly fees that, if you invested them in a pension or the mortgage payments on a well-chosen property instead, would enable you to retire at fifty and dedicate the rest of your life to trying out the gymnasia aboard Caribbean cruise ships	A fiver a go, including chips and a Wagon Wheel in the café afterwards.
Swimming pool full of crystal-clear water heated to body temperature and surrounded by potted palms, and the promise of a freshly squeezed juice in the sun room afterwards	Swimming pool full of hair, plasters, wailing toddlers and occasionally their bowel movements, surrounded by screaming parents and dead verrucas

It's up to you.

Feeling the burn

There are classes now to cater for every taste. They all, naturally, advertise themselves only in the most glowing of terms, but it is always wise to avail yourself wherever possible of accounts from women who have experienced them firsthand, for thereby often hangs a tale.

Aerobics

The good thing about aerobics classes is that they appeal to women at all stages of life and fitness. That means that when you walk in you can choose your place in the hall according to your needs and physique. The fit, bronzed, made-of-equal-parts-whalebone-and-sinew-and-already-lightly-jogging-on-the-spot-to-warm-up, naturally athletic types, doin' it because they luvvit, are all right up front in the first two rows, like the teacher's pets they are. The next few rows are taken up with wannabes – they've got the healthy glow and almost as lean a look, but not all of them are jogging quite as springily as the ladies in front, and you suspect that quite a few of them chow down on a daily warm chicken salad with resentment in their hearts and not the glee of women whose bodies truly are their temples. Tough self-disciplinarians, doin' it because they must.

After them, normal people, who are doin' it because they should. Beyond that, it's fat, fatter, fattest towards the back, barely doin' it at all, until the very last row appears to be populated by manatees in Spandex who only stub out their fags when the teacher comes in and cough a lung up at the end of every grapevine.

The teacher is a piece of work. She walks in – no, they never walk in – she *bounds* in, still bursting with energy, despite the fact that she has been aerobicising for fourteen hours straight and spent her lunch hour doing a fun run in an eighty-pound gorilla costume. She makes Sally Gunnell look like Jabba the Hutt.

She introduces herself as something like 'Dinah – as in Dinah-mic' and apparently she is the energy train and you are on board. The thought flits across your mind that a more appropriate analogy might be that she is the nuclear power station and you are the exposed workforce, but the music has started and you're off and sweating, and so you must content yourself with muttering, 'Dinah? Dinah? Nobody's called Dinah, you lying strip of sinew, except for the least interesting character in Enid Blyton's *Circus of Adventure*. Do you think we're all fools or what?'

You can't think much more after that, because the effort of keeping up even with the chain-smoking manatees becomes too exhausting. As you sweat, twist, turn and stumble, occasional thoughts do struggle to the surface of your confused and overheating mind – how much it would cost to liposuck away half your body and save yourself this trouble, how good it would feel to run along the row in front of you with a flick-knife, dragging it across every taut bronze hamstring as you pass, whether you could get up a petition to have a special arrhythmic section set up where you could stop pretending to be able to exercise in time to music – but, by and large, the hour passes in a slow and wretched blur of bewilderment and fatigue.

Swimming

Swimming is great: it burns plenty of calories (even more if you are bad at it – the more inefficiently you move through the water, the more energy it takes, creating a rare win–win situation for the malcoordinated), tones muscles, improves aerobic capacity and provides a workout for the whole body.

Everything associated with swimming, however, is a profound and abiding misery. You are lucky if you get out of any pool without impetigo and claw marks on your shins from panicking children whose parents are inadvertently insisting on swimming lessons with the local paedophile.

And the preparatory work alone is exhausting. Find a swimming costume that is cut high enough to create the illusion of slim thighs, but not so high that it creates a four-buttock effect that can be seen from space and bisects you as soon as your legs frog for the breast stroke. And make sure it has a sufficiently strong tummy-control panel and bust support for your needs without making it feel like you are trying to swim in an Edwardian corset. Then you have got to shave this, wax that, trim the other. You won't know what you have missed until it gets wet and yet more children start screaming and panicking at the sight of it.

If you normally wear glasses, it is also odds on that at some point during your swim, or crab-like scurrying to or from the water's edge, you will bump into a middle-aged pervert (as distinct from the paedophile, who is busy adjusting waterwings and hiding his semi-stiffy underwater) who will take this as an opportunity to clasp you jovially by the upper arms, frott briefly against you and invite you to join him for a Rohypnol-spiked drink in the pub afterwards.

Altogether, a dispiriting experience whose risks are not sufficiently counterbalanced by reward.

Kickboxing

Kickboxing is great, in many ways. It burns about eight million calories an hour and if you are a woman who has a lot of pent-up aggression, booting the air and shouting 'Hi-ya!' a lot is the perfect way to let it out. If, however, you naturally incline towards a life of peace and passivity, booting the air and shouting 'Hi-ya!' a lot while surrounded by a load of women whose adrenaline rushes may at any point lead them to turn on you suddenly in an all-female re-enactment of *Lord of the Flies* can be both embarrassing and dangerous. Take up yoga instead.

Yoga

Yoga is calm. Yoga is tranquil. Yoga is a state of mind. Yoga is also guaranteed to get you farting like a tuba. That at the end of every class, as you lie down for the final meditation session, everyone starts parping unstoppably is a well-recognised but, due to the ascent of yoga's practitioners to a higher spiritual plane than the average punter, little spoken of phenomenon in the bendy community.

Pilates

It looks so fun, doesn't it? Rolling about on those big balls, interspersed with a bit of yoga-y stuff, leaning a bit this way, leaning a bit that way – what's not to like?

Don't be fooled. Pilates is rugby for your core muscles. You will get up the next morning feeling like you have been in an industrial tumble dryer for a fortnight. And yet it will still take eighteen months to have any visible effect. It is no good for anyone who is a fan of immediate gratification.

Team sports

Do you remember when you were at school? And before your school sold off your playing fields to developers to pay for fripperies like books and paper after Mrs Thatcher decided that it was enough that every third child learned to read and write because otherwise there would be no one to sell the *Big Issue* in decades to come? You played netball, did you not? And hockey too, maybe. And was it not a time of unadulterated misery and despair? Standing on the edge of the pitch as the wind whistled through your aertex shirt and chilled the very marrow of your bones. Blue fingers. Chapped knees. Numb feet. No hope. Being gobbed on after matches for failing to be anywhere near the ball at any of the times when a modicum of sense or competitive instinct would have told you you should be.

And now you want to go through it all again. Listen to me. The intervening twenty years may have made you look more confident, given you a veneer of maturity, and you may even be holding down a responsible job and projecting an air of competence and professionalism therein at all times. But, make no mistake, beneath it all you are the same trembling, pathetic laughing stock that you were as a schoolgirl, and this will stand again revealed to all if you set foot on another playing field with the aim of distinguishing yourself in the sporting arena. All your girlhood nemeses have used those twenty years to become even bigger and better than you. The most you can hope for is that they have now grown out of the habit of gobbing on you after defeat and that the only moisture on your face as you trudge home will therefore be the bitter tears of thirty years of failure.

Running

The treadmill is one thing. But it does nothing, nothing at all, to prepare you for how hard running outside is. It is the purest form of exercise and this means that there is no hiding place, no way to cheat. You learn that you can run for thirty-seven seconds on the flat before you have to stop. Fifty-four seconds downhill. Seven seconds uphill. There is no way of escaping these cold, hard facts, nor the knowledge that it is going to take forty-two years before you can jog happily around as if your body were not made of lead and the earth not exerting a force on your feet twelve times stronger than normal gravity, like all the other people you see on your wheezy way round the park.

Also, it makes your bum hurt. If you are carrying any excess weight there at all, you will need a brassière for your backside. And, unfortunately, these have not been invented yet.

I apologise, by the way, if naturally athletic people who enjoy an array of these activities and incorporate them willingly and easily into their daily lives, make friends and meet life partners through them and cannot contemplate an existence bereft of the endorphin rushes and the enormous feeling of satisfaction that comes with knowing you are transforming your body, instilling good habits for the future and effecting the kind of preventative measures against future osteoporosis, various cancers and heart disease that money just can't buy have felt excluded from this chapter. It has essentially been written by, for and about lifelong sloths with the energy and metabolism of a rag rug. But look at it this way: you are going to live forever, and with bottoms that you could bounce bullets off, while we gently deliquesce and slide irreversibly from sofa to hospital bed to grave. It's a fair trade, I think.

But if you are still fired with enthusiasm for reinventing your physique, all you really have to do is remember the two golden rules:

[1] If you like it, don't eat it.

[2] If you don't like doing it, do it.

What a life.

CHAPTER 9

Hair & Heels

It is a sad truth that the amount of effort required by women before they can consider themselves fit to be seen in public is increasing exponentially with each generation. Two hundred years ago, scraping the lichen off your body once a year with a rusty spoon would have been enough to catapult you to the top of the monarch's list of choice courtesans. Our great-grandmothers only had to remember to avoid rickets, but their daughters had to put on a new pair of lisle stockings, run a comb through their lice and clean the coal from underneath their fingernails before they could head off to the local tea dance and be fêted as the next Clara Bow. Nowadays, a lot of women have to give up their jobs in order to fit in the necessary body maintenance programme, filled with waxing, shaving, plucking, exercising, massaging, exfoliating and surgery.

There are some people who throw themselves into such a regime with enthusiasm. They are generally the ones who have least need of it – pearly-skinned, natural beauties blessed with glossy tresses and a peaches-and-cream complexion that causes ordinary passersby to fall to their knees and worship. Others less physically blessed give up before they begin, reasoning that a life spent in the endless pursuit of dead-skin-cell sloughing and full-body moisturising is no life at all, and they happily devote their existence to the accumulation of experience instead of anti-wrinkle creams and feeding their souls through good works for the needy instead of nourishing their hair with Pantene Pro-V. It is an admirable rejection of society's narrow vision of what constitutes the beauty ideal and the narcissistic concerns that poison our age, and an example we should all follow. Unfortunately, the facts are these:

1. *These people die hirsute, smelly and alone, virtually indistinguishable from the rats that soon begin to gnaw at their lifeless frames.*

2. *You are but one woman. Filling your face with pies and flinging your Gillette Sensor to the wind will result only in you quickly taking on the appearance of a large ball of spam that has been rolled along a busy barbershop's floor. You won't strike a blow for personal freedom, you will be the stuff of nightmares. In short, you cannot beat them, you can only join them.*

3. *Parts of the grooming regime are fun. As we will see, make-up has been around since the earliest civilisations and even taking into account the slightly masochistic nature of our sex, nothing survives that long without offering its practitioners some pleasure in the process. Although, as we shall also see, you can also take a beauty routine too far.*

Your crowning glory

The American humourist Cynthia Heimel put it best in her 1983 book *Sex Tips for Girls*: 'If you see someone with a stunning haircut, grab her by the wrist and demand fiercely to know the name, address and home phone number of her hairdresser. If she refuses to tell you, burst into tears.' (To which I would only add: don't limit yourself to haircuts. Grab people with good shoes, good clothes and good bags and don't let go until they have cited provenances for everything. Hell, if they just seem to be leading fun lives, follow them around until you work out how it's done. And when gene-splicing becomes a quotidian reality, make sure you wrest details of her parentage from every tall, slim, attractive woman who glides past you in the street and demand a cell sample for your personal use before letting go of her well-turned ankles.)

One way or another, all hairdressers are frightening beasts. You have to work out the pros and cons of each type of salon.

Posh haircuts

Pros: Decent coffee, clean towels, gentle shampooing, possibly even a scalp massage, followed by a haircut that takes account of the shape of your face and your hair type, highlights that complement your colouring and a final look that doesn't make you want to decapitate yourself before you leave the shop.

Cons: The shampoo girl may have gentle hands, but she is spitting in the sink as she lathers because you are so ugly. Yes, she is. The stylist hates you too, because you are asking him to expend his time and skill on your miserable scalp, a procedure he mentally likens to being asked to gild a turd. You have to pay a three-figure sum in exchange for feeling this paralysed with fear and self-loathing.

High-street haircuts

Pros: Cheap, convenient and a useful insight into what Britain might look like after a Communist coup.

Cons: What you will receive is not so much a flattering, individually tailored haircut as the resentful attentions of a bored woman named Val. She will pass a pair of blood-flecked scissors over your head in a desultory fashion, while shouting orders to bored fifteen-year-old minions and dropping fag ash down your neck. The shampoo in the large and conspicuously unbranded pump dispensers is washing-up liquid from the pound shop next door and will be applied to your hair by a girl with three-inch acrylic nails who lives only to lacerate and pulverise your skull until you have to take most of your head home in a bag.

It is by reason of some mental quirk in the female psyche as yet unexplained by neuroscientific research that no woman has ever risen up and said to a shampoo girl, 'Every day I manage to take a shower and lather, rinse and repeat without bringing tears to my eyes or open wounds in my flesh. I do not, therefore, believe that it is necessary for you to treat my head as if it had done you some great personal wrong. You appear to have mistaken blameless me for someone who needs to be killed over a sink. If you would like, I can give you the number of an excellent therapist who may be able to help you with some of your deeply entrenched anger management issues over time. But for the moment, please desist, or I will have you charged with grievous bodily harm.' But we should.

Your mum's haircuts

Pros: When you are little, you have no choice in the matter. Your mother decides your hair is too long (for her taste – you may be gesticulating wildly at the illustrations in your *Rapunzel* and *Sleeping Beauty* Ladybird books, all to no avail), plonks you in a chair in the middle of the kitchen floor and has at you with the family scissors. If she is of a warm, maternal disposition, she will wait till you have passed out from shaking your head from side to side in protest and then complete the shearing. If she is not, she will bring your dissenting actions to a rapid close by jabbing you in the side of the head with the scissors and threatening to Van Gogh you if you don't stay still. Nevertheless, after a few years of ritual humiliation and eye-watering pain at the hands of hairdressers proper, you will start to hanker after these simpler times.

Cons: A woman's hair is an important cultural marker, traditionally respected as a symbol of her fertility and femininity. This is felt from the first days of school, when the girls with the longest hair are de facto the prettiest and most popular. If your tresses do not stream out behind you, a shimmering pennant of proto-womanliness fluttering in your wake as you run round the playground, you might as well be dead. Or clever.

Early experiences which have the mother–hairdresser treating your hair less as a an integral part of one's female identity and essential element of girlhood and more as a pelt that must be periodically shorn in between changing the beds, making the tea and belting your backside for impertinence, may make it hard to reconcile the conflicting messages received at home and from wider society and set up some psychical problems to be overcome in later life. Not, of course, where maternal interventions are concerned, for the first time.

In the fairly likely event that your mother could not be relied upon to help you evolve into a cutting-edge, fashion-forward, relentlessly on-trend beauty, you had to look elsewhere for help. Your babysitter was the prime candidate, as she was of the same generation, but just those crucial few years older than you and likely to be obsessed with hair, make-up and clothes and only doing the job in the first place so that she could pay for her cosmetic and wardrobe requirements.

The apprentice to Michelangelo could not have studied his master's art more carefully than you did Gina the Babysitter's. There was backcombing to conquer: could you too create a coiffure so large it has a different postcode from your head? Despite the fact that you had short hair that covered your scalp in a light fuzz and not her fabulously thick tresses that fell (when left unabused by Elnett) in ravishing swags and hanks to the shoulders? Could you replicate with felt-tip pens the streaks she imparted to her crowning glory with coloured gels and mousses? No, you could not. Between that and the backcombed fuzz, you looked like an extra from *One Flew Over the Cuckoo's Nest*. But it was an inordinate amount of fun trying, and if your Gina was one of the good ones, she managed to keep a straight face when presented with your efforts and your fragile ego remained intact.

A little later, teasing and backcombing fell out of favour and was replaced by spiral perms. Girls with hair as straight as pikestaffs spent days sitting smothered in stinking lotions – at home if they had an appropriately skilled auntie prepared to work their chemical magic in the front room or at the hairdressers, going out of their minds with boredom if not – to induce the coveted curl. If it worked, you were cool until it dropped out (the curl, not – unless you were very unfortunate or had a really stupid aunt – the hair), past the powers of even the strongest mousse and most dexterous scruncher to revive it.

For many women, memories of the scrunchy are, like all those arising from life's most important and complex relationships, still difficult to talk about. But scrunchies were extraordinary. They bred like a well-feasted gremlin after midnight. I had three, and I had no hair. Other girls' collections ran into the thousands. People had to move house and convert garages to accommodate them. And then they were gone. No one knows where they went. An elasticated graveyard? The lost city of Atlantis? A concrete bunker in an undisclosed location in the Nevada desert, awaiting the day when they become ripe for reinvention? Who can say?

Women and their war paint

Cleopatra used crushed carmine beetles mixed with ant eggs to redden her lips. When a woman is prepared to use pulverised invertebrates to enhance her looks, two things become clear. One, she probably deserves her reputation as one of the most dedicated seductresses of all time and two, the battle to separate women from the desire to acquire the latest make-up has probably been lost from the beginning.

The Egyptians were wholly committed to the cosmetic arts and invented much of the slap and other aids to beauty we use to this very day.

Eye, eye

When not carving sphinxes and constructing pyramidal tombs for dead pharaohs, the Egyptians turned their energies to grinding up semi-precious stones for eyeshadow and coming up with the world's first kohl. They applied the latter with a notoriously free hand, the like of which would not be seen again until Nick Rhodes and the rest of the New Romantics started publicly demonstrating an allegiance to the black stuff once again. The Egyptians made theirs with antimony, burnt almonds, lead, oxidized copper, ochre, ash, malachite and a blue-green copper ore called chrysocolla. Durannies had things slightly easier and were able to get the bulk of theirs ready-made in Boots.

The Elizabethans preferred henna and blue crayon for the eyes, which could also be made to sparkle – though possibly not for long, given its remarkably toxic qualities – with belladonna drops. The blue crayon could also be used to emphasise the delicate veins on the bosom, which were, slightly queasily to the modern sensibility, quite the erotic stimulant for the period's menfolk. Still, always useful to have a two-in-one application feature wherever possible.

Smelling sweet

There is nothing like living in the middle of an African plain to prompt the rapid invention of perfumes to mask the stink and oils to counter the terribly drying effect of burning sand on skin.

Charmingly, this fascination felt for perfume from the time of the earliest civilisations has been replicated in microcosm down the ages ever since, by the obsession – that unaccountably seizes every little girl at some point between the ages of seven and nine – with making the world's most beautiful potion from rose petals. On the grounds that children today are in danger of losing many of the gentle arts of yesteryear to the competing attractions of eBay-trading, ASBO-collecting and deleting porn from their Myspace profiles, I set out below the time-honoured method of making rose-petal perfume at home.

- Gather beautiful rose petals from park or garden.

- Fall in love with rose petals and become filled with joy at the thought of capturing their beauty in another medium, distilling their essence into a scent that will enable it to live forever.

- Fill jam jars with water.

- Add petals and breathless anticipation.

- Watch as the petals and your dreams wither and die.

- Throw out brown petals and murky water and most of your childish hopes. Resign yourself in some small but fundamental way to a lifetime of similarly wretched disappointments. The next will come when you first start to thrill to the beauty advice in *Jackie* magazine and waste an entire summer sitting out in the sun with your hair plastered to your head by the juice of half a lemon. You believe it will make you into the kind of blonde that Raymond Chandler described as capable of making a bishop kick a hole in a stained glass window. It actually makes you into a sunburned magnet for wasps and about as blonde as a bag of soot.

Getting lippy

If you had mislaid your beetles and pestle, you could tint your Egyptian lips with red ochre and water, which makes you feel for any rogue gingers out there who must have been crying out for a tawnier palette. But this was not to be until much later on, when people really got to grips with what vegetable dyes and grease could do for a girl's pout.

Until the sixties, lipsticks had names like 'Red', 'Jolly Red' and 'Really Jolly Red Indeed' and were made to a special government formula that rendered them indelible to ensure that no one could safely have an affair with anyone wearing a white shirt and distract his attention from the war effort. Nowadays, you can buy any colour in any finish you want – there are even lipsticks made with diamond dust, for heaven's sake. No wonder the country's moral backbone has collapsed.

Nailing it

Egyptian nails also got the red ochre treatment or could be tinged yellow or orange with henna, a process that lives on accidentally through hippies and teenagers who wish to go brunette but are unwilling to shell out for professional dyejobs.

Blushing maidens

Red ochre was pressed into service once more as blusher by you-know-who, and the Ancient Greeks used a crushed-berry-and-seed paste, but by the sixteenth century, women were gaily painting on the illusion of youth and happiness with vermilion and cochineal.

Use of a little something to heighten one's natural hue has always been one of the more fraught areas of cosmetic employment, neatly summed up by the famous exchange between Marge Simpson and her mother as the former prepared for a date:

> Marge: [pinching her cheeks] Couldn't we just use rouge for this?
> Mrs Bouvier: Ladies pinch. Whores wear rouge. Try to break some capillaries, dear.

Nowadays, however, obvious blusher is taken less as a sign of prostitution than as a sign that you need to rethink your bathroom lighting.

Good foundations

The earliest foundation users were the ladies of Ancient Greece, who evened out their skin tones and prepared for the application of seed 'n' berry cheek paste with a light dusting of white lead powder from bosom to hairline. Several accounts have survived down the ages of Greek historians and philosophers whining and worrying about how women could use cosmetics and perfumes to lure men into marrying them without them ever knowing their true looks. Given the facts, one must deduce that either a) Greek historians and philosophers may not have been quite as bright as history pretends or b) what they were objecting to was not, in fact, the deceitful artifice, but the fact that by the time she stopped bothering to put her face on every morning, what was standing before him was not a woman who had been secretly ugly the whole time, but a wife now dying of lead poisoning, a process which frequently takes something of a toll on one's looks. In fact, between that and the belladonna drops, it's a wonder any woman before 1900 made it through a heavy weekend.

Foundation creams made primarily of said white lead powder remained popular well into the seventeenth century. The Elizabethans called it ceruse and mixed it with egg white, although this dried out quickly, went grey and cracked as soon as you opened your mouth to say, 'Oddsbodikins, I feel a bit crap. I hope I'm not getting a cold or anything.' By 1661, the clever boys at the Royal Society had noticed that people who worked in ceruse manufacturing were prone to cramps, blindness and death, but as they had much more important work to do with gravity and stuff than saving their wives and other womenfolk from a lingering and painful demise, it wasn't until a hundred years later that Lady Coventry received the dubious distinction of being recognised as the first officially identified victim of such poisoning. After that, the market for starch- and alabaster-based face powders really took off.

The only other way to improve a complexion was with a home remedy known as puppydog water. It was a home remedy only in homes with a robust approach to animal husbandry, as the main ingredient was indeed roast puppy. And wine. The phrase 'against animal testing' rarely appeared on seventeenth-century labelling. I suppose it's worth bearing in mind that the bestial glandular secretions pumped into various Hollywood stars and celebrities over the years are probably not entirely voluntarily donated by the pigs/sheep/whales in question either. But still. Roast puppy. Jesus.

Now, of course, we have more skin-coverage options than the human mind can encompass. Powders, liquids, liquid powders, powder liquids, mousses, sprays, light-reflecting, shine-inducing, shine-reducing, for every type of skin from smooth-and-doesn't-even-need-any-bloody-foundation-in-the-first-place to acne-ravaged lunar landscapes and everything in between.

Lotions and potions

The Elizabethans and following generations were (as you might expect from those pox- and plague-ravaged times) particularly keen on beauty washes and lotions. Those who couldn't afford local apothecary prices for orange flower water and apricot cream could always turn to May dew (collected on 1 May, preferably under an oak tree) and cowslips steeped in hot water to get rid of freckles and wrinkles.*

Like most fun things, make-up use decreased in the Victorian age. Lip salves with a bit of vegetable dye, silver litharge and muriatic acid mixtures to get rid of freckles and arsenic solutions to take care of facial hair were about your (toxic) lot. Luckily, before everyone became too depressed by the unadulterated visages on show, the Edwardians arrived and people were able to get back to using face creams, rouge and even decidedly racy delights like *papier poudre*, flower-petal lipstick and mascara made from burned matchsticks.

A girl's gotta have it

You can save yourself a lot of time, trouble and internal psychological strife as a mother if you just accept from the beginning that no matter how non-gender-specifically you have brought her up, no matter how many pairs of trousers and sensible wooden-peg-filled toys you've bought her, no matter how far-flung the outer darkness to which you may have banished Barbie, one of the first things your little girl is going to do with a packet of Smarties is use them as lipstick.

Once the instinct has been awakened, the life's work begins. The product names may change, but the pattern is the same for every generation.

---

* For those who refused to stick the family pet on a spit or kept sleeping through the May morn, the Restoration offered a fun alternative for disguising an imperfect complexion. Beauty spots were all the rage and, delightfully, meant far more than simply twizzling an eyebrow pencil into the side of your upper lip. They could be made of red or black taffeta or leather and stuck on with glue. You could have moons, stars, suns, castles, birds, animals, fish, coaches, horses, diamonds, circles ... I can't help but feel it's an unjustly neglected craze and surely ripe for reinvention, like the Krankies. Whose amusingly contrasting silhouettes, incidentally, might make the ideal inaugural patches with which to bring the fashion roaring back.

Smarties lipstick soon gives way to rummaging through the make-up bags and boxes of every female relative within a fifty-mile radius. Cousins are prevailed upon to donate old mascaras, aunts persuaded to pass on knackered lipsticks that still have plenty of mileage in them for people prepared to scrape the remnants from the bottom of the twisty stick bit. And grandmothers are a veritable treasure trove of cast-off golden compacts with rings of powder still adhering to the edges inside, to be applied with the impossibly soft circles of flesh-coloured fluff provided.

The real excitement begins, of course, when puberty and pocket money meet. In my neck of the woods, everyone began with Cover Girl or Constance Carroll because:

a) They were vivid, viscous and vicious.

b) They were the cheapest by some distance.

c) They were sold in corner shops and markets made up of hundreds of little concession stands, each cheaper, tattier, glitzier and more glorious than the last, where you could buy clothes, belts and earrings along with your make-up and generally emerge at least ten times more fabulous as when you went in. Unlike Boots, which had smartly clinical aisles and sales assistants who knew you were only there to shoplift the good stuff.

d) We didn't care that a Constance Carroll lipstick turned green within six days of purchase or that you couldn't get Cover Girl eyeshadow off with a belt sander. We were young, impetuous and unbowed by virulent allergic reactions.

Legitimate purchases amongst teenagers are, of course, supplemented by the aforementioned shoplifting and by an enthusiastic adoption of the concept of shared ownership. If one girl in a group had a lip gloss or a gold eyeshadow, they all had it. By the same token, of course, if one girl had impetigo or conjunctivitis … But, hey, it could have been worse. At least we weren't dousing ourselves in arsenic and caking ourselves in lead.

Magazines which included free gifts were also a valuable source of cosmetic loot. Frosted-pink lipstick from Rimmel! Eyeshadow trios in tones more commonly seen in distress flares. Accompanied by sponge applicators so cheap and unyielding that they gave you friction burns! Make-up bags made of plastic seemingly rescued from a landfill site! Mascara that dragged your eyelashes out by the roots! Sometimes it was hard to express our excitement. Usually this was because the giveaway that week was lip gloss so sticky that opening your mouth required two hefty friends and a crowbar. And even then, the glutinous strands would web your mouth like the melted cheese on a pizza, so anything you wanted to say would be preceded by minutes of sticky spluttering. My dad ended up using most of mine to mend tiles.

It is a glorious thing to live your teenage years at a time when the fashion in make-up is perfectly matched to the exuberance of youth. Happy the sixties teenager who could trowel on the metallics and mascara and know she was only doing herself good. And as for the eighties – well, was there any greater fortune than to live your most vital years in that unique time in history when you were not just permitted but all but required by statute to have a fluorescent face? All notions of choosing your make-up to suit your colouring and face-shape were abandoned. Cool girls swept on their bright-pink blusher with a brush the size of a baby's head and an enviably insouciant grace. Lesser mortals stabbed at their faces with stubby fingers and left two fuchsia stripes where they hoped their cheekbones might one day prove to be.

I followed every magazine's instructions to line the lips in
pencil, fill in with lipstick, blot, powder, repeat and finish with
lip gloss. My mouth was so heavy by the end, I had to prop
my head up with a stick. I improvised a version of the blue
mascara recommended by every beauty editor by mixing a
cast-off azure eyeshadow from my cousin Katie with water
and trying to apply it with the thin end of my comb. The
price of beauty, it turns out, is two scratched corneas and an
embarrassing trip to casualty.

The height of sophistication

At fourteen, however, a measure of sanity returned to us all. Some
kind of switch flips in the collective female psyche and the urge for a
more sophisticated, less garish look becomes felt. One abandons slavish
adherence to one-shade-suits-all facial fashions and begins to assert
one's individuality.

In my neck of the woods, we decided this was best achieved by a
mass obsession with Body Shop unguents. We used to descend on our
local branch every Saturday like locusts on a cornfield and strip the
shelves. Every Monday morning the entire school stank of dewberry
and White Musk perfume. Teachers had to be carried out on stretchers.
Your worth was judged by the size of your Barbara Daly blusher brush
and your dedication to the exfoliatory arts. At the height of our fervour,
you could have chucked broken glass in marmalade and we would have
bought it, as long as you called it 'Orange Facial Scrub' and promised
us suitably sloughed skin. When I think of the money I wasted on that

shop's gunk I could cry. If you could translate tea tree oil shampoo into pension contributions, I could have retired by now.

In your twenties, you become genuinely more sophisticated (and solvent) and able to tailor your purchasing to products and colours that help you to accentuate the good and ameliorate the bad. It is, on the whole, a relief not to have to improvise, take pot luck with stolen goods or accept the occasional bout of unidentified burning rash as a necessary evil in the pursuit of beauty any more, but you do occasionally miss the collective enthusiasm and camaraderie that existed around the face-painting project. Putting on your make-up in the peace and tranquillity of your own bathroom has its charms, but from time to time you miss the screaming laughter and excitement of eight girls crammed into a bedroom passing one pearlised lipstick and two shimmering shadows round and trying to get their mascara on safely before someone jogs their elbow and takes their eye out.

In your thirties, make-up becomes a matter of maintenance, a joyless process more akin to panel beating and plastering than the enjoyable enhancements of yore. In a highly irrational and unhelpful development, it becomes too upsetting to look at your face in the mirror, even though this is the only way you can begin to improve it. Every month you resolve to break out of this mental deadlock and follow the example of your friend who wears three different types of foundation every day: one for her cheeks, one for her 'oily T-zone' (vexed subject of the remaining twenty per cent of *Just Seventeen* articles that weren't devoted to men bobbing their love antennae at you) and one for her neck, all blended seamlessly with one of those wedge-shaped applicators you marvel at briefly on cosmetics counters but never actually get round to buying.*

---

* It's impossible to imagine what she does when she goes out – strips her face back to the bone and starts again from scratch with epidermis she's grown in petri dishes from Nicole Kidman's skin cells gathered from Balenciaga's changing-room floor and sold illegally over the internet, probably.

But at the moment you are still locked in the downward spiral that even on your bravest days sees you do no more than crack open your trusty all-in-one foundation compact and drag a layer of fine grit across your face with a sponge so feculent it will probably function as the mixing vessel from which the fatal crossover strain of avian flu will eventually emerge.

The make-up bag

The importance of the make-up bag has been obvious from the very beginning. Even the Egyptians kept their cosmetics in special boxes that they could take to parties so they could discreetly fix their faces whenever they chose. Which was probably quite often, given how many touch-ups the modern woman requires even without the problem of perfumed oils running down her ninety-per-cent-kohl face all night. History does not, unfortunately, record whether the Ancient Egyptians were as generous with their emergency loans as their counterparts today, but it is pleasant to imagine cries of 'Oh my God, I've run out of crushed beetle! Charmian, can you lend me a burnt cockroach?' 'Oh, I love that myrtle and calamus oil you've got! Can I try a bit? I'm blistering the walls with my BO here …' and 'Jesus, has no one invented wand mascara yet? Where am I supposed to get oxidised copper at this time of night?' ringing down the ages.

A woman's make-up bag is an archaeologist's guide to her cosmetic evolution. The upper stratum is the useful, currently used stuff – sensible lipstick, basic mascara, concealer and a nearly finished foundation that's going to run out just before you can get to Boots.

Next layer: thirty-two back-up mascaras, eighteen leaking lip glosses and emergency lipstick that doesn't really suit you but is too expensive to throw away.

Next layer: evening versions of the earlier strata. More expensive, more glittery and more lovely. You look better just for owning them. They do not, however, help you solve the conundrum that has pursued women down the ages: how to meet a man for a date at 7 o'clock on a summer's evening. This is late enough for proper flirting and therefore proper make-up, but still light enough to cause him to recoil in horror from Amazing Clown-faced Woman if you do pitch up in full slap.

Next layer: untouched eyeshadows, lipsticks, etc. that you will never use but that are too, too gorgeous to give away. You feel vaguely guilty about denying them their beautifying destiny, but you cannot be parted.

Next layer: 702 congealed, dusty and broken tubes, pots, jars and compacts dating back to your prehistory and that you could never throw away because they contain too many memories – of summer holidays, childish passions, first discos, shared secrets, private hopes and public proclamations, eternal friendships pledged and broken, magical kisses and terrible snogs – and it would break your heart to lose them. It's sticker syndrome all over again.

Clobber: from Primark to Prada

Like hair, clothes mark your place in the pecking order from day one. Pixie boots, legwarmers, ra-ra skirts, Sasparilla jeans, batwing sweaters and anything slashed, spangly or sloganned from Chelsea Girl, Tammy Girl, Miss Selfridge or Dorothy Perkins were good. Anything else, from anywhere else was bad.

Do you realise that anyone over the age of twenty-five today is a member of what will probably be the last ever generation for whom the purchase of a new top or skirt was accompanied by a sense of occasion? The advent of Primark, H&M and all the other discount retailers has changed everything. Girls can pile into shops every weekend now and heap their baskets with a month's worth of outfits for a tenner. They buy clothes like we bought sweets – instead of enough cola bottles and Space Dust to last you for a week, they stock up on vest tops and skinny jeans. You have to fight the urge to pin them into a corner and make them listen to the tales of deprivation from your own childhood, like some post-war matriarch driven mad by the profligacy of these exuberant new 'teenager' creatures with their 'pocket money' and their 'Elvis Presley'. But we did do things differently – we did! For a start, there was no Sunday trading. Saturday shopping was an intense experience, an expedition that was planned all week. And clothes were expensive. I feel faint when I remember paying £18 for a pair of flowery shorts from Chelsea Girl. Of course, I thought they were the most gorgeous things that human endeavour had ever created at the time, but £18! And the label said '100% dishrag. Will fall apart at first wash, if withering glances from mother don't destroy them first.' That seems an incredible price now, and if you translate the 1988 terms into today's prices … well, you must excuse me while I go and have a little lie down.

But that's what you did. You saved up for months to buy some coveted piece of glittering Lurex or stonewashed denim that your mother would never, ever agree to pay for, and half the fun was in the delirious anticipation of acquisition. When one of my friends wanted to buy black satin trousers from Tammy Girl, we couldn't have had more fun awaiting the momentous purchase than if she had been buying the Koh-i-Noor diamond. As was frequently the case, however, ownership of said item turned out to be slightly anti-climactic. She had, of course, only set her heart on them because they were the closest thing Lewisham Centre had to offer to the shiny, skin-tight trousers worn by Olivia Newton John at the end of *Grease* and which were so instrumental in her conversion from Sweet Sandra to Sexy Sandy. Lisa, and the rest of us, had invested a lot of hope in the transformative power of black satin trousers and we were collectively quietly devastated when she remained as bespectacled and covered in puppy fat as she had been before she parted with £36 – three Saturdays' wages! – for the supposedly magical trousers.

Woman, know your place

If, unlike the Primark-gobbling yoof of today, we had to learn harsh lessons in deferred gratification, at least we knew the joys of generational distinction. Which is to say, at least we grew up with mothers who knew their place. And that place was Marks & Spencer. Once a year. They went there to buy a new pair of black court shoes and a couple of elasticated skirts. If they were feeling particularly frivolous, they could supplement the crazy spree with a coffee in Army & Navy before going sensibly home and sensibly deciding to take one of the skirts back. It was all deeply reassuring and gave daughters – nay, the world – a tremendous feeling of security and stability. It was, quite clearly, a middle-aged uniform and marked wearers out as having kindly vacated the sexual arena, leaving it clear for the teenage-you to find a space there, test it out and have some fun before it was your turn to don the low-heeled shoes and forgiving waistbands and become that stately breed of woman whose job it was to look after foolish children, tell them off and watch *Coronation Street* in sartorial comfort.

These days, mothers and daughters – even grandmothers and granddaughters if you live in an area where teenage pregnancy is a particularly popular lifestyle choice – are frequently found raiding the same shops. It must blur some mental as well as physical certainties. I don't think I would have coped too well with having a mother who kept sabotaging my flailing teenage attempts at iconic individualism by dressing indistinguishably from me. In fact, I think I would have had some kind of breakdown.

As with make-up as you get older, so with clothes. In your teens, you can get away with anything, either by virtue of youthful effervescence and a svelte frame or thanks to the kindness of your elders, who will look at you with forgiving eyes and gallantly refrain from pointing out that in your batwing jumper, puffball skirt and footless neon tights you look like something Miss Selfridge threw up on. In your twenties, it is a matter of developing your own style and taste rather than mindless following of your clique's rules, and hoping your disposable income keeps up with your desire to do so. In your thirties, your sartorial options begin to narrow and, with the cruel irony of fate that you are coming to know so well, although you are more likely to have enough money to buy whatever you want, you start to choose your clothes increasingly on the basis of whether they help you disguise the horrors and showcase any remaining highlights and less and less on whether you have any actual liking or regard for them at all.

Instead of spending happy weekends shopping with your friends and falling in love with various items, you perfect the art of standing at the top of escalators, scanning four hundred square feet of retail space and announcing that there is nothing for you here. At the back of your mind, a tiny hope begins to crystallise that by the time you are forty the kaftan will have made a roaring comeback.

Underwear

We should all take a moment right now to proffer a small prayer to whichever particular deity we habitually contribute our fortunes to for his/her/its great providence in ensuring that we were born into the post-corsetry era.

If you were living under Elizabeth I instead of Elizabeth II, you would be strapped into a buckram-stiffened bodice designed to flatten your frontage and keep you sitting up straight. As a further aid to squashed-bosomed perpendicularity, you could insert a busk down the front, which is described by Randle Holme, a later observer in the seventeenth century, as:

> 'A strong piece of wood or whalebone thrust down the middle of the
> stomacher to keep it straight and in compass, that the breast or belly
> shall not swell out too much. These busks are usually made in length
> according to the necessity of the person wearing it: if to keep in the
> fullness of the breasts, then it extends to the navel; if to keep the belly
> down then it extends to the honour.'

In other words, if you had a spare tyre you could look forward to a lifetime of being unable to sit down without a near-cliterodectomy from a jagged piece of whalebone and spending the next four hours picking splinters out of your fanny. So just think on that next time you are moaning about visible panty lines or having to squeeze into a pair of Spanx pants.

Your first bra

As previously noted, for most of us, the greatest female rite of passage is the buying of the first bra. With impressive disregard for the physical realities of the situation, you bought it simply when you deemed yourself old enough to do so. It didn't matter whether you had the requisite 30AA boobs or a chest so concave that you looked like John Hurt post-alien hatching, you bought it when you were thirteen and you wore it, either with pride or cotton wool balls.

Some of us snapped on its increasingly limp, frayed sinews for years as our capricious hormones gaily ensured that although we exuded pints of grease and sprouted pus-filled spots with the best of them, we would never bust gloriously forth like our friends (and even more often, our enemies) and require an underwired upgrade. Normal girls, of course, quickly entered the world of proper bras, in all their lacy, satiny, padded, unpadded, balconied, half-cupped, frilled, flounced, embroidered, sexy black, slaggy red glory. Forget GCSE results, the biggest day in our school calendar was the day the first intrepid fourth year explorers got the train into London and discovered Knickerbox. Life was never the same after that.

From there you evolve into one of two types of women. Either you become the proud owner of innumerable matching sets of expensive lingerie, housed in their own drawer and supplemented by quality white cotton bras and knickers that remain dazzlingly bright because you would no more think of putting them in a non-white wash than you would think of not rinsing the plates before you put them in the dishwasher.* Or you become the less proud but infinitely more understandable owner of fifty-two pairs of knickers which are mentally divided into 'normal day wear', 'period' and 'one step away from floor-cloth'. And three grey bras. And a black one. Somewhere.

It hardly needs adding that Type 1 Woman also has a small drawer full of pristine stockings, suspender belts and garters, while Type 2 owns a large cupboard full of tights knotted into one giant nylon ball, buried somewhere in the middle of which, legend has it, exists the unladdered pair.

And while we're on the subject of tights, let me just add another note to the list of things your mother never told you: namely, that if you are the possessor of thighs that meet at any point below your crotch (and let's face it, if you are someone who has enjoyed a meal at any point in the past fifteen years, then yours probably do), walking for any length of time in patterned tights will result in the kind of chafing that can enable you to see your femur by midnight. The friction they

---

* Freak. Freak, freak, freak, freak, freak.

generate is unbelievable. Fishnets should come with a health and safety warning. So have a care.*

'Pampering'

By which I mean the panoply of more or less painful and humiliating services offered to women under the entirely misleading heading of treats – massages, facials, manicures, pedicures, mud wraps and, above all, the various forms of depilation that abound.

Of the last, waxing has a special place in every woman's personal history of beautification. I avoided the practice for many years, relying instead on a blend of hacking away at my flesh with a rusty disposable razor and slathering the more delicate regions with stinking hair-removal cream and trying not to puke as I scraped the hairy coagulated mass off with the wholly inadequate spatula provided, ten minutes after the recommended waiting time. However, one of the many things your mother, science lessons and all the other supposed sources of vital biological information for a girl fail to tell you is that just as men become hairier with age, so do women, and some more than others. The day I woke up to find a fetching line of pubic hair running up to my navel as if it were the advance party for further colonisation, I thought, 'That's all I need – a hairy waist!' and started booking myself in for regular strippings at the local salon. The first time I went, the grim-faced beautician in

---

* It's a toss-up as to whether this is preferable to the pain involved in going tights-free in summer. Although the intercrural sweating mitigates some of the thigh-chafing, you have also got the blistered toes and shoe strap lacerations on your Achilles tendons to contend with. I am working on a patent for invisible casings in breathable clear plastic for feet and giant flesh-coloured plasters for inner thighs, which I predict will transform our summers in years to come. I need £50,000 for start-up fees, so if you would like to have a hand in protecting the delicate lady-flesh of future generations, please send investment monies to antiabrasions.co.uk and I'll get to work.

charge took one look, turned towards the back room and shouted, 'Stoke the fires!' She has been locked in monthly battle with my apparent biological destiny to become Mr Tumnus the Faun ever since. Last time she brought in her brothers to hold me down, and a blowtorch.

As to the rest – manicures, pedicures, facials, massages etc. – there is no starker illustration of the truth that in life you get what you pay for. Pay through the nose and you will end up with beautiful nails, rejuvenated skin and a soaring sense of wellbeing coupled with a deep feeling of relaxation. Don't and you will get a bored sixteen-year-old sawing at the ends of your fingers and toes until she reaches bone, a heavyset woman slapping bear grease on your face while she describes the identifying features of her latest vaginal infection to her colleague in the next cubicle and a retired SAS trainer pummelling your muscles until they each lodge an individual complaint at the European Court of Human Rights.

Mud baths and seaweed wraps are relatively safe. Pointless, and designed only to separate from their money the kind of fools who believe that the stuff being slathered on was indeed gathered that morning from the bottom of an untouched moonlit pool and blessed by Kylie Minogue and not dug that morning from the cat pee-soaked flowerbeds of the owner's back garden in Hounslow, but safe.

Shoes, shoes and more shoes

Ah, shoes – women's Achilles heel. A recent survey by *Grazia* magazine found that the average woman spends nearly £80,000 during her shoe-buying lifespan. Eighty thousand pounds! If we conservatively estimate the average shoe-buying lifespan (that's the time between the moment a girl first says to her mother, 'I am leaving this Sensible Shoes for School and the Orthopaedically Wary emporium and heading for the glittering stacks in Crippling Stilettoes R Us, do not follow me,' to the day she sighs with relief and realises that fleece-lined slippers will now get her happily from bed to sofa to death) at fifty years, that works out at £1,600 a year!

Women's love affair with shoes is well documented. Even though we are in full possession of our mental faculties, we will not only totter about with our entire body weight thrown onto three square inches of foot flesh, while our toes fuse into one giant, throbbing stump, risking fractured ankles with every step, but we will do it with smiles on our faces. The affair has flourished down the ages because of one simple fact: there are diets aplenty in the world, there are complicated operations involving stomach stapling, bone grafts and eighteen months in a Stryker frame, but shoes are the only thing in the world that make you look taller and slimmer instantly. And you don't have to bugger about getting medical certificates saying you qualify to have them. You can just buy them. Brilliant.

Handbags

Now, don't get me wrong. I love handbags. I have eighteen of them, each with a precise but slightly different purpose and suitability, as I am tired of explaining to my boyfriend every time he complains about the fact that he has nowhere to hang his coat. But I think the most expensive cost about twenty quid. To me, a handbag is an impulse buy, something you get to cheer yourself up when nothing else in the shops fits. So there are two pieces of information I have to hand that both distress and confuse me.

The first is the news from a recent survey that the average woman (she is beginning to annoy me), ports a daily handbag 'n' contents combination worth £500. I could empty my entire wardrobe, jewellery box and current account into mine, and still need to add a cheque for £376 to bring me up to scratch.* The second is that, if this is what

---

* Unless old bus tickets and mismatched gloves suddenly emerge as the frontrunners in the search for alternative energy sources, of course. Then I'm sitting on a gold mine.

normal women are carrying around with them as a matter of course, how can I learn to cope with the knowledge that there are untold numbers of ladies out there who must be spending oh so much more? Even if I owned all the money in the world and had global control of everyone's mints and presses, I don't think I could spend thousands of pounds on anything that I couldn't live in or drive away. But I may be in a shrinking minority. The designer handbag market is growing at a geometric rate. Before long, you won't be allowed out of the house without £8,000 worth of ostrich skin and tasselled padlocks on your arm.

So there you have it. The modern woman, taken from top to toe, is a crazy lady crippled by her shoes, bankrupted by her accessories and periodically doused in mud and covered in hot wax, who voluntarily plucks hairs out by the roots, spends a fortune on unguents she doesn't need and bras she will never wear and won't throw out make-up that is harbouring new strains of fatal disease because it reminds her of tear-stained, joy-filled nights crammed into the fetid lavatories of suburban nightclubs with her friends. And yet, somehow, they keep letting us get jobs, own property and have babies. For God's sake, whatever you do, don't tell anyone about this.

CHAPTER 10

Sometimes It's Hard ...

Becoming a Woman

Admittedly, our generation manages to put it off for longer than any other in history, but at some point we all have to grow up. We can postpone the traditional markers of maturity by getting married, buying property and having children later than our mothers and grandmothers would have dreamed possible, taking sabbaticals from work whenever we have a bit of money saved, filling our twenties and even up to our late, late thirties with fun, frolics and friends instead of adult burdens and responsibilities, but eventually we must succumb.

So when do you finally become a woman, an honest-to-God, no-getting-away-from-it grown-up? Well, there is actually a checklist. It's set out below. When you fulfil sixty-five per cent of the requirements outlined, then you'll be a woman, my girl.

1. You find your first honest-to-God wrinkle

This is preceded by years of increasingly anxious inspection of your face in unflattering bathroom light, during which time you begin to realise that, for all your bloody moaning and groaning during your teenage years, you always knew, deep down, that the mirror was your friend. Yes, you saw spots and pores that spewed more oil than Kuwait and a face that was about as painfully unlike Debbie Harry's or Sheena Easton's as it was possible to be, but you knew, in your heart of hearts, that the former flaws were just temporary aberrations skittering across your springy young face and the latter was really something you could learn to live with without too much trouble. The basic material was good.

Cut to twenty years later and the basic material is starting to give you sleepless nights. The genuine bloom went off in your twenties, but you dealt with that. But now you can't even fake it with shimmery powders, daily exfoliants and sticks of subtle shine swept across your once naturally glowing cheeks. Partly this is because your epidermis stubbornly resists revivification, preferring instead to devote its energies to developing incipient crow's feet, tiredness lines that don't quite disappear after a good night's sleep and a certain burgeoning whiff of death and decay. And partly it is because, frankly, you can no longer be frigging arsed.

I exaggerate about the death and decay aspect, of course. Most of this perceived corruption in your thirties is just in your head. But you also know that the reality is, as they say in *Trainspotting* of an impending heroin withdrawal, in the fucking post for sure. It is that realisation that marks the beginning of your long-awaited adulthood and a gradual but increasing avoidance of mirrors and other reflective surfaces. Fifteen years from now, you will be spending most of the day commando-crawling across the floor to avoid them. And because the texture of cheap carpet will be the one remaining substance on earth that makes your skin feel young and vibrant by contrast once more.

2a. You stop being able to drink alcohol

One moment you are happily knocking back the booze with the best of them and shrugging off the results the next day with a swift coffee and bacon sandwich before starting to get ready for the next night's binge. The next, you are having one glass of champagne at someone's engagement party and spending the next day groaning for an ambulance and/or the sweet release of death.

Yes, falling alcohol tolerance is a sure sign that you are reaching maturity. It is your body's way of telling you that you are now officially old enough to cope with most social situations and times of stress without resorting to artificial aids and stimulants, that your liver is no longer as capable of regenerating itself after your mindless abuse as once it was and that you should be making carefully thought-out, ideally procreatively-aimed decisions about sex with sensible men and not falling into a gin-soaked bed with the best-looking bastard in the vicinity.

It is a hard and unwelcome lesson to learn. I suggest you keep drinking to avoid having to think about it too much.

2b. You start to look forward to a cup of tea

This is closely related to the disappearance of alcohol from your life. Nature abhors a vacuum, so something must rush to fill the void. A lukewarm mug of PG Tips soon becomes the last word in sybaritic indulgence. At home, you sigh with pleasure as you sink into an armchair with it. You indulge in mildly hysterical thanks if someone brings you a cup of the divine libation at work.

Biscuits too take on the kind of luxurious aura you previously reserved for expensive weekends away in country house hotels, paid for by adoring merchant-banker boyfriends. With any luck, you won't start to ponder how your life ever narrowed to this sharp and tragic point.

3. You get called 'Madam' in shops

The first time this happens, it is quite confusing. You look round, checking for the imperious dowager or aged crone that the shop assistant has decided to serve instead of you. You look back. Light dawns. You see yourself for a moment through the girl's seventeen-year-old eyes, which is like looking down the wrong end of a telescope. You stifle the urge to reach down her throat and bring out her innards in your fist. You realise that the only way to deal with the situation is to smile graciously and imagine that she regards you with respect and awe, hope and aspiration, that you are imbued with a golden glow of success in her mind and are not simply another faceless proto-mum amongst the endless stream of grey-faced automata with whom she deals every day.

As well as 'madam', you also start being referred to as 'that lady' by children whose interest you have, for whatever unfathomable reason, piqued and who are now intent on pointing you out to their frankly uninterested mothers. It is, of course, even more disquieting when you realise that you are older than said mothers.

On the plus side, this stage also coincides with the stage at which you realise that, for the first time in your life, you are not afraid of teenage girls. From whatever age it is that consciousness first dawns, they have been terrifying beings – loud, raucous, self-confident, overbearing, bitchy, cackling, loathsome, colourful, gorgeous, over-numerous, giggling, mocking, riotous, shrieking, mesmerising, haunting, strident, unruly, grating gaggles who would as soon refrain from flicking you into the gutter as they passed as they would from stealing the latest eyeliner from Superdrug and who only gained in terrorising splendour when you reached that age yourself. The smouldering fear and awe lingers for years after you emerge from the teenage fire, and you instinctively cringe throughout the next decade whenever they pile onto the bus or approach on the pavement, expecting at any moment volleys of ridicule and the avalanches of scorn and derision to be heaped upon your innocent and yet somehow blameworthy head once more. Until one day, one ordinary day that begins much like any other, you find yourself walking past the loathsome fiends … and barely registering them. Your feet stutter to a halt as you digest what has just occurred. You saw them – and dismissed them. They are but children. They are but total cretins. What they say cannot affect you, you wise and fabulous woman of the world. You are free. You are finally free. If you can set aside forty-eight hours for the hangover, you should have a drink to celebrate.

4. You have a baby

You know you are on your way to being a grown-up when you look around at your friends and realise that none of you has had a pregnancy scare in years. In fact, quite the opposite – they are all taking folic acid instead of the pill and desperately praying every month for their period NOT to arrive, otherwise they are going to have to stop paying the mortgage and start funnelling all their cash into IVF instead.

Whatever way you look at it, producing a member of the next generation is quite a definitive marker of adulthood. You actually made a baby. Even more impressive than that, you gave birth to it, either by letting it claw its way out of your nether regions or by letting someone slice through layers of muscle, fat and uterine wall and wrench it out by hand. Either way, kudos, and I think we can all agree, you are now many miles into a forced march to maturity. Yes, you can be a young mother, an energetic mother, a mother who still spends all her disposable income on shoes and impractical jackets, but the fact remains that from now on, when push comes to shove, you are likely to put the needs of your beloved squalling infant before your own. The capacity for such self-abnegation is the very essence of adulthood.

5. You become a godmother

This is almost as frightening as becoming a mother. Not only are you old enough to have friends who are sprogging up, but you are also clearly old enough to have the kind of life that makes them think you are a suitable person to be given a hand in their offspring's spiritual development. And to buy them age-appropriate presents for the next eighteen years. And hold them over a big, water-filled marble font without dropping them to their deaths. They think, in short, that you are old enough to be charged with responsibility, not just for yourself but for others.

You may need to sit down for several days while you come to terms with this sudden and by no means welcome revelation.

6. Look around your kitchen

AWARD YOURSELF POINTS FOR OWNING ANY OF THE FOLLOWING:

- matching plates — 1 pt
- matching utensils — 2 pts
- matching utensils stored in a pot marked 'Utensils' — 3 pts
- a full set of Tupperware — 4 pts
- a butcher's block — 4 pts
- a breadmaker — 5 pts
- a breadmaker that you actually use to make bread — 6 pts
- a breadmaker that you actually use not just to make bread but to make brown bread with nuts in — 7 pts
- a larder — 8 pts

• a drawer full of oddments	3 pts – plus an additional point for every one of the following oddments therein: freezer bags, plastic clips for sealing freezer bags, fairy cake casings, string, matches, candles, scissors, Sellotape, painkillers, sticky-roller-lint-removing-thingy. Plus an additional 10 points if you know that they are there and 20 more if this is because you deliberately put them there so that you can lay hands on them in a leftovers/gardening/power cut/children's party/cat hair emergency. Award yourself 800 superpoints if you have a spare sticky roll for the sticky-roller-lint-removing-thingy. You are amazing.
• a Welsh dresser	900 pts

Add up your points. If they total 27 or more, you are indubitably A Woman.

7. You have a present box

The gift-based equivalent of the oddments drawer. It contains presents for upcoming birthdays, Christmasses, weddings, christenings, bar mitzvahs and housewarmings. It is a mature recognition of the fact that you cannot rely upon one weak human mind to remember all possible celebrations and festivities, nor on one weak human scheduling programme to find the time to buy an age-occasion-and-strength-of-relationship-with-recipient-appropriate gift at the last minute. Or the spare credit card capacity.

8. You carry a spare bag in your handbag

One of those nylon ones that folds up to nothing in your handbag, but which can be whipped out at a moment's notice to provide instant extra luggage capacity at times of unexpectedly heavy purchasing sprees. This kind of foresight and preparation for common but not certain eventualities is very, very grown-up.

This also goes for umbrellas, tights and tissues. But not, I repeat not, for condoms. See (2).

9. Snow = Bad

Snow is no longer fun. It ruins your hair, requires you to carry three changes of shoes in your bag at all times and makes the trains run late.

10a. Olives = Good

You may consider yourself a die-hard olive-hater – green, black, pimento-stuffed, they are all just little pellets of vile-tasting vegetable flesh to you. Let me assure you that at some point in the next few years it is going to be as if a little dial inside you has suddenly clicked over from 'Yeeeeeeuuucccchh' to 'Yum' and you will start falling on them at parties as if they were manna from the very gods. I'm told that much the same thing happens to men with regard to whisky. It goes from being a fiery liquid that turns your head red and throbbing to the elixir of life. Nobody knows precisely why, but it is thought to have something to do with providing a useful guide at parties as to who might be ready to embark on a joint mortgage and who might just be more suited to a shared cab ride home.

10b. Salad = Even Better

When you spoke as a child, when you understood as a child, salad was a joke. And not a funny one. To be offered it as a garnish or side portion was an outrage, an insult. To be offered it as a meal was unthinkable. If anyone had told us that there would come a day when we would welcome it as a viable repast, we would have regarded them as either a pathological liar or an unadulterated idiot. If you had added that you were not talking about salad poked reluctantly down the throat as a loathed but effective aid to weight loss, but salad as a thankfully received option on a hot summer's day or tasty alternative on days when a sandwich feels just too stodgy to be borne, we would have run, legs pumping like demented pistons, far and fast from the crazy with the nightmare visions and the senseless stories.

But – turns out – it's true. Who'd have thunk it?

11. You can't remember the last time you had a really good laugh

Take a moment. Think back. Do you remember how funny – how truly, madly, deeply, gut bustingly funny – everything was when you were young? I used to spend hours a day at school laughing with my friends, whom I believed to contain the distilled essences of Joan Rivers, Phyllis Diller, Charlie Chaplin, Les Dawson, Groucho Marx, Oscar Wilde, Dorothy Parker and Gary Wilmot. Now I'm lucky if I crack half a smile during a *Friends* re-run, and even then it's usually tempered by a single salty tear sliding down my face as I remember that Courtney Cox was forty by the time she finished the final season and still looked like a particularly fresh-faced twenty-five-year-old.

The other side of the coin, of course, is that although everything was funny then, it was also tragic. As soon as anything went wrong, the school stage was filled with figures bemoaning the awful fate that had befallen them, the devastating betrayals and crimes perpetrated against them (usually involving stolen scrunchies and broken-heeled shoes) and lying draped over PE benches, gasping with limitless, uncontainable sorrow and grief. The highs and lows of existence at that age cannot be sustained over an entire lifetime. You would end up a mass of burst blood vessels.

But we should make an effort to retain at least some of the highs, and luckily this is perfectly possible, as long as you stay in touch with enough of your friends from those heady school days, because the joyful fact of the matter is this: reminiscing about the time Abby Smith trapped both nipples in her locker because she wasn't used to having boobs yet will be just as amusing in the retelling as it was at the time. Why, I'm laughing now. You just need to get your girls round.

12. You become assertive

You are in a shop. You are in a hurry. There are four people ahead of you in the queue, each with a purchase requiring more information and detailed discussion with the single serving shop assistant than would be necessary if the purchaser were in fact buying a pharmaceutical company from a multinational conglomerate. The shop assistant is cross-eyed with boredom and profoundly uncommitted to the concept of working for a living. She is moving at the speed of a snail tracking through molasses. At one point, you suspect she is actually going backwards. There are three other assistants standing nearby, one picking at her nails, one admiring herself in the mirror and the other gazing vacantly into space, possibly working on a simplified proof of Fermat's Last Theorem, possibly not. Quite possibly the only useful thing they are doing is raising a neat philosophical point: if an assistant is not assisting, does she make a sound when you kick her up the useless bum?

So you take a step forward out of the queue and say in a calm but indisputably raised voice, 'Excuse me, but do you think one of you could help serve?' The blood pounds in your head, your world reels, you are flooded with the sudden fear that all over the high street shop assistants have sensed your words and are now sniffing the air like murderous hounds ready to hunt you down and tear you limb from daring limb. But this does not happen. Instead, one of the three stooges rolls her eyes, reluctantly detaches herself from the group and installs herself behind the till, where she serves with as bad a grace as has ever been seen since time began. But still, there are now two cashiers working where only one existed before.

Congratulations. You are now an adult.

Ditto if you have ever been in a pub or café and uttered these words: 'I'm sorry, do you think you could turn the music down just a bit? My friend and I can't hear ourselves speak!' Double ditto if you emphasised the word SPEAK.

13. You end a relationship not because you are unhappy, but because 'it isn't going anywhere'

This is a definite harbinger of maturity, as it marks the first time you understand that, at some level and for some things, time is running out and you have to start planning for a future that exists some time beyond next Friday night. It feels weird and wrong, because it is weird and wrong. It is wholly unnatural to have to end a relationship when you are still having a perfectly pleasant time and are months, maybe even years, away from wanting to tear each other's eyes out. But you do it anyway, because deep down you know that he is not the man with whom you want to share the rest of your life/custody of the children if things don't, after all, work out. And your treacherously rational mind knows that if you spend time letting the relationship run its natural course, you will sabotage your chances of meeting Mr Really Right and popping out babies, should you in future years desire to do so.

It is the first of many head-not-heart-led decisions that will eventually see you sitting at the kitchen table with a man and saying, 'You have to take this promotion because we have to pay for a wedding within the next year so that I can be pregnant before I'm thirty-five, which means we also have to move house in the next eighteen months to somewhere with a nursery and a guest bedroom for my mother because I can't cope on my own if you're working all the hours God sends because of your new job, and by the way I think my entire system just went into meltdown and I am about to choke to death on the roiling tide of life that is suddenly sweeping towards me, please help me, I think I'm drowning.'

Or words to that effect.

14. You get married

Getting married is huge. It may be more of a milestone on the flinty path to adulthood than having a baby. After all, you are not just professing enough confidence in yourself and in your ability to choose a suitable life partner, and you are not just declaring yourself ready, willing and able to embrace the concept of permanence, compromise and the sealing off of all further sexual options until you die, you are also stumping up a serious wodge of cash to do so. And agreeing to wear a proper frock. And to let all your family and friends meet each other. These are all immensely mature and frightening things to do. In fact, are you sure you have entirely thought this through? Couldn't you just live together for a bit longer? At least until you have got your oddments drawer in place? As a general rule of thumb, I would suggest not making any eternal vows or taking any steps of extreme religious significance until you at least know where you keep the spare batteries for every remote control in your home. You know it makes sense.

15. You buy your first pair of control pants

It used to be that big knickers or tights alone could smooth sufficiently the gentle but unsightly bulges that ruined the line of your best skirt or favourite trousers. It used to be that you had the time and inclination to flatten your stomach via a five-day crash diet before you went out on a hot date or to a big party or a posh do.

Now you are fatter, busier and increasingly aware of the fact that every day you do not indulge in a half carton of Chunky Monkey is a day you're not getting back. You don't go out on hot dates any more. You are either coupled up or entering a stage of life in which dates no longer generate the frisson of delight they once did. They no longer even pretend to offer a tantalising cornucopia of possibilities, but hold out the near-certainty of being stuck with a forty-something management consultant still looking for 'the right woman' – which loosely translates as 'anyone who will indulge me regularly in my nappy and breastfeeding fetish'. All of which means you are no longer able to work miracles by the donning of ordinary undergarments nor are motivated enough to starve yourself beforehand in order to dazzle without them. Exit the diet. Enter the control pants. You never look back, although if you did you would only see a delightfully redistributed bottom sans VPL and a dramatically thinned thigh. Ta-daah!

16. You take pleasure in hanging the washing out

Well, not actually in hanging it out. That was, is and evermore shall be a task that redefines the word tedious. But you begin to find yourself taking a step back from the line when you have completed the job and feeling a deep, inexpressible satisfaction at the sight of towels and pillowcases flapping in the breeze. Ah, the healthful, old-fashioned, sun-bleaching, economical airiness of it all! The lovely smell it will have when you bring it in! You may even begin to nod sagely and congratulate yourself on the good drying weather. Only women feel this. There is no turning back to childhood now. It's a long, slow slide into the grave from hereon out. Let's just hope it is flanked by gorgeous piles of freshly laundered, snowy-white linen when you get there.

17. You enjoy gardening

An interest in gardening sneaks up on you. Most children can be coaxed into growing mustard and cress on a damp flannel, particularly as it doesn't know it shouldn't grow in rude words and will happily sprout into a verdant 'fuck off' if you take the time to sprinkle it into position correctly when you first embark on your great horticultural experiment. But even in the first years at primary school, it was only really the girls (and the very nicest boys) who took any interest in the annual daffodil-bulb-growing competition, because instead of the almost instant gratification offered by garnish-rearing, you had to tend to your bulb for months, keeping it warm and moist in darkness at first and then moving it to brighter and brighter spots on the windowsill so that it could acclimatise properly and reach its full potential. It is hard to avoid the conclusion that we were exercising some primitive form of proto-maternal instinct.

Perhaps fortunately, both the maternal instinct and the interest in gardening generally goes into abeyance for a good few years after that, otherwise the world would be full of seven-year-old single parents (because, believe me, even those nice boys are too caught up in British Bulldog and Buckaroo tournaments to pull their weight in the Wendy home) and exhausted prepubescents trying to dig over vast allotments with tiny plastic trowels.

But it returns, stealthily. Maybe you are living in a flat with a communal garden and find yourself nipping out now and again to pull off a few dead leaves here and there, or prune back a bush that's hiding a much nicer plant behind. Then maybe you move to a house with its own scrap of garden. At first you are glad that it is decked or paved over, but then, oh so gradually, a hankering begins, which soon grows too big to be denied, for a set of matching pots filled with matching plants to sit by the door. And perhaps a bigger one for herbs, which will save you money in the long run, after all, and be far more ecologically sound, when you no longer have to buy them in extortionately priced plastic packets from the supermarket. Some bulbs would be nice for the spring too. I mean, it's not really a home without some daffodils and tulips bobbing cheerfully about the place, is it?

And once you are in the habit of popping down to Homebase, you quickly get caught up in the pleasures of buying whole trays of little, coloured, flowery plants that take instant root in your pots and at the base of the tree out front and spread so merrily that your heart cannot help but lift at the sight of the carpet of campanula nodding and dancing in the breeze when you come home from another shit day at the office. Look what you did! You bought some flowers and enabled them to make more flowers! You are a genius! You are a god! You find yourself able to talk to your mother and grandmother about snapdragons, the value of shade-loving cyclamen and the grief of losing every one of your sweet peas to slugs.* Your relations look at you fondly and then nod at each other with the wisdom of ages. They know a resurgent maternal instinct when they see one, and they are already knitting bootees in their minds.

N.B. This is, of course, not to say that all gardening urges are a sign of imminent procreative activity, nor that you must experience the latter before the former. I simply say that the two are linked more often than one would find if it were merely the laws of chance at work.

Given this, it may also be instructive to note what type of gardener you are. Ideally, you should be constitutionally capable of pottering. If not, you will be like my mother, whom I can see through the window as I type at the dinner table at home. The woman into whose Bran Flakes we daily crush eighteen Valium just to enable her to open the post safely is zooming about the garden, apparently operating some sort of scorched-earth policy and aiming sharpened bamboo canes at the faecally profligate cats who have violated the integrity of her lobelia. If this were 1974, I would phone social services and demand that any offspring she had in the next three years were taken away at birth and given to someone more suited to the long-term task of childrearing.

---

* I know whereof I speak. Born and bred in Catford, my horticultural experiences were largely limited to picking used hypodermics out of window boxes and stepping over homeless men kipping in the bushes in Lewisham Park. Now I have eighteen pots filled with dwarf narcissi and two hydrangeas that are bigger than my house. I don't know what you're supposed to do with them in the way of repotting or pruning or anything, but I operate on the principle that if they really want to live, they will find a way to tell me what they need. If my theories about proto-maternal instincts are right, I may be more like my mother than I thought possible.

18. Coasters, enforced use of

Do you now have furniture that you paid good money for, instead of rickety pieces of loading pallet cast off by your parents or left behind by previous tenants who did not want the stink of damp and slumlord to penetrate the new one-bedroom flat they somehow scraped together the money to buy? Furniture that you want to protect from wear, tear and hot mugs of tea? Have you bought coasters? Do you use them? Do you force guests, smilingly but firmly, to use them when they visit? Do you think these are the actions of a flighty young miss, hellbent on reckless living, a creature of rash and juvenile impulse, careening through existence heedless of the morrow? Or do you think you might just have taken one giant leap down the path that leads inexorably to Reactionary Old Fart Towers?

19. You discover a penchant for polyester

You start looking at the labels on clothes to check that they are machine-washable before buying them. You think of writing letters to manufacturers who put in their 'Everyday' range items which announce themselves to be dry clean or handwash only. Letters that begin: 'What kind of a life do you think I lead? Who are these people who can wear these fragile, gossamer clothes which require individual manual attentions or daily trips to the dry cleaners as a matter of course? Are you perhaps under the illusion that you are designing for the pre-war upper classes who are desperately looking for some way to occupy the servants in their large and comfortably overstaffed homes? Do you imagine that I own a selection of tweenies who have nothing better to do after they have riddled the parlour fires than wash a week's worth of stinky jumpers in the downstairs copper? Have some sense, man, do. I've been wearing the same pair of jeans for three weeks. I have to hit them with a pan to get them to crack at the crotch. I think my bras are giving me MRSA and I've forgotten what the bottom of my laundry basket looks like. For all I know, it could be the last resting place of Shergar and Lord Lucan. Have. Some. Sense.'

20. You experience your first fashion revival

You can comfort yourself all you want with the thought that in today's high-speed whirligig of a world, the time that elapses between an original trend and its reinvention by a later generation is becoming laughably short, but still – the first time you set foot outside the door and bump into a gaggle of youngsters wearing clothes you remember having the first time round is enough to send you hurtling back inside and bolting the door against the sight. Talk about intimations of mortality.

And it has recently been very much our turn. Footless tights have made a comeback. *Coloured* footless tights have made a comeback. Leggings too – albeit worn in a cowardly fashion, under dresses and things, instead of bravely, as a legitimate item in their own right, as we pioneers did – populate the high street once more. And off-the-shoulder tops and batwing sleeves have had a brief second moment in the limelight. There were even reports of puffball sightings, but these remain unconfirmed by any reputable source, and commonsense would dictate that even in what is in evolutionary if not fashion terms the very short space of twenty years, girls have developed sufficient additional intelligence to avoid this particular trend like the hellish barbarism it was and will always remain.

But this should not encourage complacency. For the protection of your own mental health, you should be aware that we are only ever one hot new designer away from disaster. Beware the enthusiastic bundle of talent born in 1984 and leaping fresh from Fashion Academy full of ideas on how to rework the fascinating styles s/he has read about in history books for the coming season. Beware the day s/he pulls her/his hair into a directional side ponytail and gets to work. The streets will be filled with legwarmers and fingerless gloves quicker than you can say 'Rubik's Cube motif on a neon ra-ra skirt'. You will have to shop blindfolded. Or with that spare bag from your handbag over your head.

21. You become a cat person

You may have been a cat person all your life. If so, you can skip this bit. I am talking here to people who have spent most of their lives unable to see the appeal of any walking repository of fleas, fur and faeces, otherwise known as the family pet, and blind to any possible charms inhering to the feline variety in particular. You have spent years listening to friends' and colleagues' stories of how their cats walked, then sat, then curled up, then jumped around a bit, then sat again, twitched, purred, licked its genitals and so on and on and on, ad infinitum and nauseam. You wonder how the teller and the audience can be so genuinely enraptured with these tales. Cats, you reason, are, after all, wholly independent, notoriously fickle animals who will curl around the legs of anyone who will give them food or a warm cushion for the night and happily stalk off into the sunset the next in search of a better offer. They have none of a dog's loyalty, neediness, pleading eyes when you leave the house or naked happiness when you return.

What you realise with age, however, is that the last thing you want cluttering up your home, which already heaves with tasks undone, is an animal that creates yet more work and responsibility. You have a boyfriend or a husband and maybe children who need you, make demands on you, look at you with pleading eyes and (maybe, depending on their ages and temperaments) roll about with delight at your return to hearth and home. There are already more drains on your time and emotional and psychological resources than you can comfortably handle. You fully understand those women who disappear on a trip to Sainsbury's one day and go off to build a new life for themselves in a Spanish coastal resort and hot-pink bikini instead.

Suddenly, the existence of a living being in the house who doesn't demand anything from you but the opening of a tin once or twice a day, who provides a comforting presence without getting under your feet or leaving tea stains all over the kitchen counters and who will occasionally curl up on your lap and let you soothe your frazzled nerves by raking his soft belly with your fingers comes to seem a prize beyond rubies.

Cats are blessedly silent. They are independent, preferring to come back to their warm beds with you, certainly, but by their very natures providing you with that margin of error that other domestic residents cannot – namely, that if you did finally snap one night and locked everyone out of the house while you drank bottles of brandy, wept copious tears and watched your entire boxset of *Sex and the City* DVDs backwards, they would not only survive but return the next day as if nothing untoward had happened. No questions, no reproaches, nothing more than a light feed and a snooze by the radiator. They are blank slates onto which you can project any emotions you need to decant from yourself at the time. They are empty vessels into which you can pour as much or as little love and interest as you have to spare on any given day. They will watch you do the ironing or fill the washing machine as if it were the most intriguing thing they have seen all week, imparting a pleasing sense that you are not engaged in a repetitive domestic chore of mind-numbing tedium, but in some kind of stage show spectacular, possibly involving trapezes, sequins and erotic burlesque. You come to realise, in short, that cats are brilliant. But you need to be a woman of a certain age before you can truly appreciate their gifts.

22. I don't know what you would call this one

It is a deeply weird, twisted psychological quirk in women that resists all rational explanation and can best be described as: the tendency, when you live with someone, to take advantage of his absence from the house to do a vast and comprehensive set of washing, ironing, cleaning, dusting, vacuuming and tidying before he gets back.

Why? Why? In God's name, why? You should be performing all such drudge work in front of him and with great sighing, commotion, looks of martyrdom and combative remarks like 'Get off your arse and help me' and 'You should be doing fifty per cent of this and you don't even know where we keep the lavatory brush, even though it is in very much plain sight next to that thing whose rim you keep peeing all over, namely THE LAVATORY. So why don't you try picking it up some time?' But instead, you wait for him to go out of the house. Your efforts go unnoticed, you perpetuate the myth of the Shitcleaning Fairy, he avoids his share and you hate him even more. What's the point?

It is something to do with the need to have an uninterrupted run at hateful jobs around the home. You can immerse yourself in the tasks at hand and at some level forget that there is another, better world out there in which you would not be scouring the bath in your bra and knickers but drinking margaritas by the sea, *mamasita*, which makes things that much easier. There is the knowledge that there isn't a lumbering beast behind you, undoing all your good work as you go along, like a cable TV man digging up a recently resurfaced road. There is the satisfaction of knowing that the finished product is all your own work and that it will remain pristine for at least the few hours left until he comes home.

But even with all that taken into account, when weighed against the lost opportunities for ostentatious suffering and sacrifice (to be translated into meals out, jewellery, the moral high ground or victory in the next familial or financial decision to be made, according to individual taste and priorities), training, blows struck for relationship equality and deconstruction of the pervasive Shitcleaning Fairy myth, the scales still surely thump down heavily on the side of madness.

23. You turn into your mother

The phenomenon is, of course, well recognised and features many of the qualities and lunatic characteristics outlined above. 'Turning into your mother' is, after all, practically synonymous with becoming a nagging shrew with a fully equipped kitchen who becomes drunk and violent on a glass of Bucks Fizz at Christmas and strangely euphoric at the sight of a free shortbread biscuit with her hot beverage in the M&S café, thinks nothing of lambasting sluggish shopgirls* and ordering muzak to be switched off and who owns so many spare bags that she has to keep her handbag in one of them in order to be able to carry them all. Her friends have scattered to the four winds, so her sense of humour has atrophied so thoroughly that the most she can muster in the way of riotous merriment is a few dusty barks of hollow laughter at *Dad's Army* repeats.† She has endured fifties, sixties and seventies fashion revivals, her underwear is made by Govan shipbuilders and her life is fully machine-washable. Oh, and she loves her cats far, far more than she loves you. In fact, it's probably time to start periodically checking the will.

But over and above this, you will start to notice the very small, idiosyncratic ways in which you personally are turning into your very own, hitherto inimitable mother. It may be hand gestures or pained

---

* Incidentally, I'm told by various unrepentant and much-loved battleaxes of my acquaintance that after retirement, this particular activity can rapidly take on the nature of a religious calling. A trip to local emporia resembles nothing so much as the scene from *Notting Hill*, but instead of Hugh Grant walking down Portobello Road as the seasons change, you see an impressively bosomed woman sailing stately as a galleon along the high street, shop assistants shifting and blossoming from recalcitrant troglodytes to captains of industry in her wake.

---

† I wouldn't start smirking if I were you. It's only a matter of years before you're doing the same at reruns of *Duty Free*. That David Pearce – he is a one!

facial expressions. It may be the sudden desire to enforce the insane and illogical rules that she once held so dear.* It may be the unexpected emergence of phrases that have lain dormant in your brain since childhood but one day start tripping off your tongue as if they have just been waiting for the right moment to emerge. 'Am I talking to myself?', 'I'm not doing this for the good of my health, you know' and 'You treat this place like a hotel' are three that have caught many a girl unawares, but you will have numerous others of your own, particular to just you and your distaff relations, hovering in the dim outskirts of your mind, biding their time, just waiting to bound into the light and issue forth from suddenly stuttering and bloodless lips. Try to think of it as continuing an ancient and venerable tradition. If you start crying, you see, you'll never stop.

Without these telltale signs, it would be almost impossible these days to work out just who is supposed to be a grown-up and when you are classed as such yourself. The irony has always existed that the truly youthful spend their time straining desperately to look older so that they can get into more clubs, pubs and trouble, while everyone else struggles equally hard to look younger, but now both ends of the spectrum are expanding. It has never been easier or more acceptable for girls to ape their elders, twenty- and thirty-somethings maintain their flights from responsibility and into the age-obscuring lands of Topshop and Primark until the last possible moment, and even the properly old are quite failing to fall into decrepitude as swiftly and comprehensively as they used to do. It's the modern mollycoddled

---

* You can try and legislate against this – I, for example, have stipulated to lawyers and my GP that if I am ever found denying my children drinks with soup or requiring them to lay the table for breakfast eight days in advance, I am to be taken out and killed immediately and my body left on public display with an explanatory placard as a warning to others – but there is no guarantee of success.

life that does it, of course. Women are no longer subject to half the ravages of age that once pursued them so relentlessly. Female health and figures now go unblighted by the suffering caused by two world wars and music hall comedy. We are all well fed – no longer required to hand over the weekly slice of ham to the wage-earning head of the household and left to nibble decorously on a cobblestone – and our richly calciumed, unosteoporotic ribs even go uncrushed by corsets. Women no longer have to carry their prolapsed innards around in a burlap sack because they fell out in the apothecary's after the nineteenth child in six months. Now, with a modicum of sense, good fortune, contraception, mammograms, smears, HRT and giant Cadbury's Fruit and Nut bars, we can banish most of the ills to which feminine flesh has historically been heir.

The current crop of famous women further muddy the waters of life, of course, and especially the ones who loomed so hugely over our formative years. The Material Girl, *Pretty Woman* Julia Roberts, Olivia Newton John in *Grease*, Michelle Pfeiffer in *Grease II* and peripheral but curiously influential Brat Packer Demi Moore et al have all spent the last thirty years looking twenty-something. I'm almost dreading the day that they can brace themselves against the weight of years no longer and our entire generation of stars – albeit with a heartfelt sigh of relief – crumbles into a dusty heap overnight. They are embodiments of the truth that the outward signs of ageing have never been more avoidable or, therefore, more undesirable. New categories, slogans and decidedly bogus-sounding chemical compounds proliferate – middle-youth, fifty is the new forty, penta-cera-peptamides – to help even the non-celebrity sisterhood push back the boundaries of age and put off the apparently evil day when a woman must admit that she is no longer an unborn foetus.

There is every possibility, then, that we may eventually go collectively mad trying to reconcile the conflict between having the freedom to act like teenagers for a vastly protracted length of time, while on the other hand being consigned to the dustbin of life and sexual attractiveness at the first sign of physical decline. Oh well. With any luck, L'Oreal will come up with another wonder cream that will not only reduce the signs of ageing, but come full of synapse-repairing peptokleptosteptocides to prevent our brains from dissolving under the strain.

Until then, we must focus on the advantages that accrue to us over the years:

- *You grow in confidence (which is a polite way of saying that you give less and less of a shit about anyone's opinion but your own and become intoxicated with the heady freedom this brings).*

- *You grow in independence (by which I mean that if you have any sense, you maintain a separate bank account for your legitimate income at all times and siphon off as much cash as possible from whoever you are shacked up with into another without him noticing or being able to prove anything if he does).*

- *You gain the ability to imbue the horrors of the playground that scarred you to the very bottom of your tender soul with a rosy nostalgic glow and recast the bone-chilling hours in condemned church halls full of dangerous fungal spores, recently paroled supervisors and moments of heart-splitting betrayal as valuable, character-forming experiences.*

You can rest easy in the knowledge that no matter how old you become, you will never, ever forget how to make a pompom. Just as you will never, ever work out what anyone could possibly ever do with eighteen inches of French goddamn knitting. And, best of all, you gain the ability to look back on your girlhood and laugh.

Finally, you must always remember two eternal verities. One, the older you get, the more chance you have of using all the handbags you've bought at least once. And two, when you are on your deathbed, surrounded by loving children, fat grandchildren and fond lunatics from your whist drive and cat appreciation evenings, you will be able to look back and say that whatever the trials, tribulations, triumphs and catastrophes that life has yielded up to you, it was always, always much, much better than being a boy.